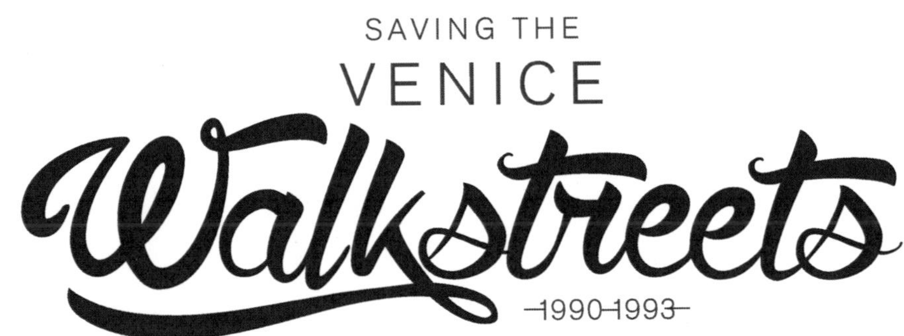

SANDY BLEIFER

SAVING THE VENICE WALKSTREETS

ISBN: 978-1-7330719-2-5
Library of Congress Control Number: 2019907973

Saving the Venice Walkstreets
Photographs of the Venice Walkstreets and residents' commentary as the Venice community, led by Sandy Bleifer, strove (successfully) to retain the configuration of these neighborhoods and to protect them in city planning records as historic and cultural assets.

Photography: Sandy Bleifer
Book Design by Michele Castagnetti / AcrylicAirlines.com

Published by Sandy Bleifer / Bleifer InPrint

www.sandybleifer.com

INTRODUCTION

Although many beachfront communities have created entertainment destinations along the oceanfront, Venice is unique in its attempt to adapt a European model: Venice, Italy. Abbott Kinney designed Venice of America as an entertainment district, so the Walkstreets, as well as the Boardwalk and the Canals, were configured to facilitate pedestrian access and recreational use. From the beginning, Venice was conceived as a place to be experienced by walking. People arrived by public transportation for the most part, and the automobile was not so pervasive at the beginning of the Century. The residential areas of Milwood and North Beach were intended as vacation homes using neighborhood friendly Eastern seaboard models including porches, low picket fences, and welcoming front yards.

The Coastal Plan circumscribing guidelines for development of ocean-side communities from Alaska to Mexico is, periodically, revised in order to preserve coastal areas and to secure public access to them. Over the years, development trends, the assertion of private property rights, and increasing sensitivity to public safety issues have surfaced. At these moments, there is a delicate balance between historical features that have been unproblematic for decades, which suddenly become questioned in terms of perceived risk management issues.

In 1990, an Interim Coastal Ordinance was put into effect with specific recommendations for Venice expressing the anticipated changes that government agencies expected to be codified in the final Land Use Plan. This caused a great deal of soul searching, and residents came to fully appreciate many of the elements of the public and private space that were now under scrutiny. Public debate ensued on a number of issues, but of particular concern were policies that impacted the configuration of sixty-five Walkstreets in the North Beach, Milwood, and the Peninsula areas of Venice. The proposed plan mandated greater access for firetrucks on the pedestrian Walkstreets, thus prohibiting any fencing or planting on the public easements residents had historically used as front yards.

My home on one of the North Beach Walkstreets was impacted by the pending restrictions, so I had a vested interest in taking action. The intent of the photographs that comprise this book was to show the beauty and eclectic mix of the Walkstreet gardens, their intrinsic aesthetic and community value for both neighbors and visitors, and how they express the idiosyncratic charm that is uniquely Venice.

I enlisted the Venice Historical Society, and we engaged a broad spectrum of the Venice community. Under the direction of Achva Benzinger Stein, the University of Southern California's Urban Planning and Landscape Department worked with the Los Angeles Fire Department to resolve the fire/life safety issues.

The photos along with the impassioned statements of Venice residents convinced the Coastal Commission to withdraw the plan and allow the continued use of the public right of way for front yards and fences. Ultimately, the protections we championed became codified in the Venice Specific Plan, which embraced the overarching values we highlighted and against which future development and construction projects must be weighed.

– Sandy Bleifer

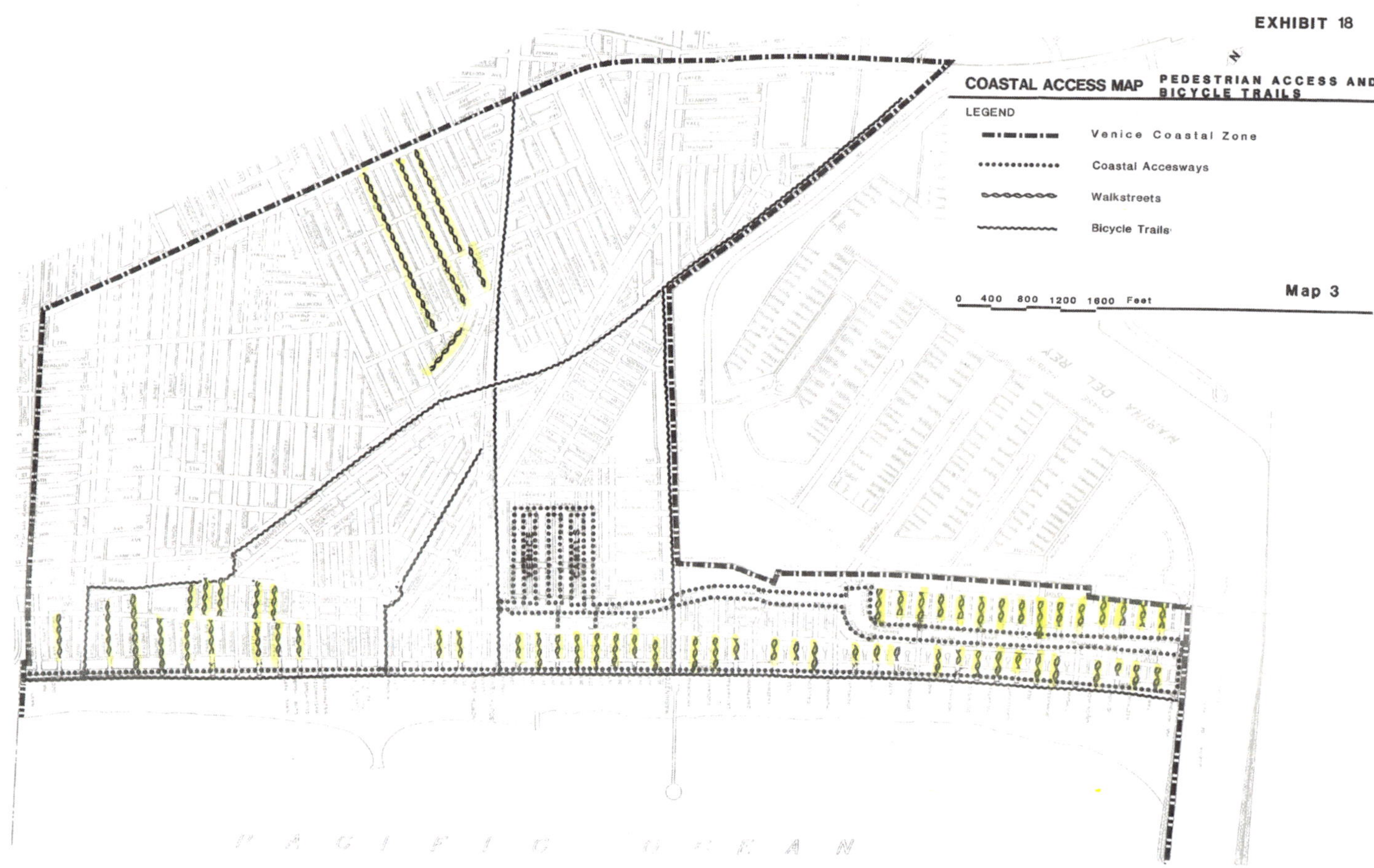

THE REASON FOR ACTING TO SAVE THE VENICE WALKSTREETS

The Coastal Plan circumscribing guidelines for development of ocean-side communities from Alaska to Mexico is, periodically, revised in order to preserve coastal areas and to secure public access to them. Over the years, development trends, the assertion of private property rights and increasing sensitivity to public safety issues have surfaced. At these moments, there is a delicate balance between historical features that have been unproblematic for decades, which suddenly become questioned in terms of perceived risk management issues. In 1990, an Interim Coastal Ordinance was put into effect with specific recommendations for Venice expressing the anticipated changes that government agencies expected to be codified in the final Land Use Plan. Public debate ensued on a number of issues, but of particular concern were policies that impacted the configuration of 65 Walkstreets in the North Beach, Milwood and the Peninsula areas of Venice.

In the proposed Plan 11.11 Implementation Strategies "Walkstreet improvements shall balance the need for adequate fire access with the enhancement of public access and neighborhood character" and went on to call for the "prohibition of fences, walls, hedges and other accessory structures for 10 feet on either side of the centerline of the Walkstreets in order to create a 20' wide lane (later increased to 28' wide) of permeable paving materials" so as to "Provide adequate access for emergency vehicles at all times..."

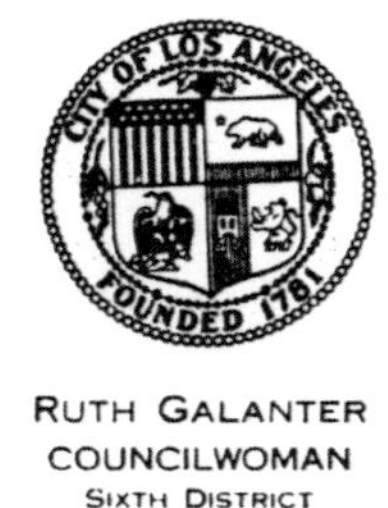

City Council
of the
City of Los Angeles
City Hall
90012

February 14, 1991

Betsy Goldman, President
Sandy Bleifer
Dell Chumley
Venice Historical Society
P.O. Box 2012
Venice, CA 90294

Dear Friends:

Thank you for your recent letter concerning the walk streets in Venice.

As you know, I share your alarm at this potential threat to our community. My Legislative Deputy, Jim Bickhart, and my Venice Field Deputy, Linda Lucks, have been working closely with your and other community groups as well as the Fire Department. I remain hopeful that we can resolve the issues that have been raised about emergency vehicle access to the walk streets. In the meantime, I have told the Planning Commission and the Planning Department that I do not support current language in the proposed Coastal Land Use Plan which suggests that "enhancement" of the walk streets is feasible. I firmly support preservation of the walk streets in their current configuration.

The walk streets are among Venice's most charming aspects. I believe the Fire Department's needs can be accommodated without altering this very special area.

I appreciate your support on this issue. Thank you for taking time to write to me.

Sincerely,

RUTH GALANTER
Councilwoman, Sixth District

RG:ahs

THE PROBLEM [WITH NEW URBAN REDEVELOPMENT], HE [ANDRES DUANY] CONCLUDED, WAS WITH OUTDATED CODES THAT ARE MEANT TO 'KEEP CARS BUT NOT PEOPLE HAPPY.'

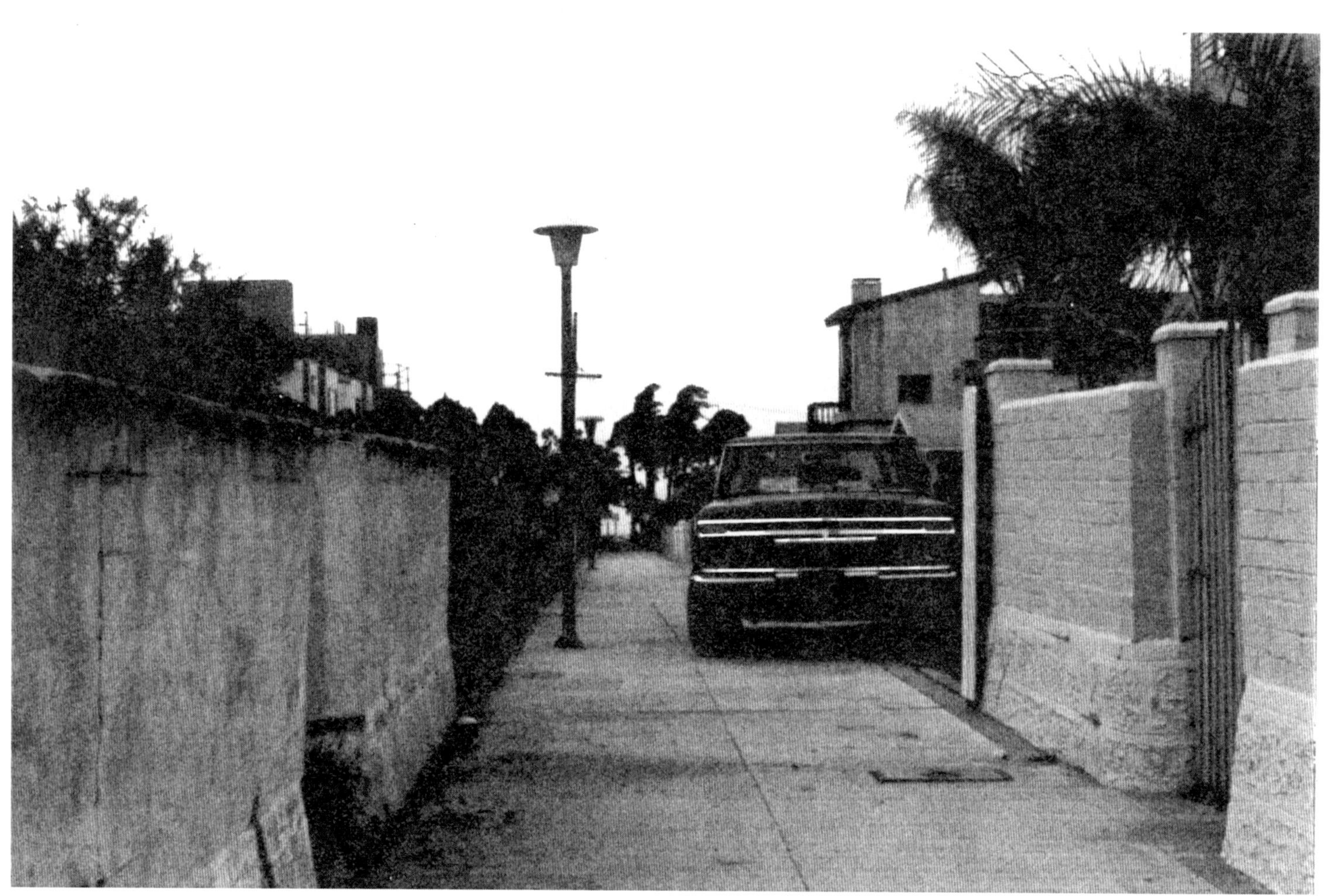

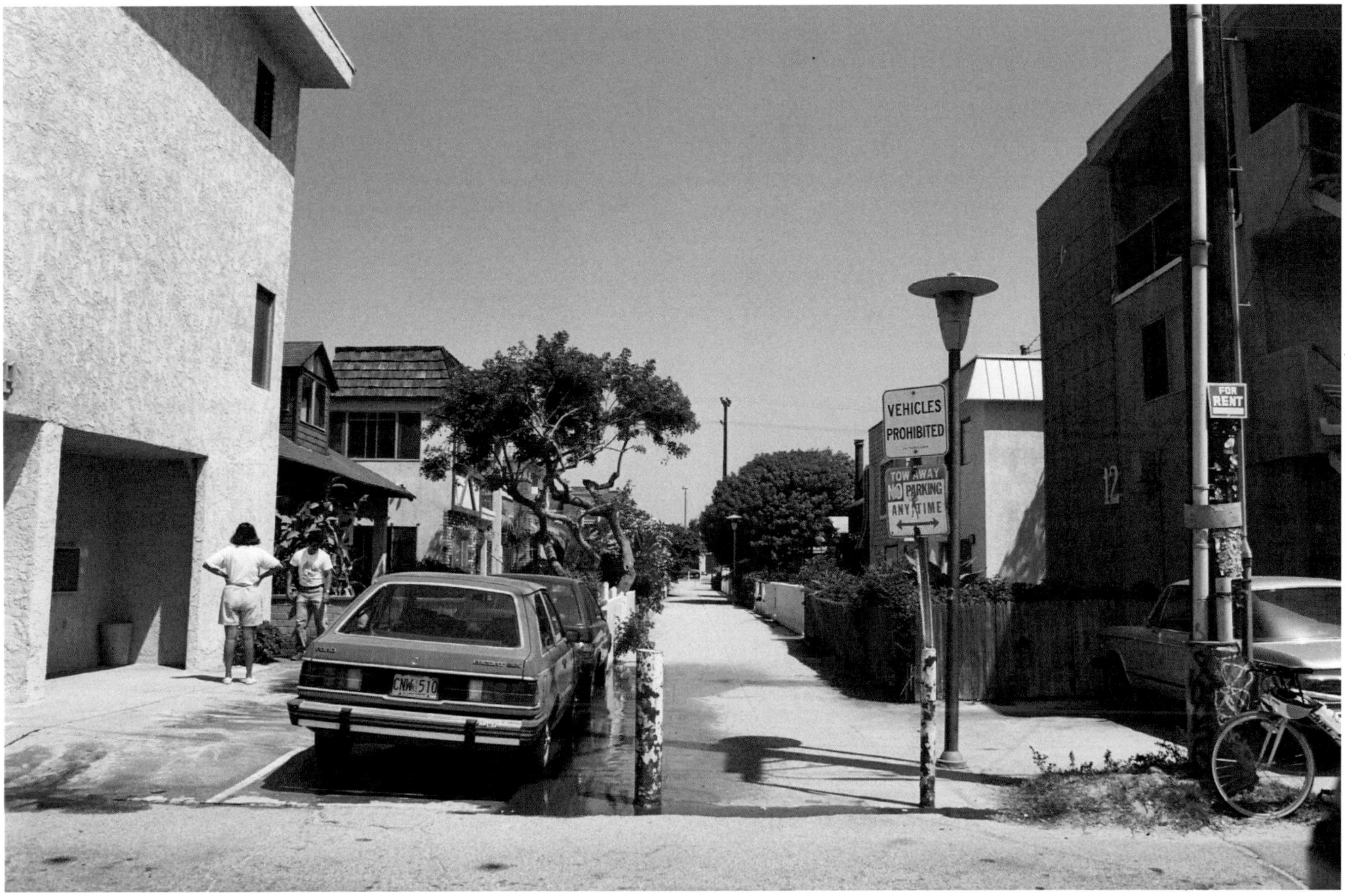

VEHICLES
PROHIBITED
TOW AWAY
NO PARKING
ANY TIME
FOR
RENT
12

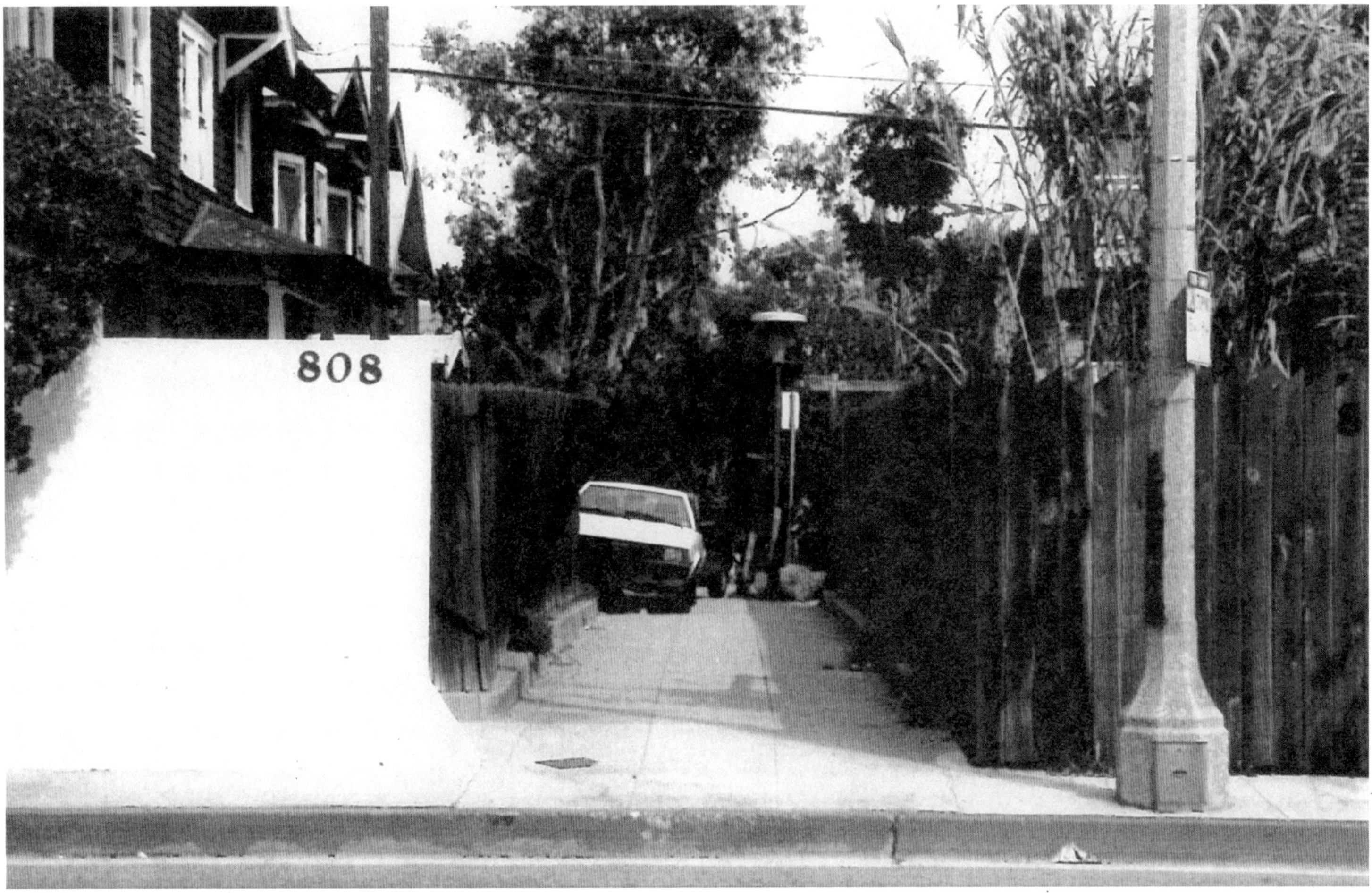

808

WHAT HAPPENS TO THE WALKSTREETS WHEN THERE IS NO FENCE LINE.

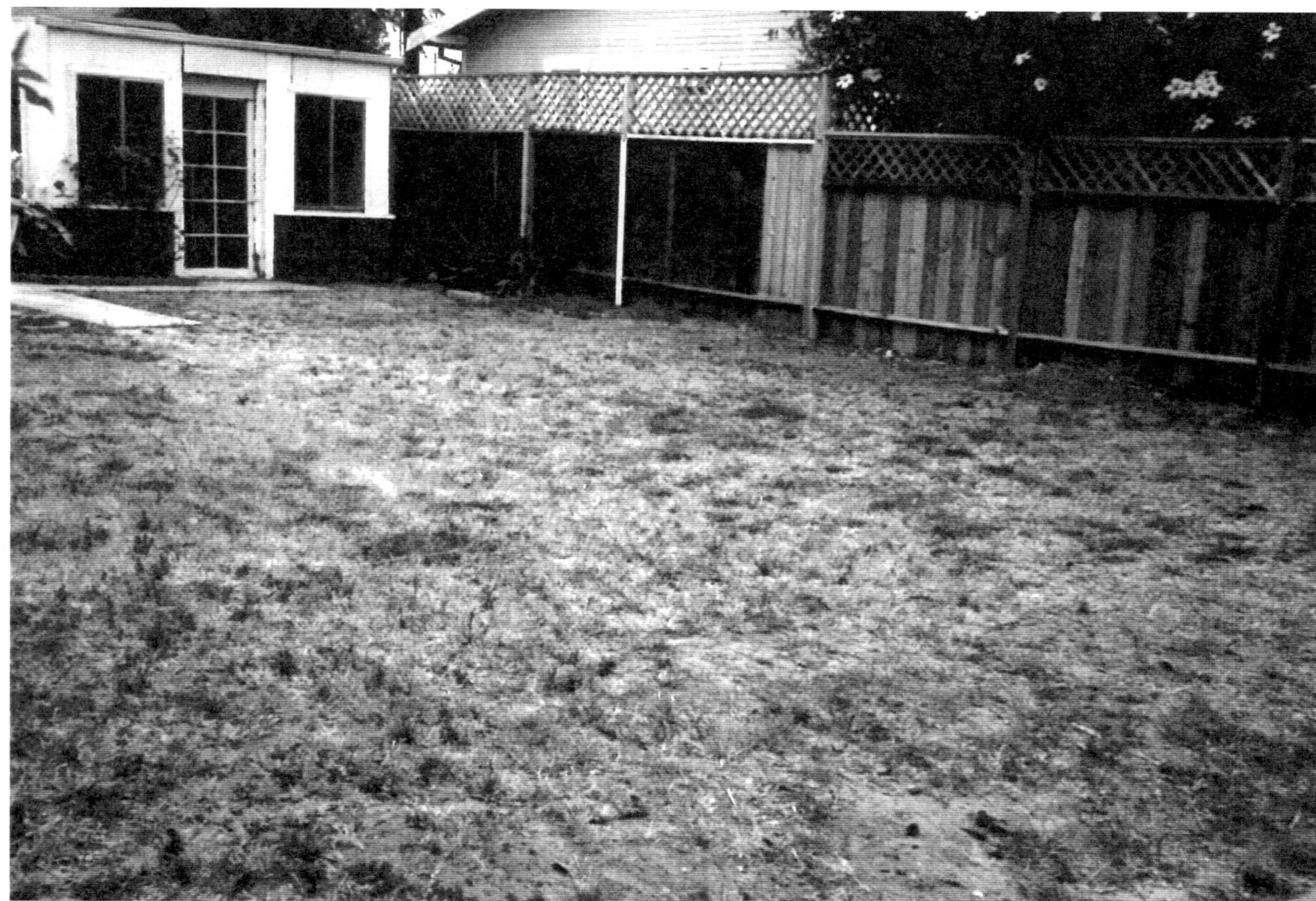

There are several examples of Walkstreet properties which conform to the proposed elimination of structural and landscape encroachments on the public right of way. Without fences or landscape to define public and private areas, a no-man's-land is created whereby owners do not invest in landscaping and avoid utilizing their front yards. It is as though the Walkstreet had become a highway for strangers and not shared with them for their private use.

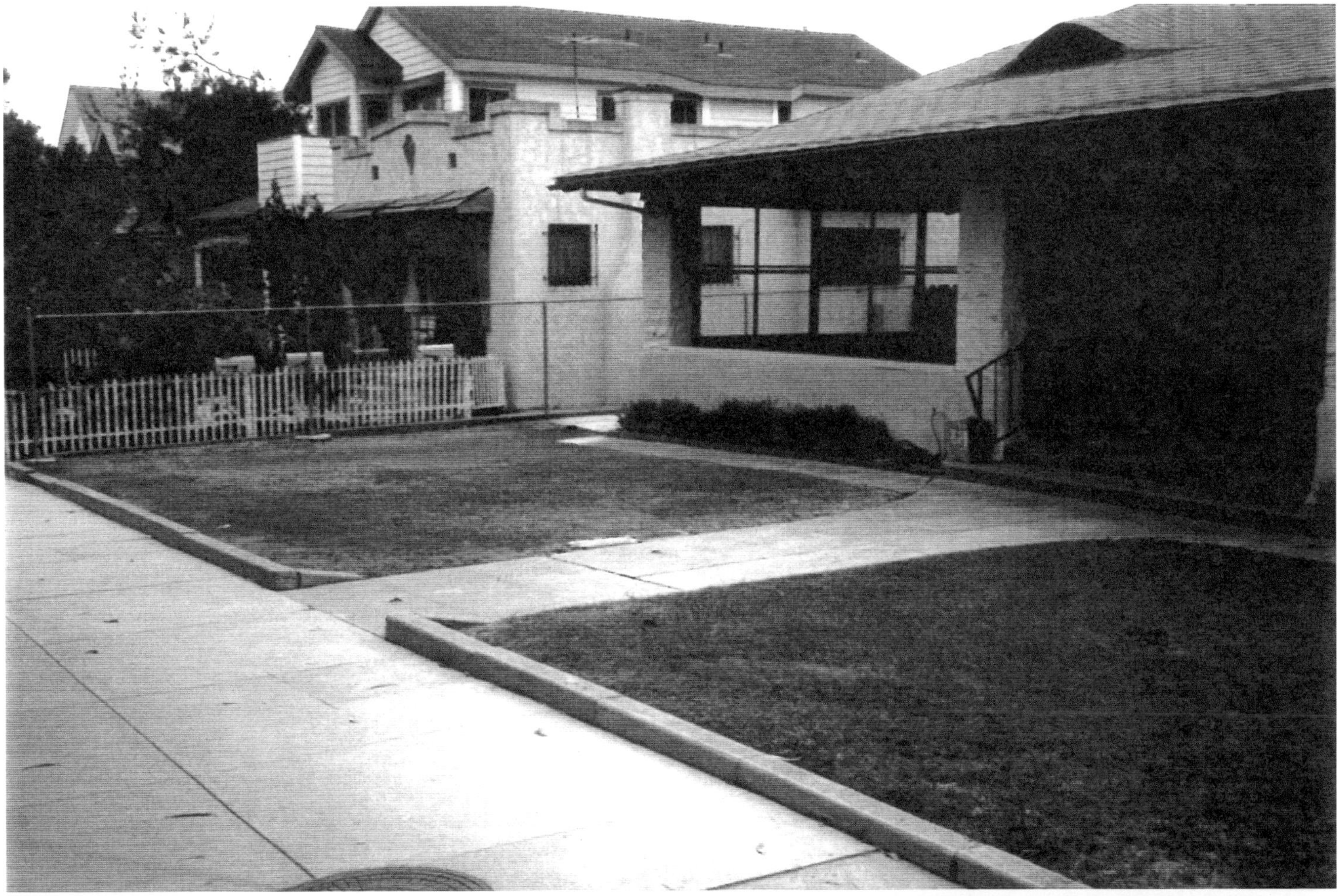

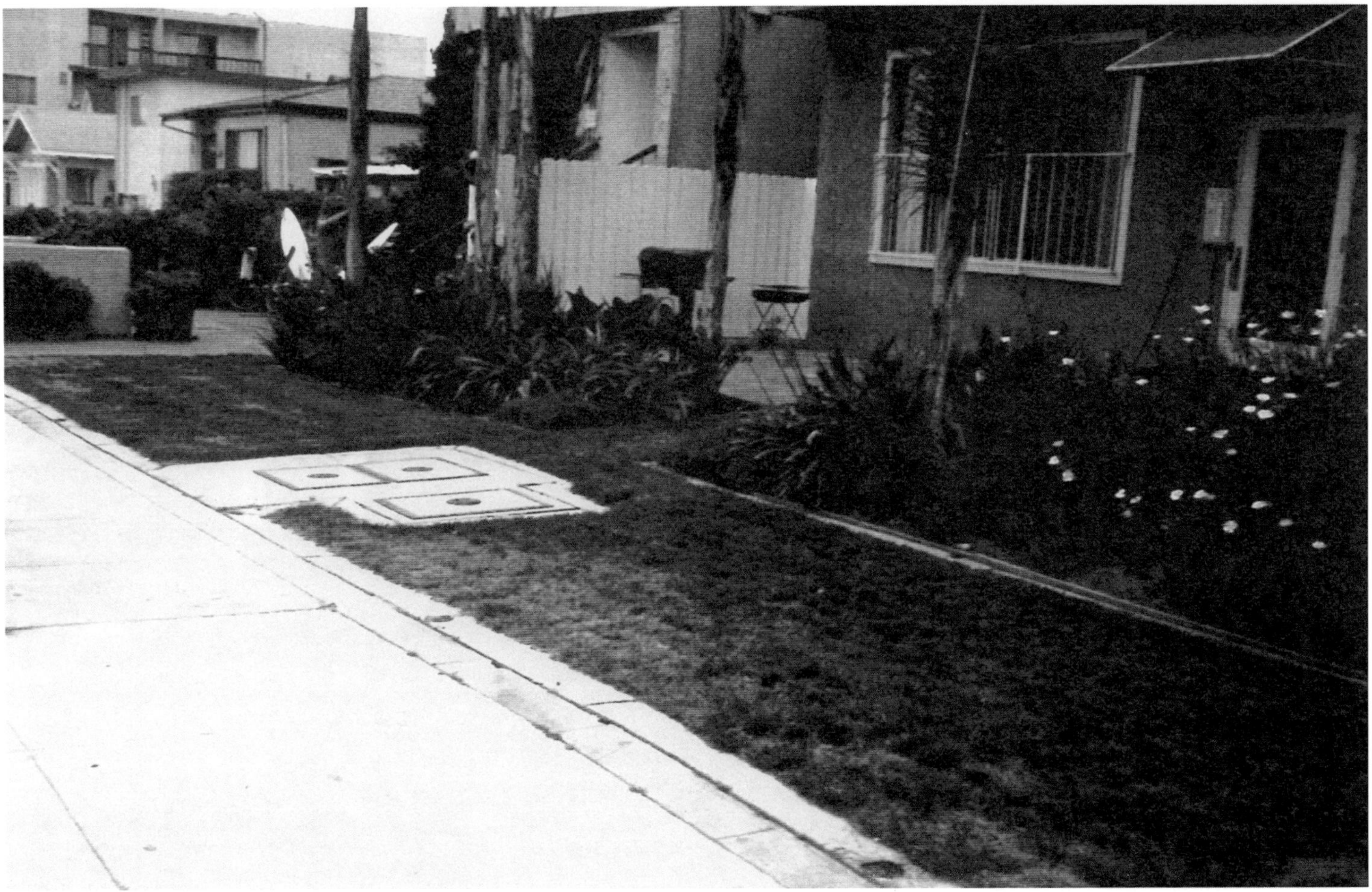

THE VENICE COMMUNITY FELT THIS WAS
A THREAT TO AN IMPORTANT COMMUNITY
ASSET AND ORGANIZED UNDER THE AEGIS
OF THE VENICE HISTORICAL SOCIETY TO
GALVANIZE SUPPORT TO GUARANTEE THE
PRESERVATION OF THE WALKSTREETS IN
THEIR HISTORICAL CONFIGURATIONS
IN THE COMMUNITY AND COASTAL PLANS.
THIS PUBLICATION IS A RECORD OF THE
SENTIMENTS AND ADVOCACY OF VENICE
COMMUNITY MEMBERS AND THE WEIGHT
OF COMMUNITY PLANNING EXPERT
OPINIONS TO SECURE THIS CHERISHED
ELEMENT OF OUR UNIQUE NEIGHBORHOOD.

PUBLIC TESTIMONY BEFORE THE CITY PLANNING COMMISSION,
January 17, 1991

The Walkstreets should be preserved with existing
encroachments for the following reasons; preservation
of the unique character, ambiance and sense of community
along Walkstreets; preservation of Walkstreets as an
historic district or historic pedestrian overlay
district; preservation of existing trees and landscaping;
maintenance of existing property values; concerns that
if encroachments are removed and therefore, walk streets
become wider, unauthorized, non-emergency vehicles would
enter and park illegally in front of Walkstreet residences;
and concern that the financial burden of walk street
improvements and maintenance would be placed on the
residents and property owners along Walk Streets."
While "..both the Preliminary Plan and the Response
documents continually reiterate the desire to preserve
neighborhood character...the Planning Department has
assumed that the ambiance of these streets can be
preserved simply by restricting their use to pedestrian
traffic. Pedestrian usage of these walkways is only one
facet of the neighborhood's character. It is, in fact,
the intimate scale of the walkways (those in the North
Beach area are 8'-10' and Milwood's are 4-1/2' wide)
which allows for a buffer zone for the residents of
gardens, patios and porches between their private space
and the public access routes. The charm of these small
gardens and the tree canopy that creates shade on many
of the streets enhance these passageways for visitors
as well. -Sandy Bleifer

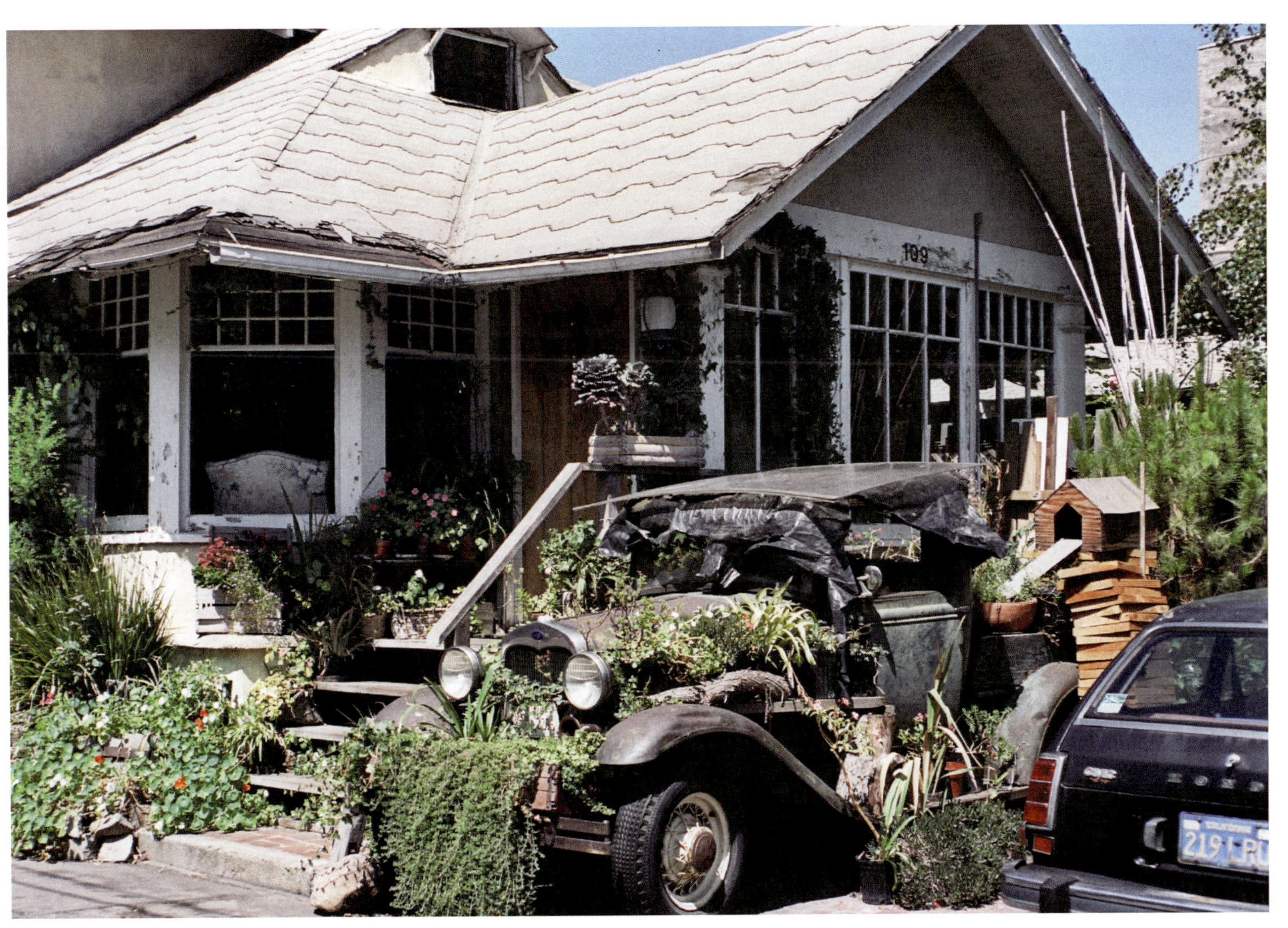

The walk streets are right out of a fairy tale...lets
not let the evil empire wipe them out! —Jock Worther

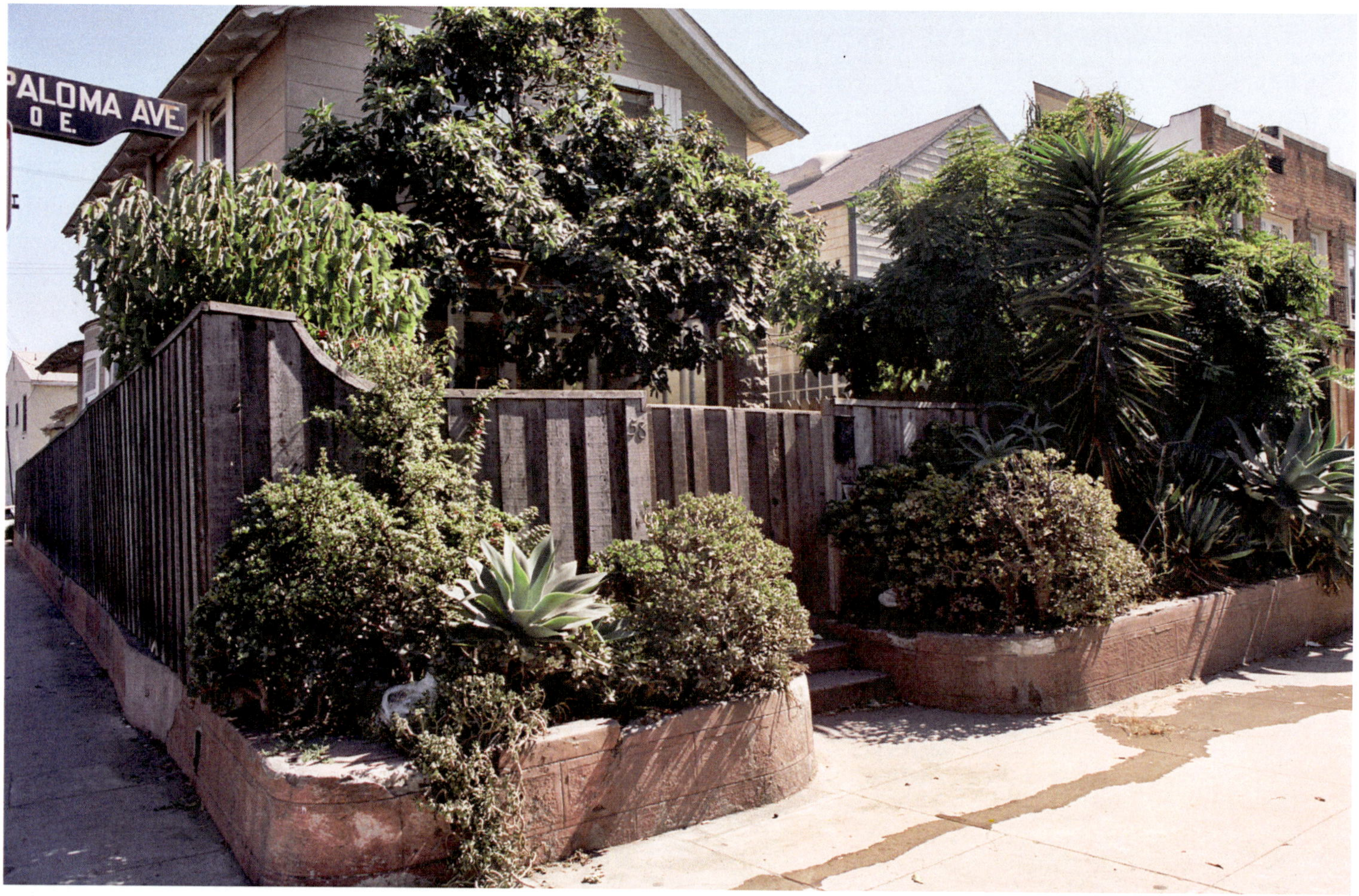

PALOMA AVE.
0 E.

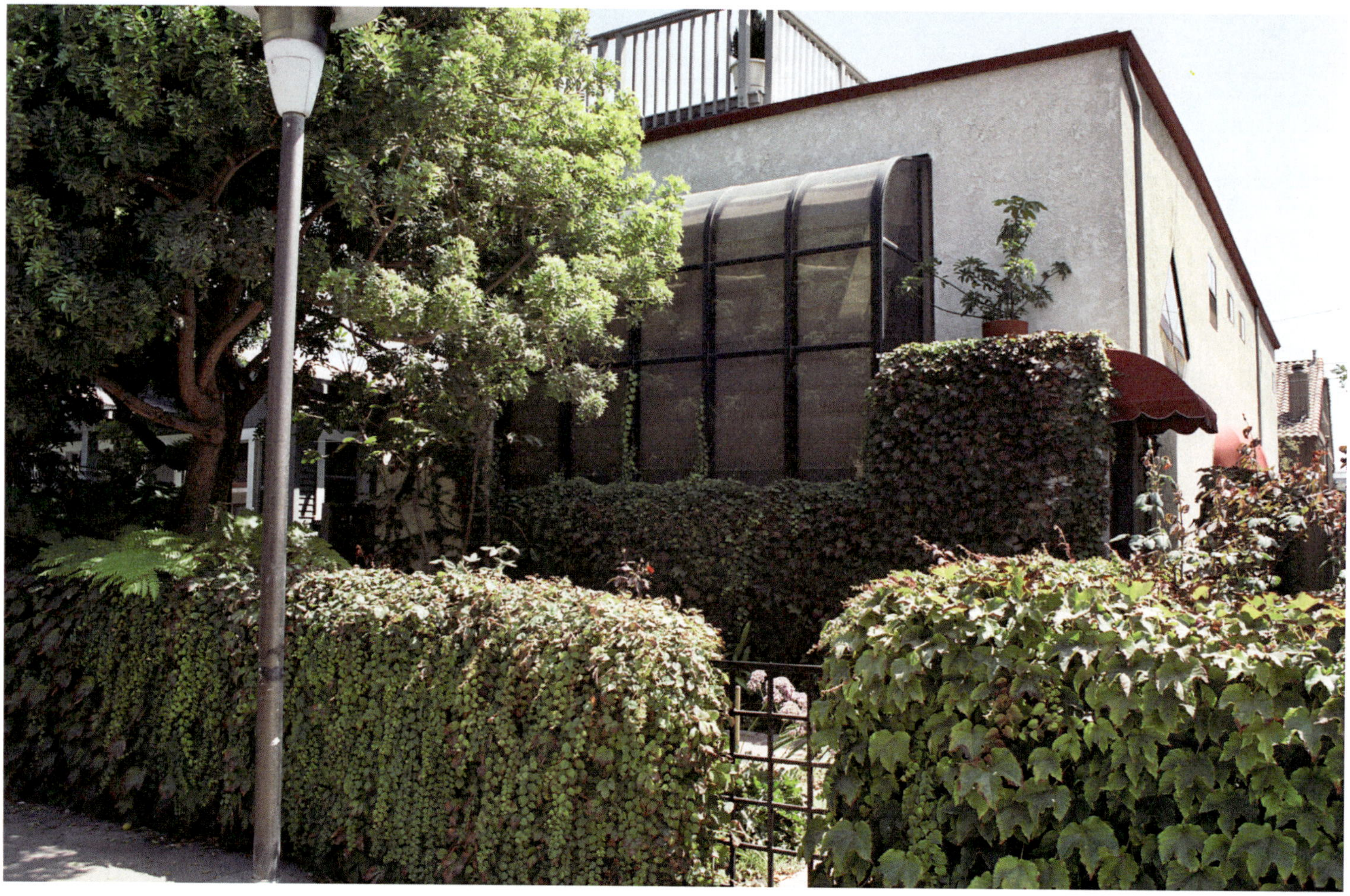

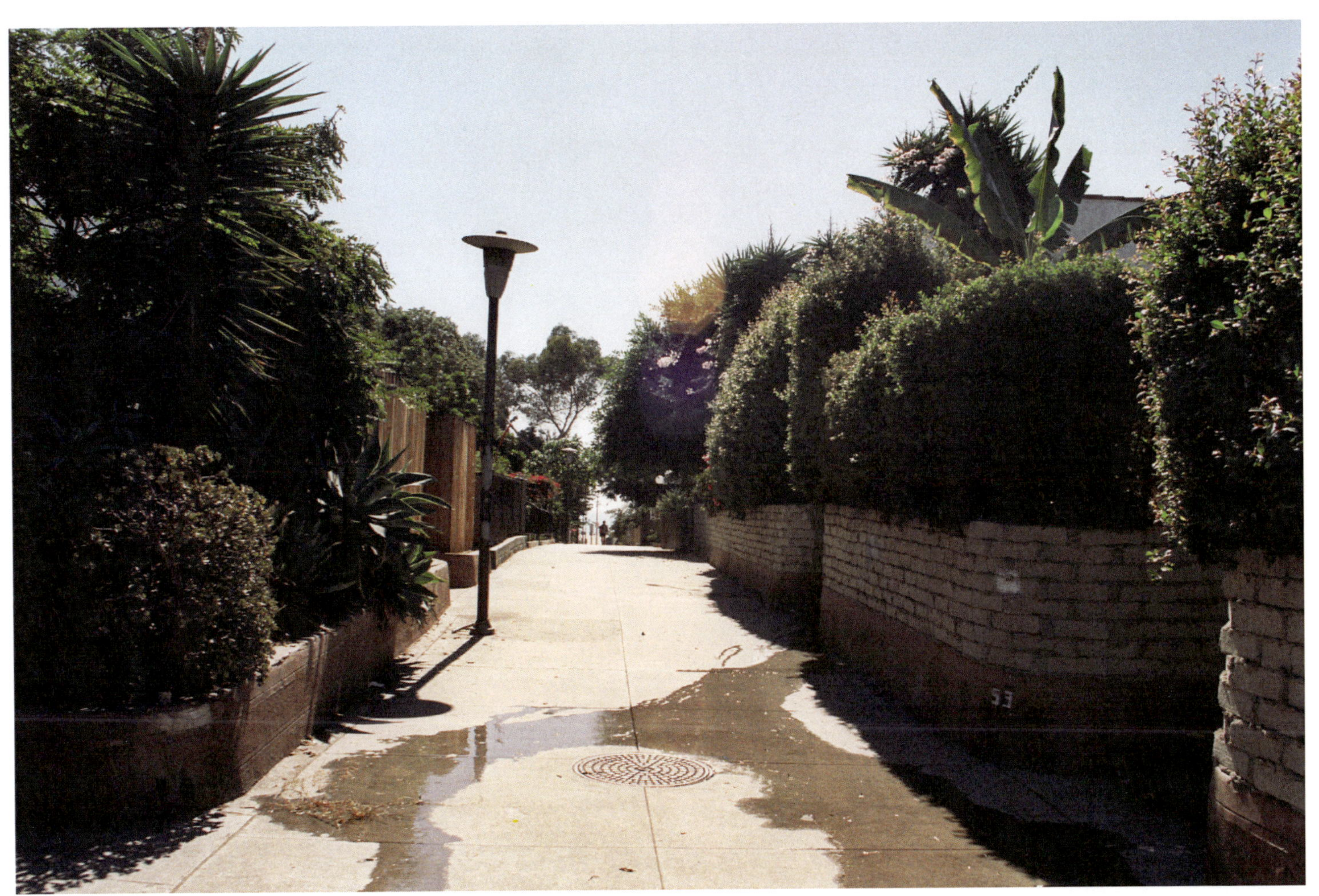

SAVING THE VENICE
WALKSTREETS
A COMMUNITY PRESERVES
ITS ECCENTRIC NEIGHBORHOOD

Abbott Kinney's design for the Venice of America as a tourist attraction inadvertently became a template for the optimal neighborhood experience recognized by modern city planners worldwide.

While the Boardwalk is a festive public space and the Canals are unique private waterfront properties, it is the Walkstreets that sustain a delicate balance between public and private space.

This reality is experienced by all who live on a Walkstreet and, when that delicate balance was threatened, the community came forward to eloquently express the almost intangible qualities that make living in Venice so special.

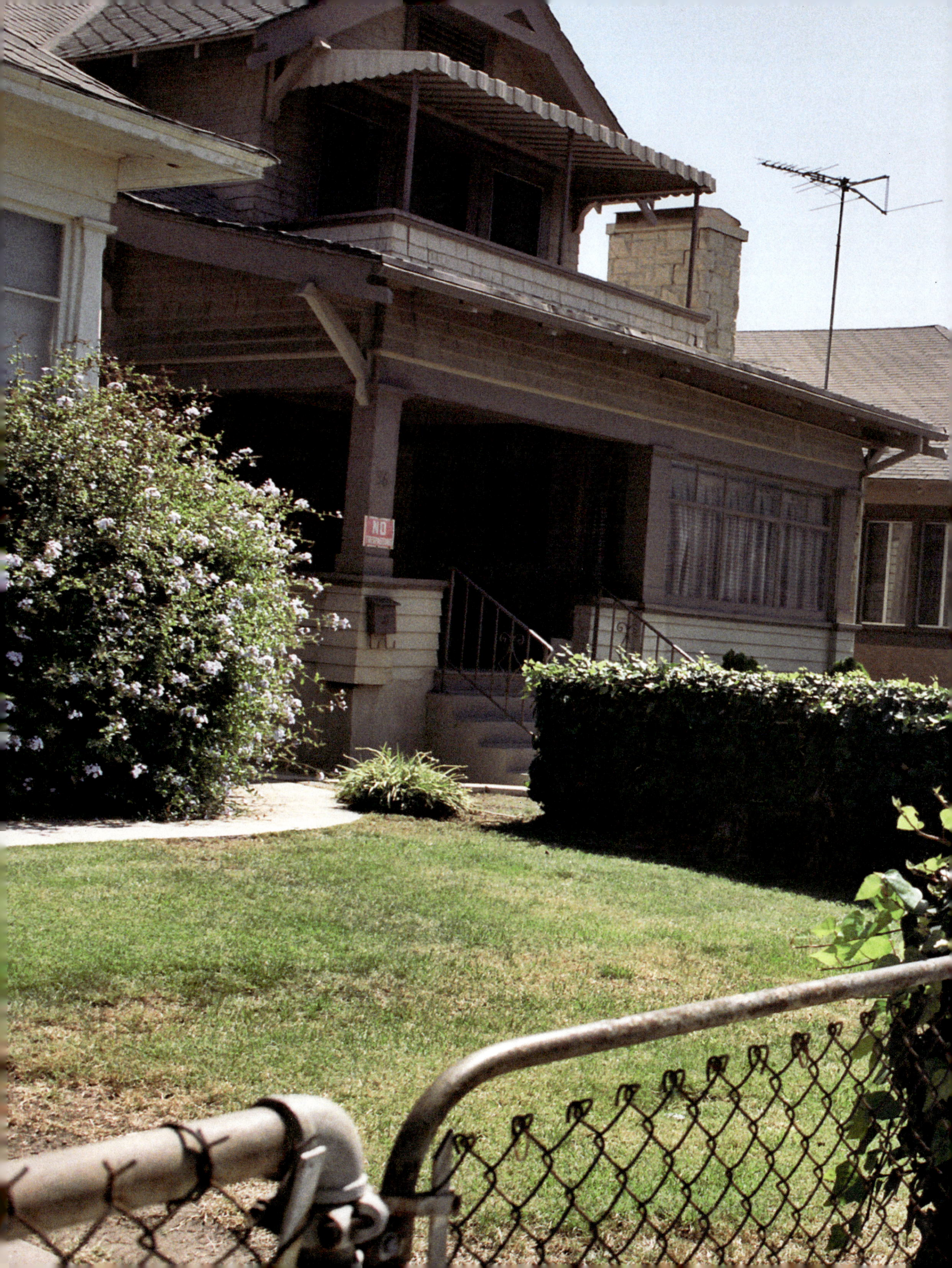

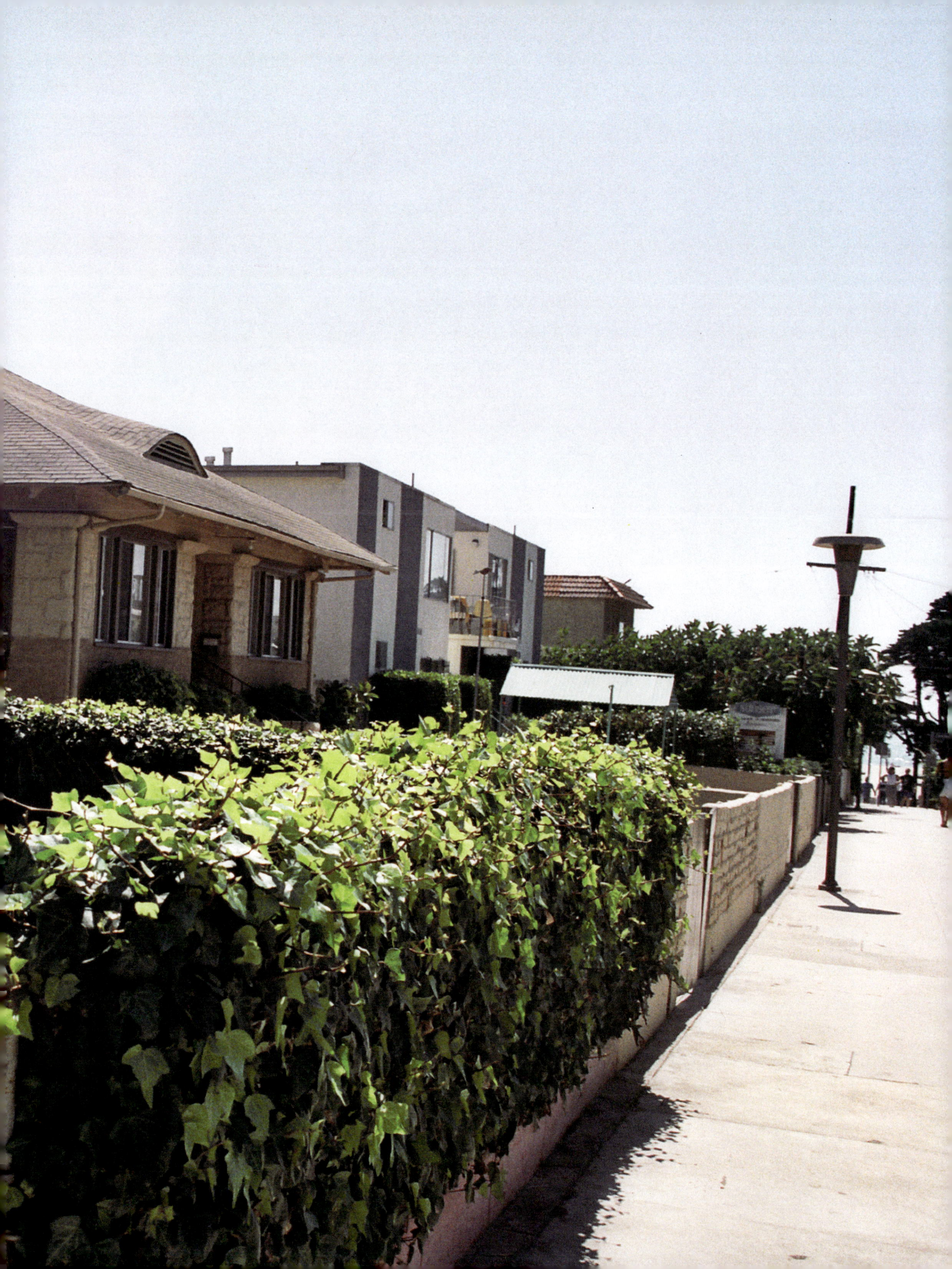

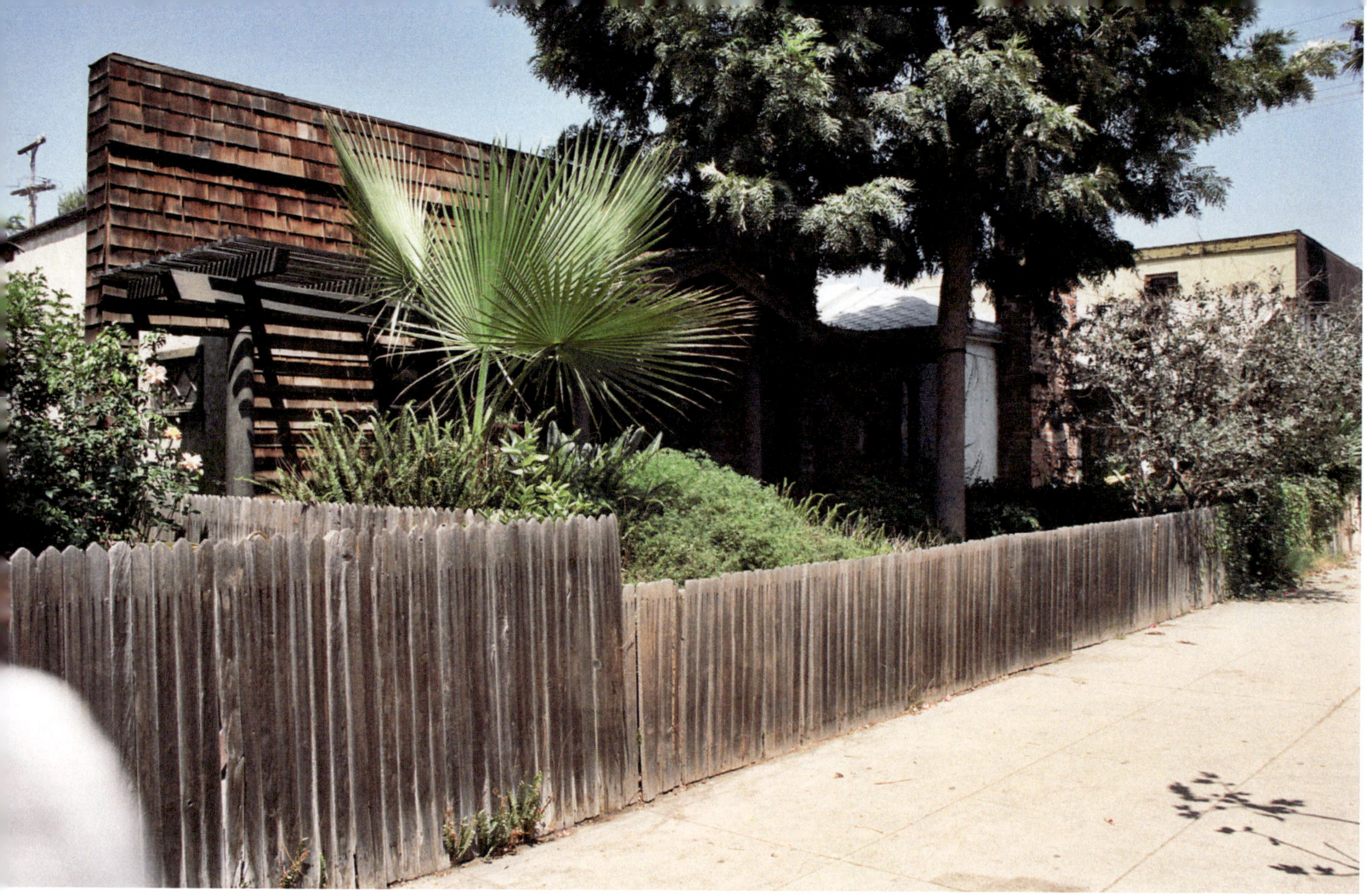

Unlike an historic or architecturally significant structure, affective elements such as space, light, and the interplay of zones of human movement v. landscaped areas are often not noticed until they are destroyed. —Walk Street Preservation Committee

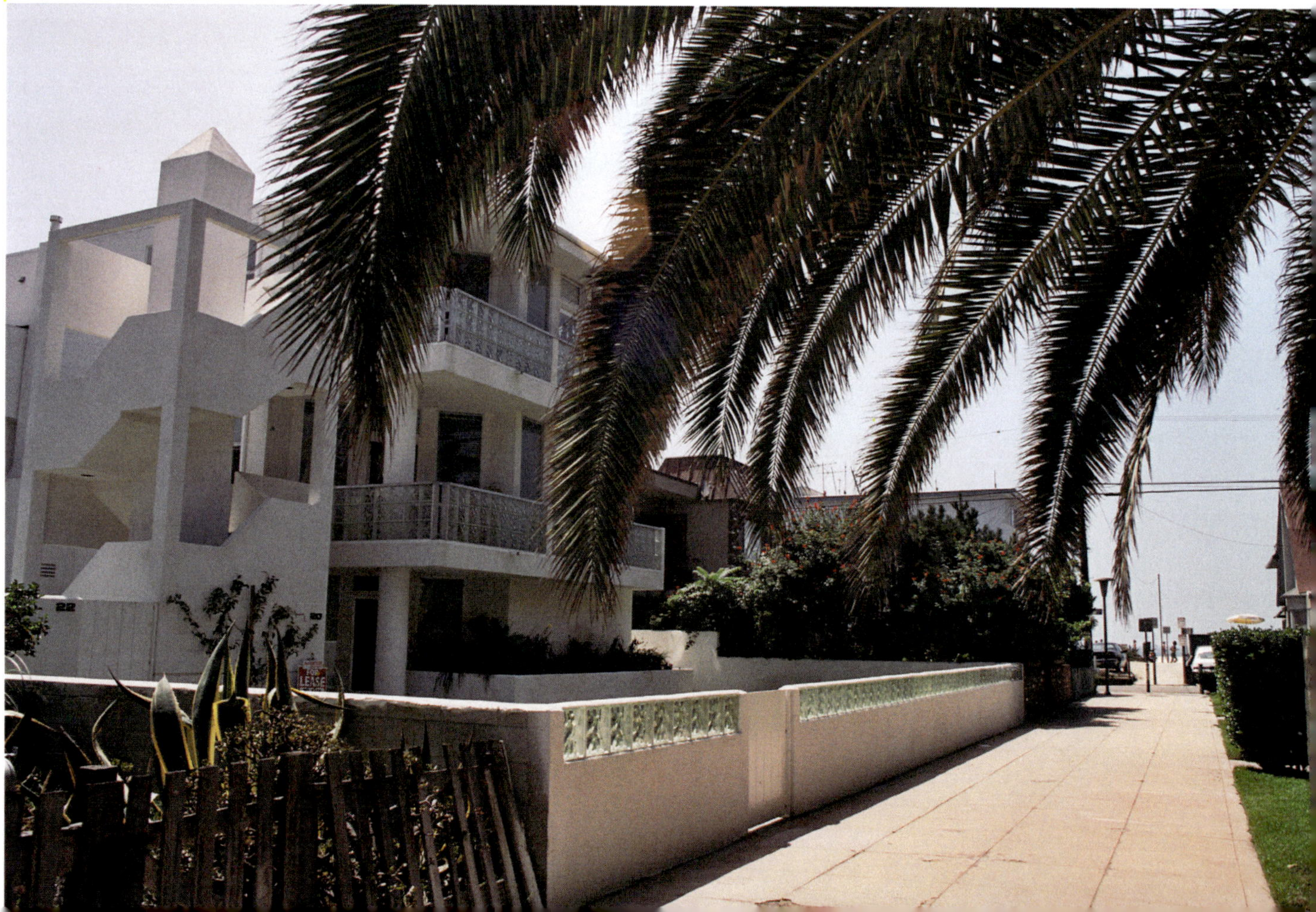

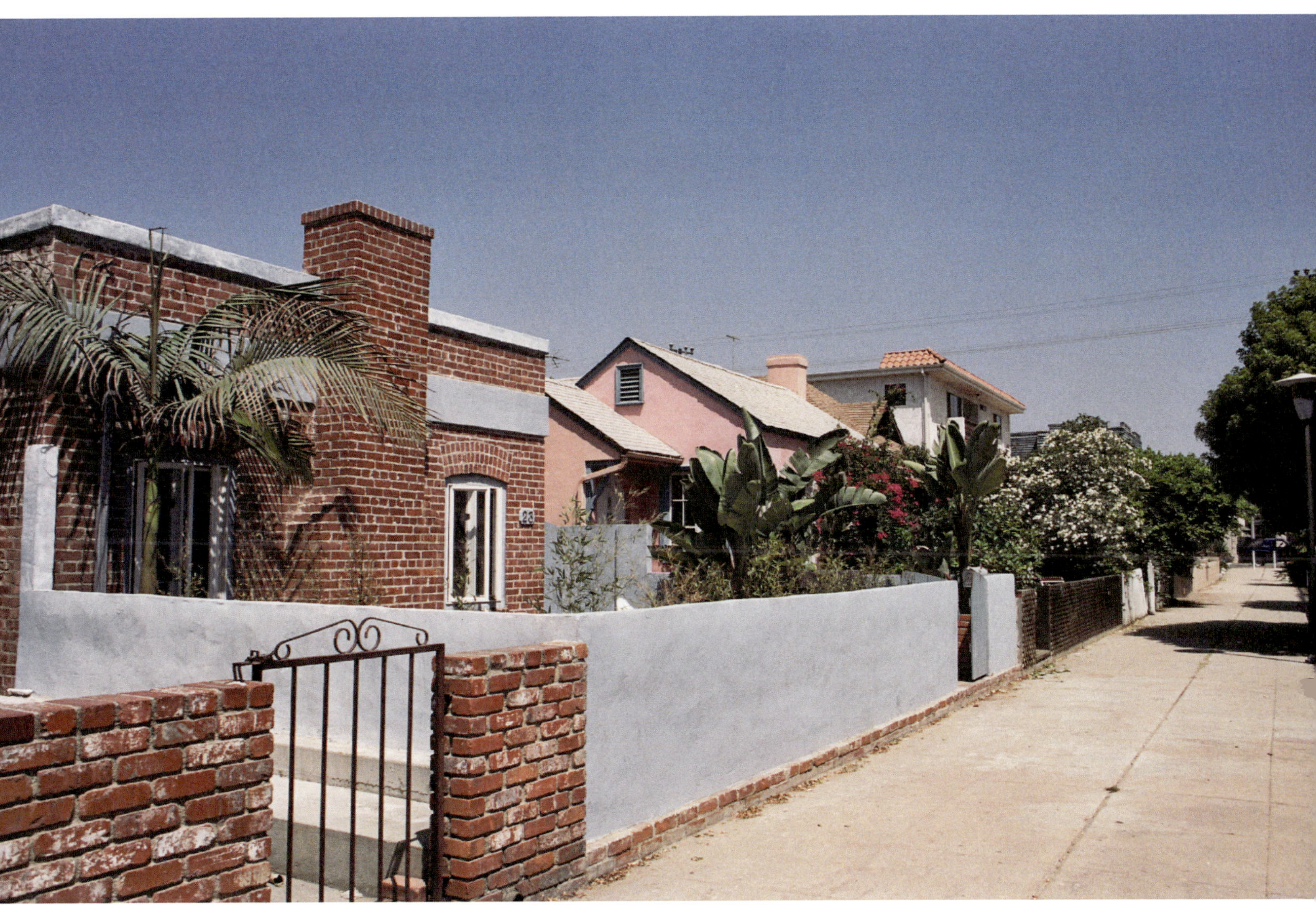

Although many beachfront communities have created entertainment destinations along the oceanfront, Venice is unique in its attempt to adapt a European model: Venice, Italy. Abbott Kinney designed Venice of America as an entertainment district, so the Walk Streets as well as the Boardwalk and the Canals, were configured to facilitate pedestrian access and recreational use. From the beginning, Venice was conceived as a place to be experienced by walking. People arrived by public transportation for the most part, and the automobile was not so pervasive at the beginning of the Century. The residential areas of Milwood and North Beach were intended as vacation homes using neighborhood friendly Eastern seaboard models including porches, low picket fences and welcoming front yards. From the earliest days of its development, Venice was designed as a place to be experienced by walking. Today, Venice continues to be thought of as a pedestrian community – unique within the Los Angeles area. The Walkstreets are a vital part of this ambiance for both residents and tourists. —Betsy Goldman, Venice Historical Society

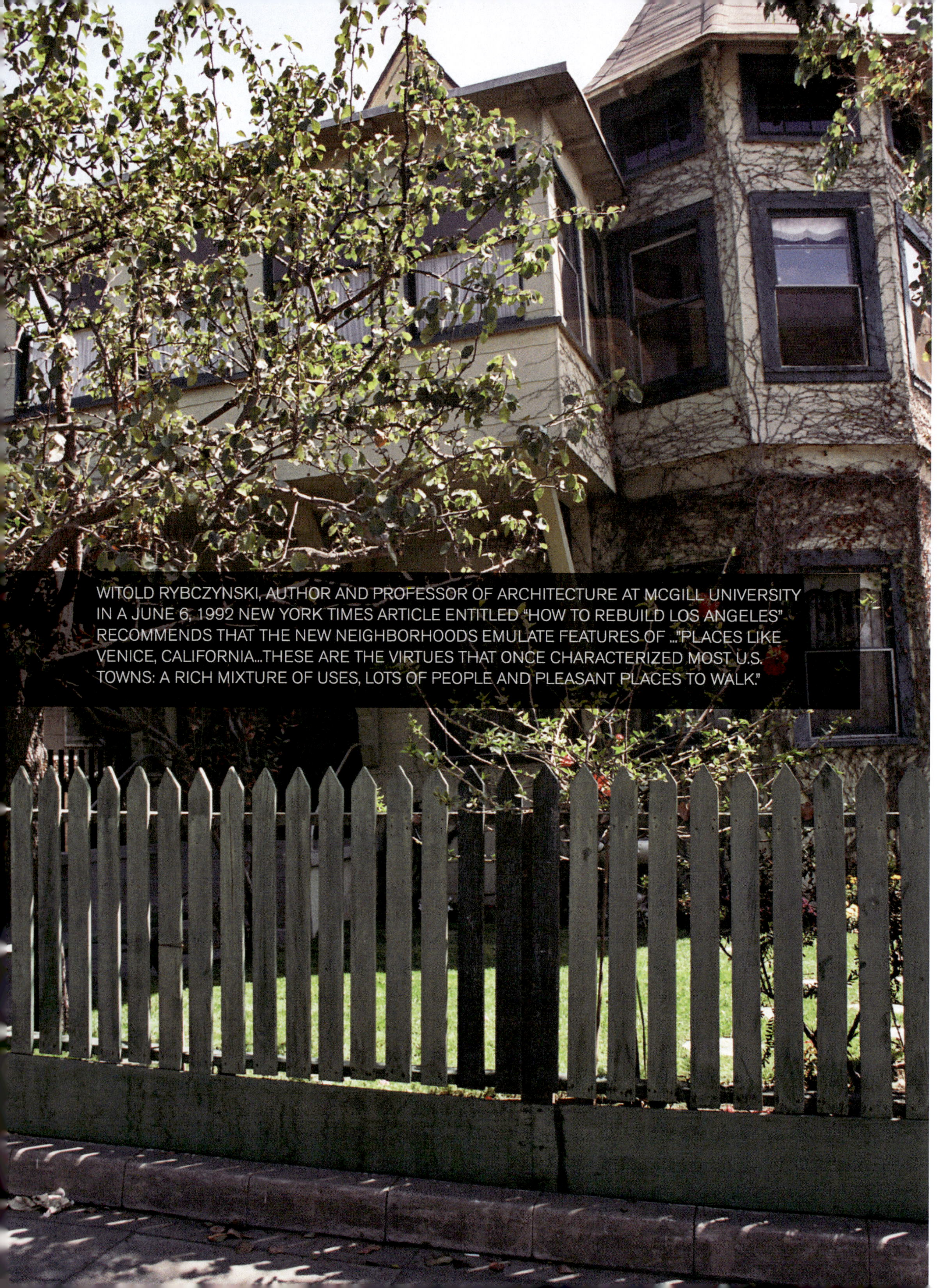

WITOLD RYBCZYNSKI, AUTHOR AND PROFESSOR OF ARCHITECTURE AT MCGILL UNIVERSITY IN A JUNE 6, 1992 NEW YORK TIMES ARTICLE ENTITLED "HOW TO REBUILD LOS ANGELES" RECOMMENDS THAT THE NEW NEIGHBORHOODS EMULATE FEATURES OF ..."PLACES LIKE VENICE, CALIFORNIA...THESE ARE THE VIRTUES THAT ONCE CHARACTERIZED MOST U.S. TOWNS: A RICH MIXTURE OF USES, LOTS OF PEOPLE AND PLEASANT PLACES TO WALK."

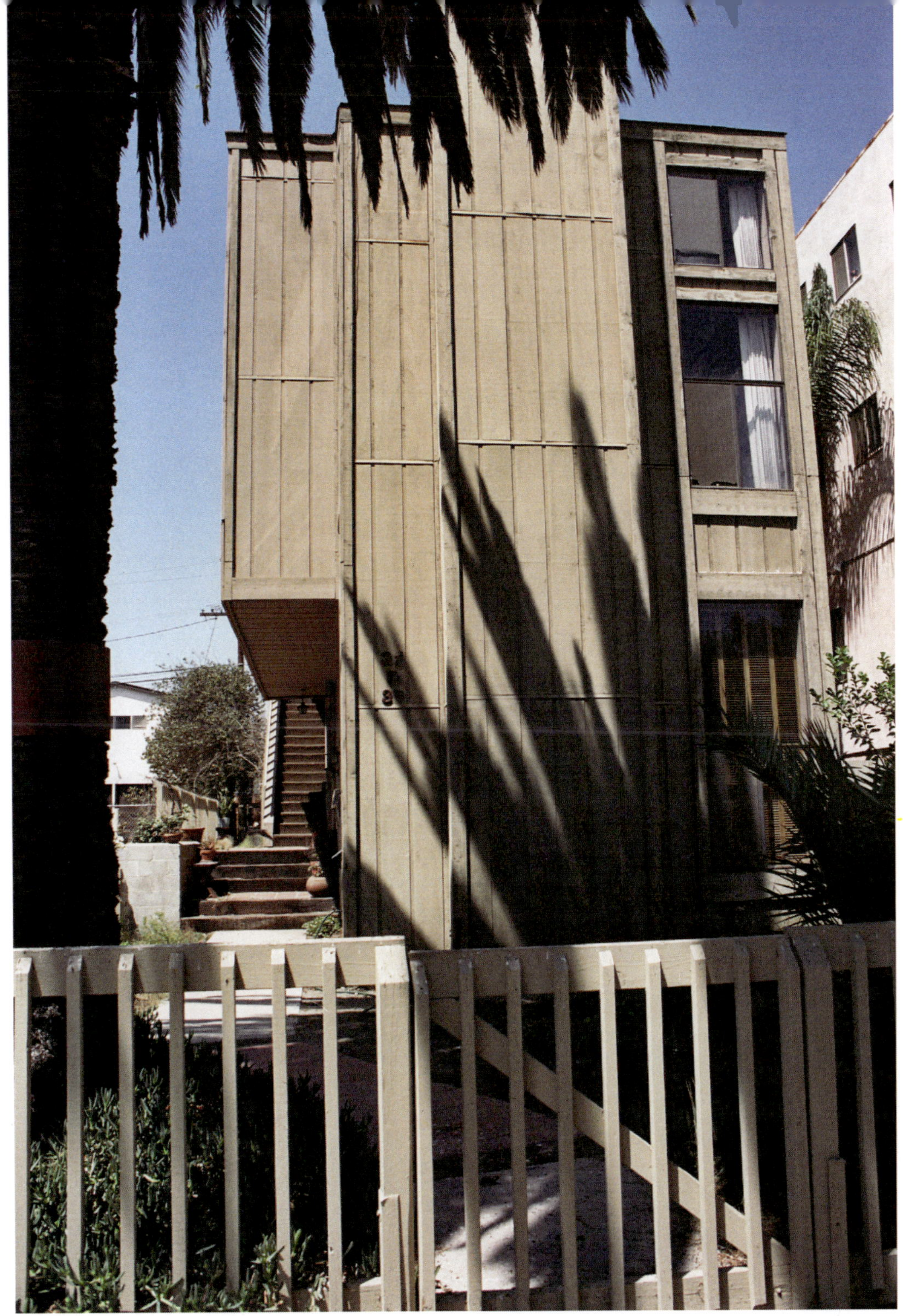

The Walkstreets are a unique contribution to city planning that is
being emulated all over the country by the planning duo of Andres
Duany and Liz Plater-Zyberk and their disciples. This is evidenced
by such rave successes as Seaside, a new development in Vero Beach,
Florida, recently reported in the New York Times and coming soon
to our very own Playa Vista neighborhood. These new communities
are founded on such radical ideas for urban neighborhoods as safe
streets, pedestrian environment — being able to walk no more than
five minutes to shopping, restaurants, entertainment, or transit —
and devices such as a notion of street wall and massing and fences
that are not visual and social barriers. In short, they are out
there proselytizing for a decidedly old style community, which we
already have , and the values which it instills by virtue of its
quality of life. —Dell Chumley, Walk Street Preservation Committee

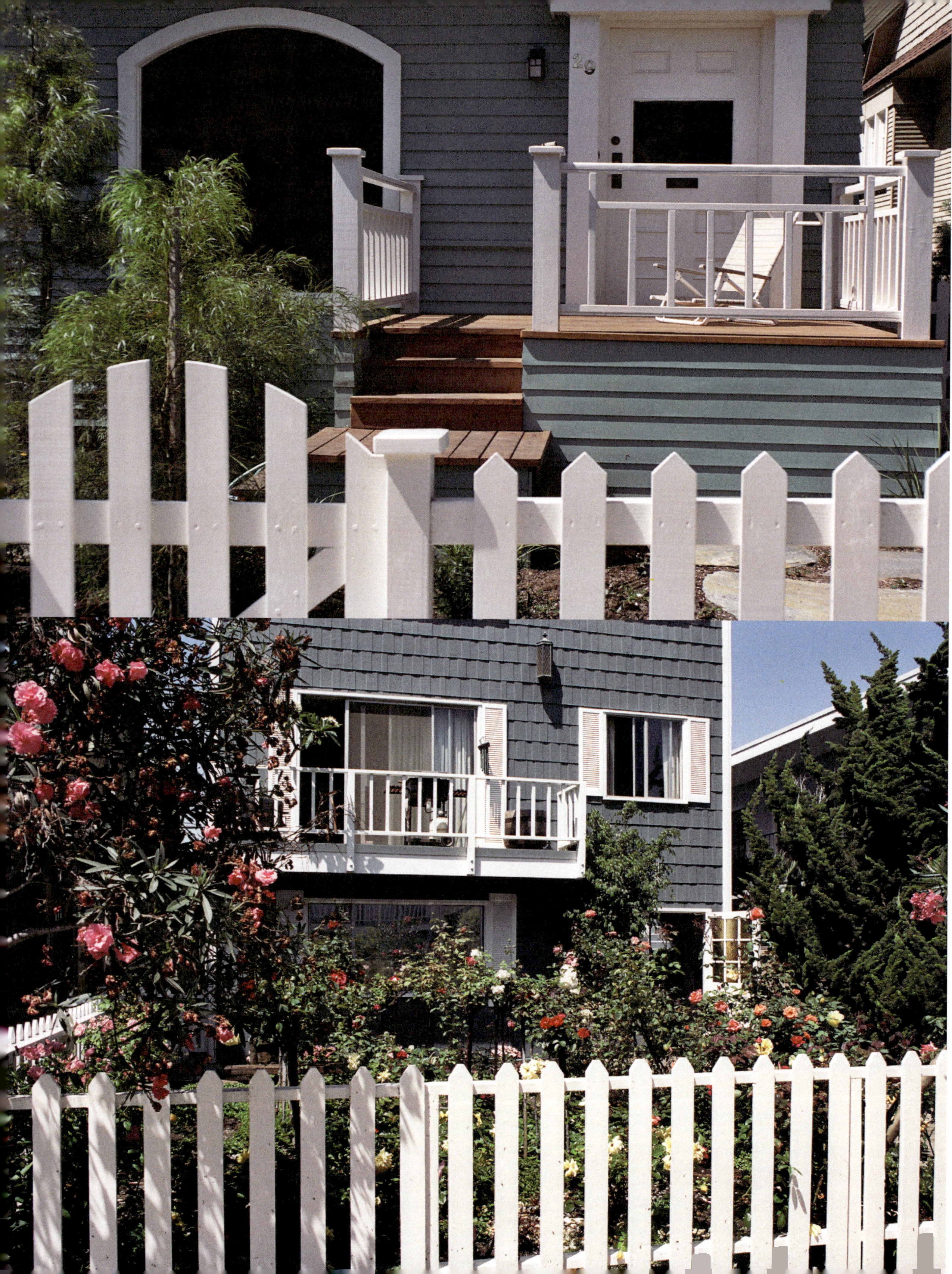

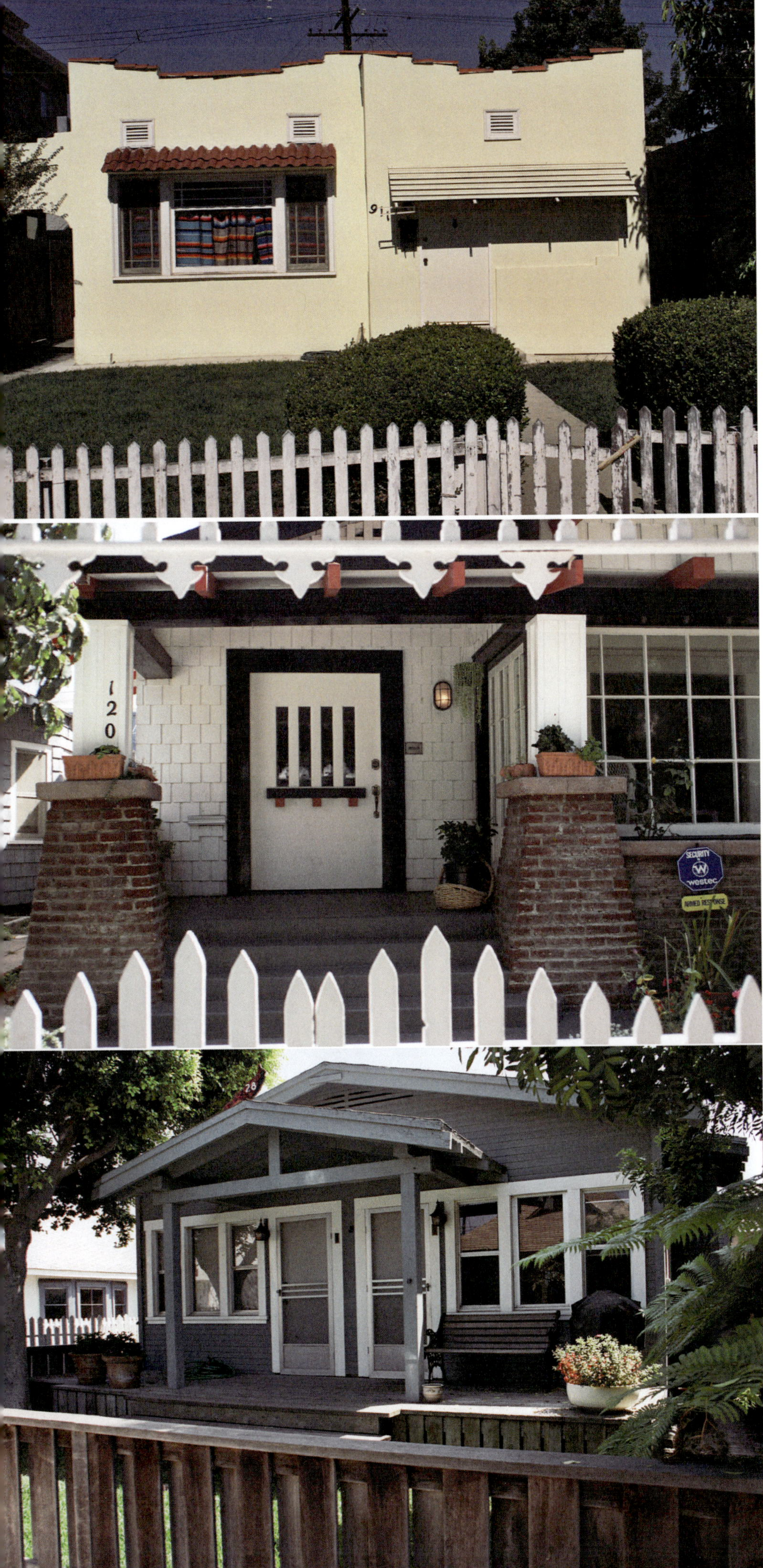

...IT IS ALSO, EVEN MORE, ABOUT CREATING A TOWN THAT FEELS LIKE A TOWN, WHERE PEOPLE LEAN ON THEIR FENCES TO CHAT, SIT ON THEIR PORCHES, WALK, MEET AND TALK ON THE STREET AND GATHER IN COMMON PLACES AS THEY DID A CENTURY AGO. SAYS ELIZABETH PLATER-ZYBERK, WHO WITH HER PARTNER AND HUSBAND ANDRES DUANY DEVISED THE TOWN'S [SEASIDE, FLORIDA] BASIC PLAN, 'THE FENCE, THE WALKWAY, THE SCREEN PORCH, CREATE AN ELABORATION OF CEREMONY. YOU HAVE A CHOICE OF REALMS RANGING IN INCREMENTS FROM THE PUBLIC TO THE MOST PRIVATE'.

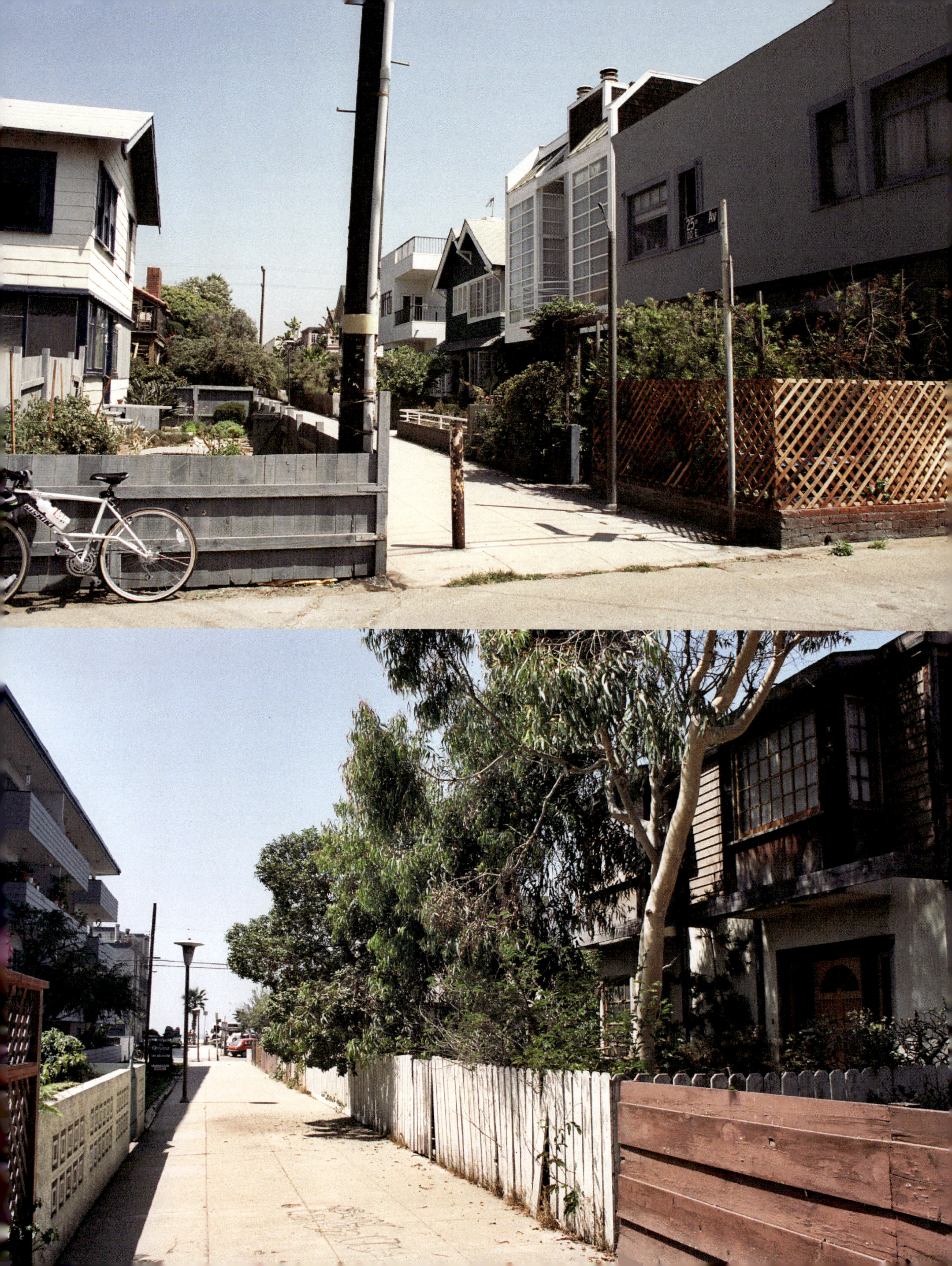

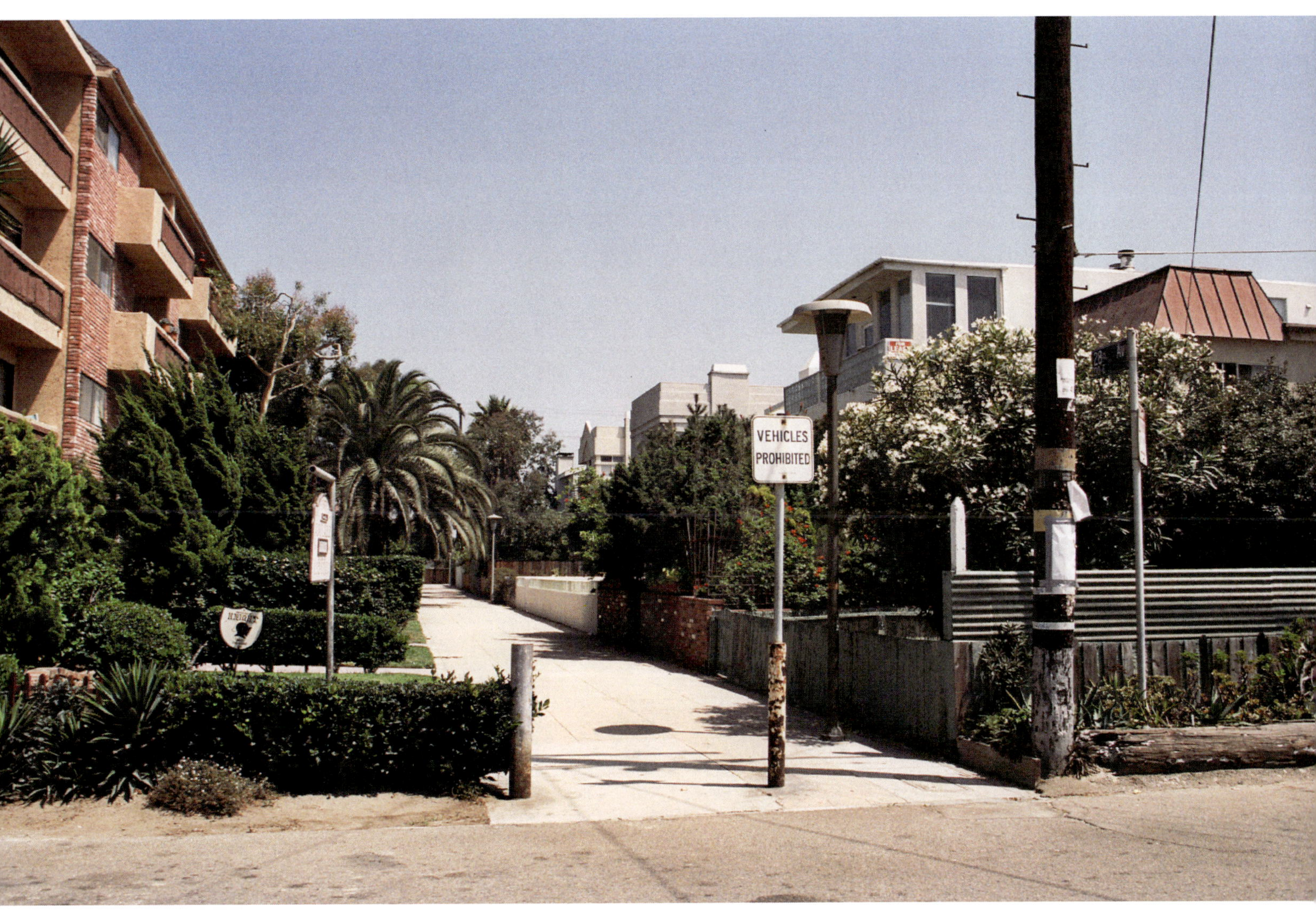

I moved to Venice to find things that are in short supply
in Los Angeles — neighborhood spirit, residential
aesthetic beauty and a more relaxed ambience. These rare
and irreplaceable qualities are all directly contingent on
having intimate narrow walkstreets. If the walkstreets are
widened, these unique qualities of the neighborhood will
soon vanish.

...the walkstreets provide a unique setting to escape the
hustle-and-bustle of Los Angeles in general and although
chaos may exist on the boardwalk and on Main and Pacific
Streets, the walkstreets remain peaceful and quiet. This
vital escape would be destroyed by widening the walkways.
—Jens Koepke

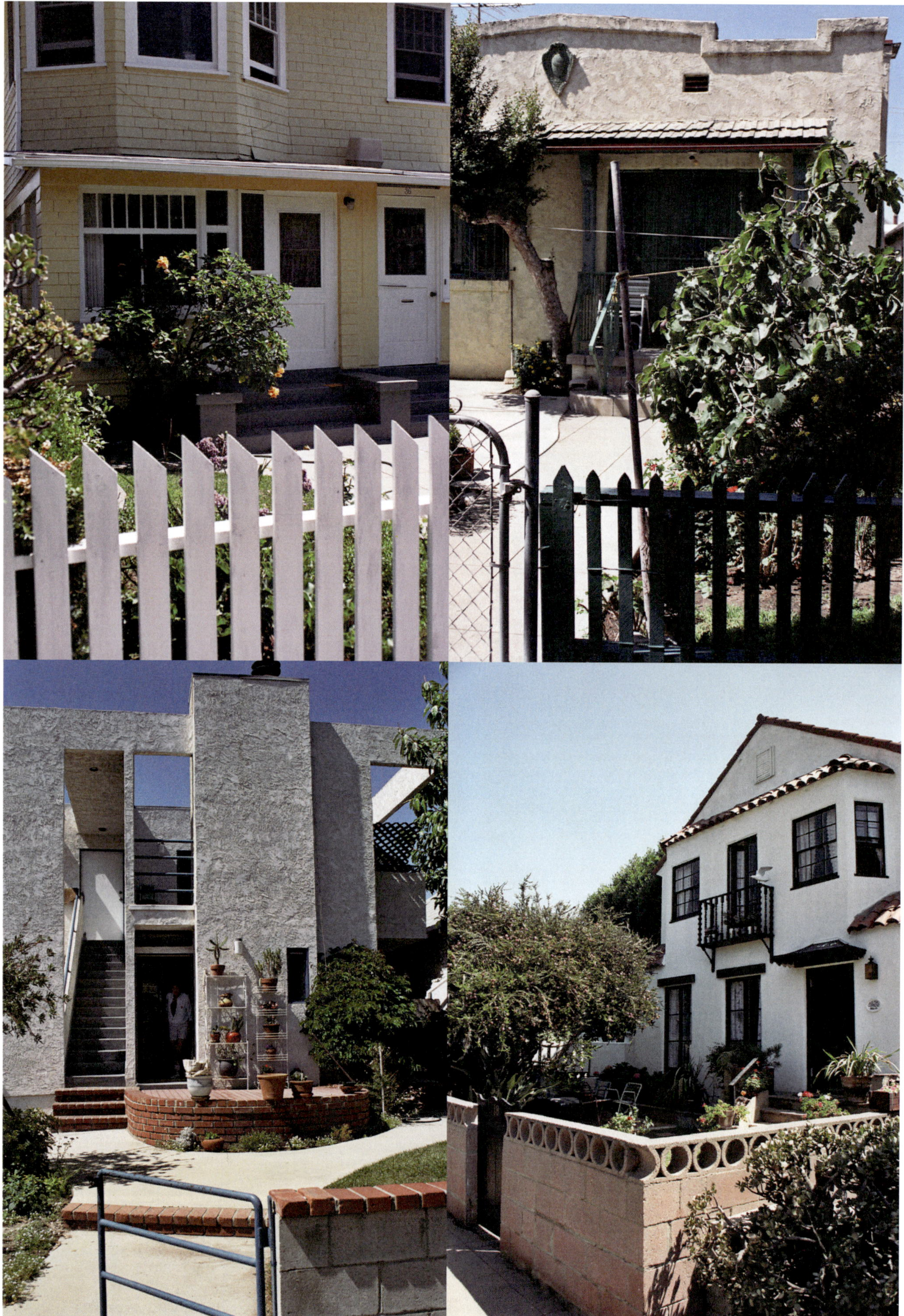

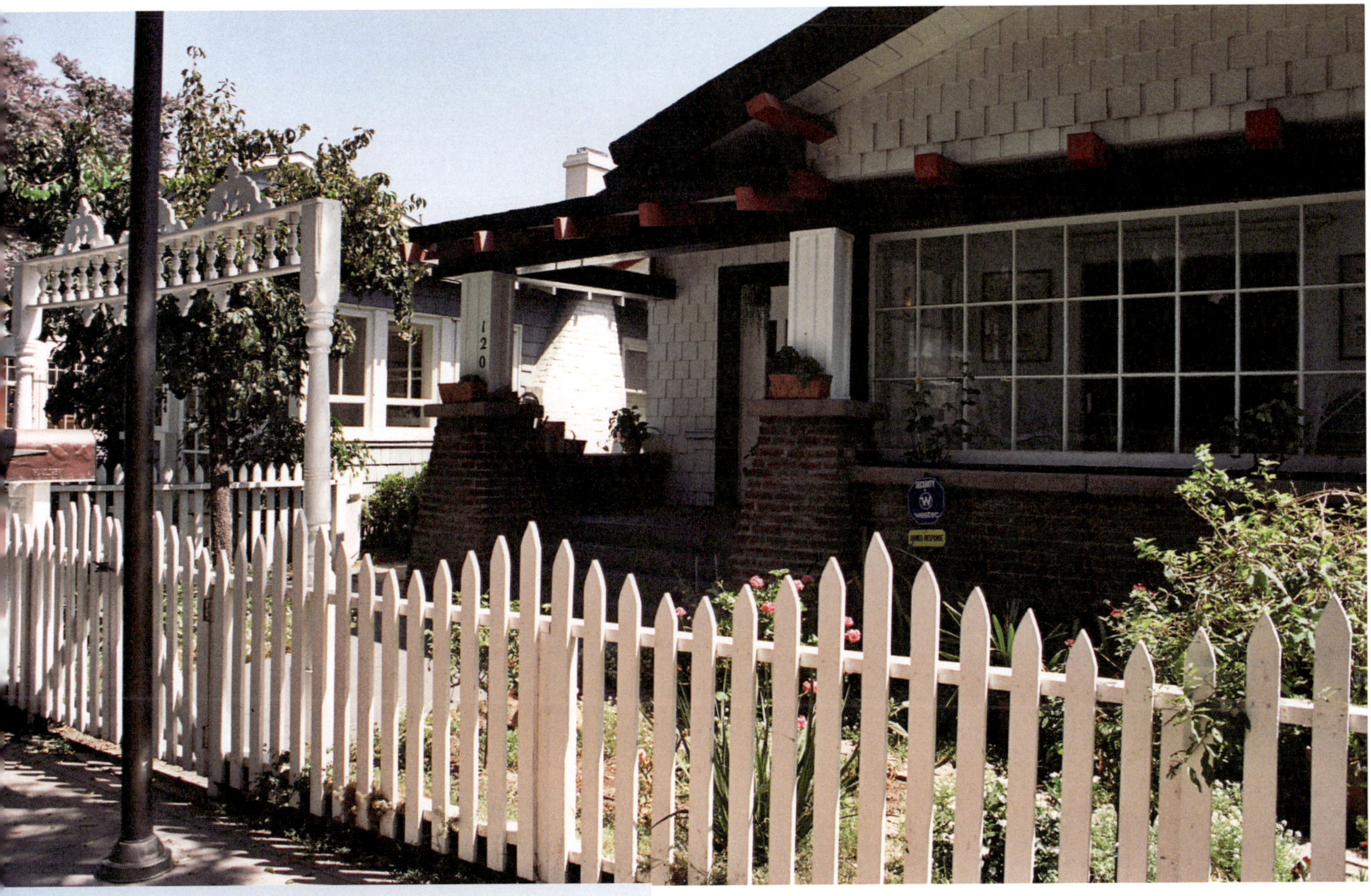

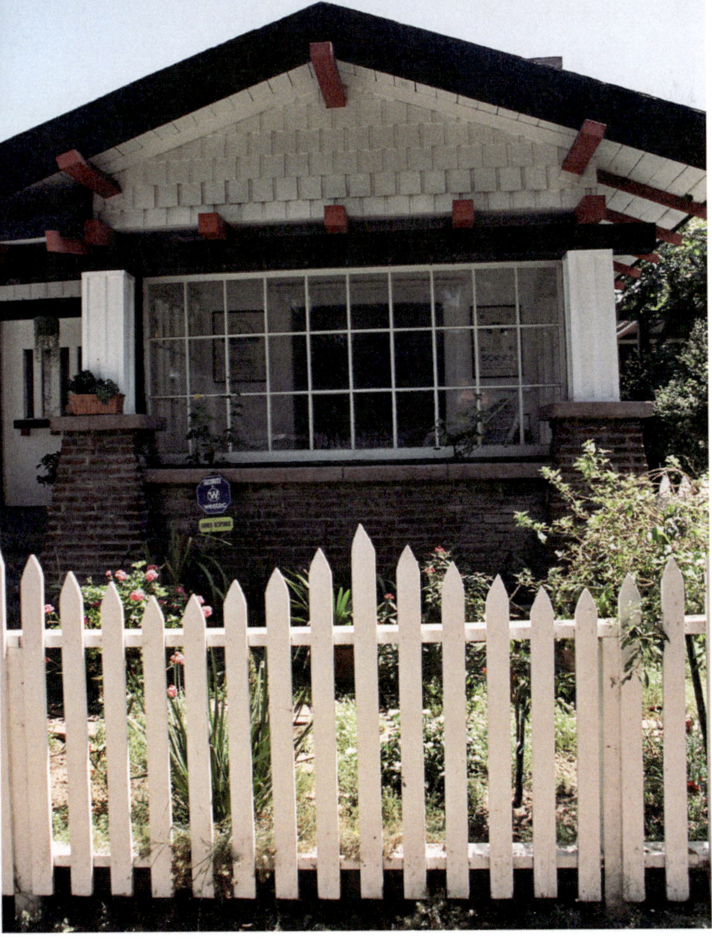

I was horrified to learn of the possibility
that Venice's walk streets could be
obliterated. I have lived in Venice for
over twenty years. The walk streets are
the heart of my community within the
traditional anonymity of most of Los
Angeles, Venice is a unique haven, a tight
knit community, to a large degree the
"plan" of the walk streets enables this
tight knit to come about. The size of the
walks and the space between houses brings
neighbors to their street for socializing.
The absence of traffic other than at a
foot pace makes the streets an ocean
of tranquility.

Numerous new forms are planned around what
Venice has already. The Atlantic Monthly
last year outlined many of these, and
I have enclosed an article about Seaside,
Florida from the current issue of The
Smithsonian. There are lots of things
needing change in L.A. – the walk streets
of Venice need preserving. –Mark Schoul

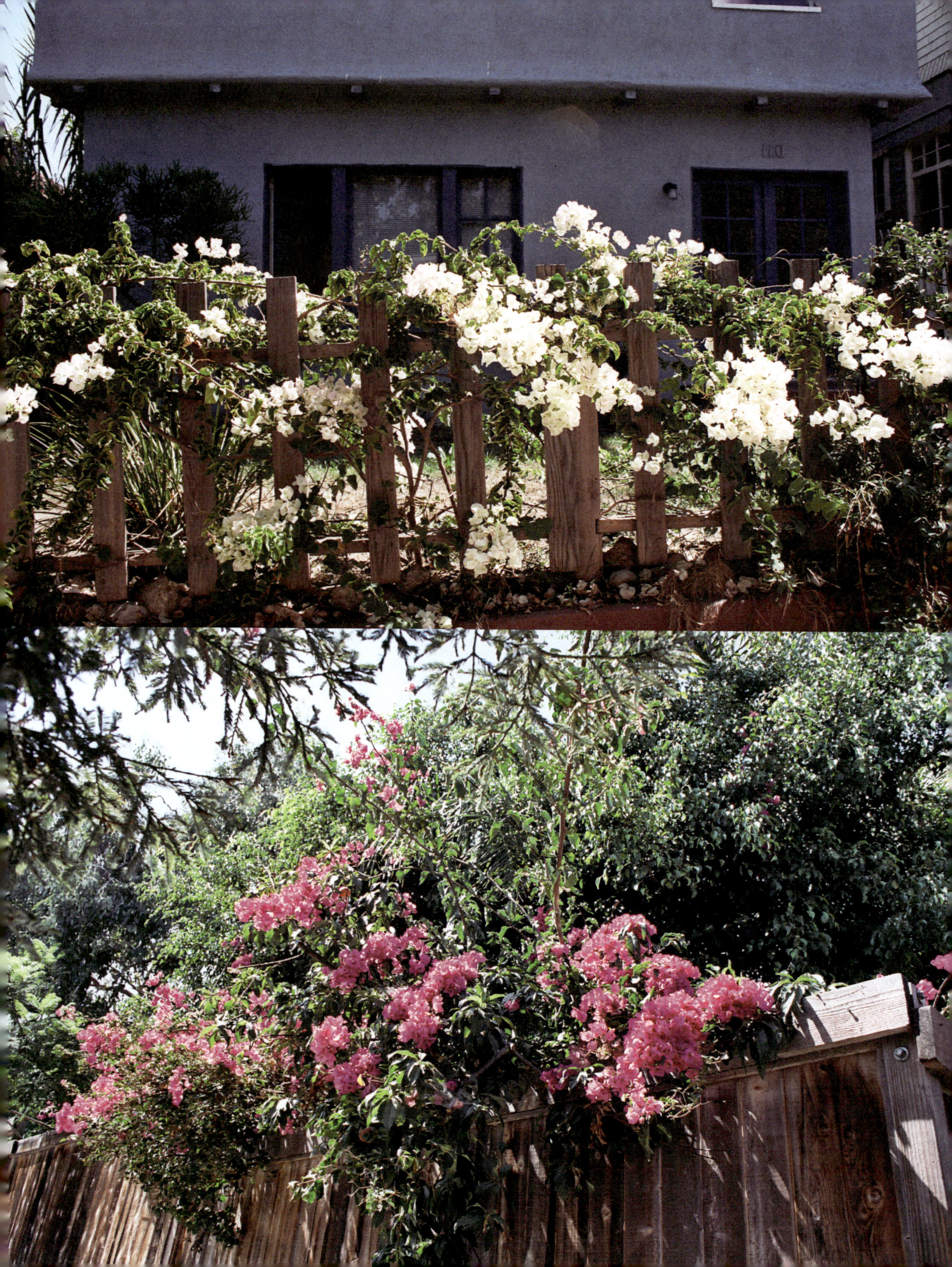

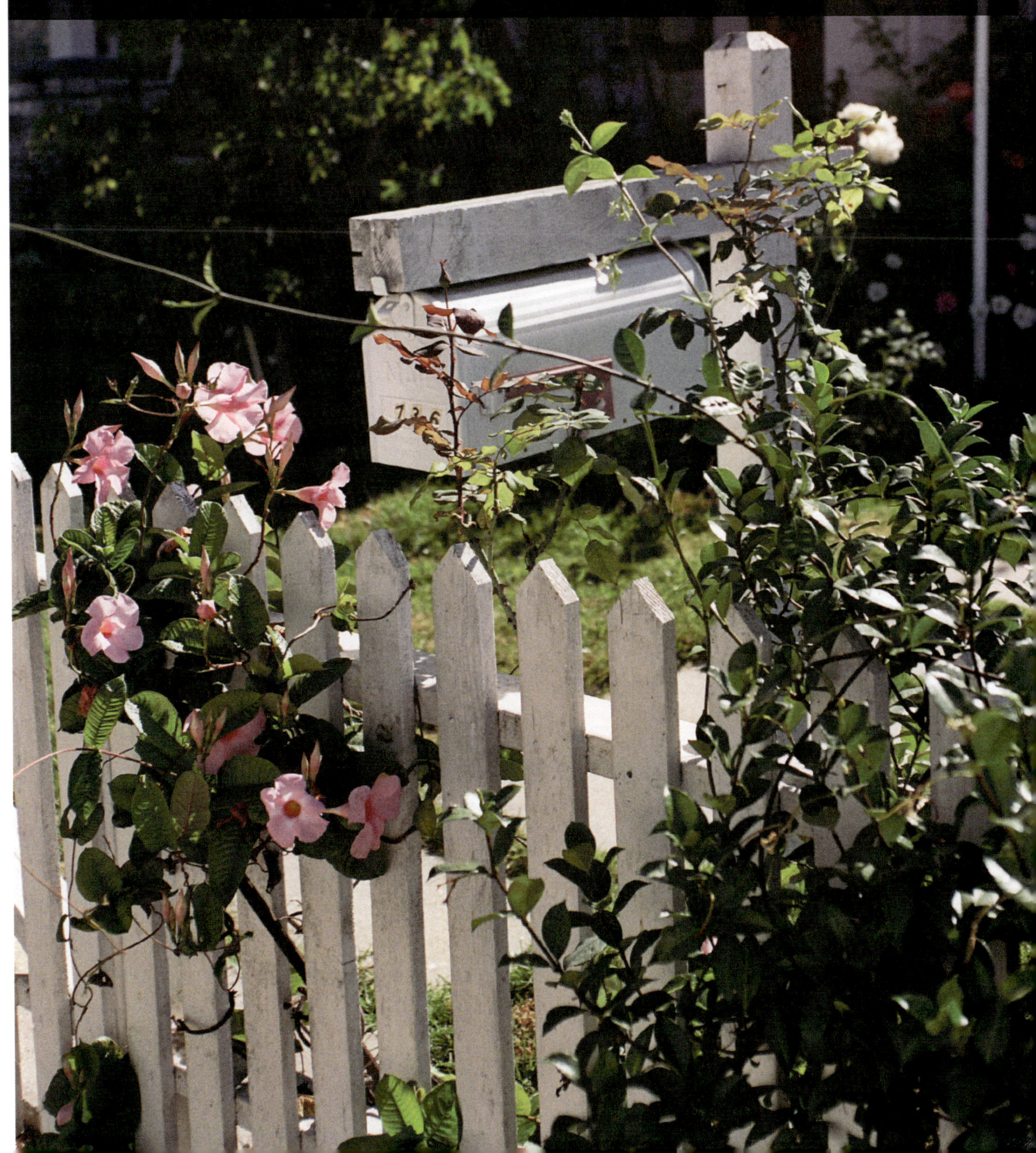
DUANY AND PLATER-ZYBERK'S TRADITIONAL NEIGHBORHOOD DEVELOPMENTS ARE BASED ON REGIONAL AND VERNACULAR MODELS. THEY BOAST TREE-LINED STREETS, SIDEWALKS THAT STIMULATE STROLLING, PICKET FENCES THAT DEMARCATE THE PRIVATE REALM, ALLEYS THAT CONCEAL GARAGES AND TRASH RECEPTACLES, AND NEIGHBORHOOD STORE, TRANSPORTATION, AND OTHER CONVENIENCES THAT ARE NO MORE THAN A FIVE-MINUTE WALK FROM HOME. -ANDREA OPPENHEIMER DEAN, "ANDRES DUANY AND ELIZABETH PLATER-ZYBERK'S EMBRACE OF TRADITIONAL COMMUNITY PLANNING ISN'T JUST NOSTALGIC, IT'S INTELLIGENT", HISTORIC PRESERVATION, THE MAGAZINE

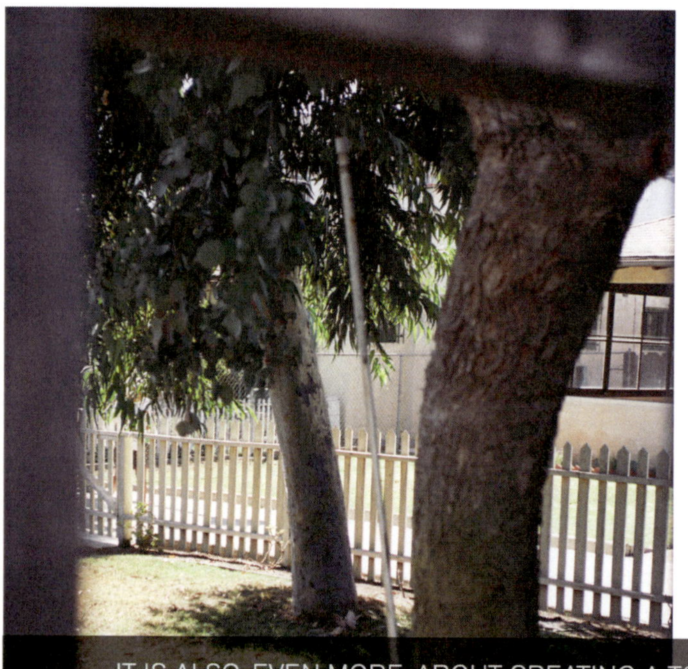
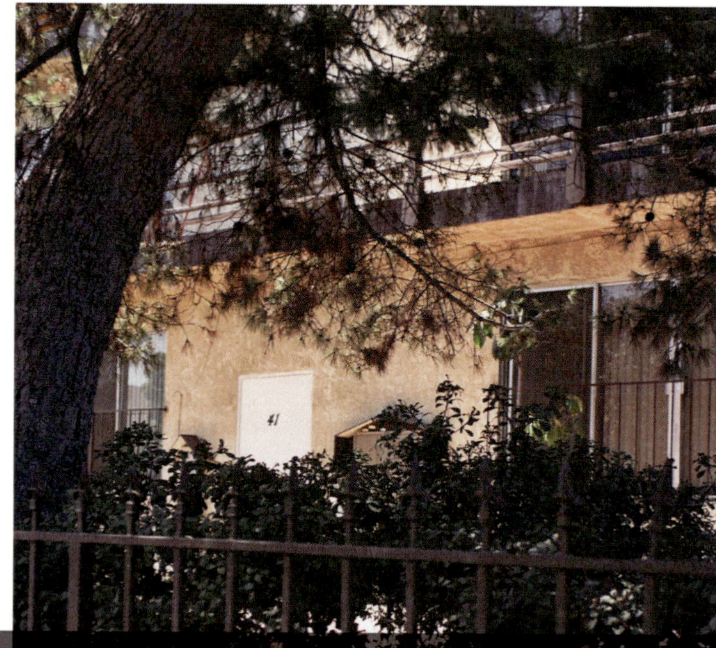

..IT IS ALSO, EVEN MORE, ABOUT CREATING A TOWN THAT FEELS LIKE A TOWN, WHERE PEOPLE LEAN ON THEIR FENCES TO CHAT, SIT ON THEIR PORCHES, WALK, MEET AND TALK ON THE STREET AND GATHER IN COMMON PLACES AS THEY DID A CENTURY AGO. SAYS ELIZABETH PLATER-ZYBERK, WHO WITH HER PARTNER AND HUSBAND ANDRES DUANY DEVISED THE TOWN'S [SEASIDE, FLORIDA] BASIC PLAN, 'THE FENCE, THE WALKWAY, THE SCREEN PORCH, CREATE AN ELABORATION OF CEREMONY. YOU HAVE A CHOICE OF REALMS RANGING IN INCREMENTS FROM THE PUBLIC TO THE MOST PRIVATE'.

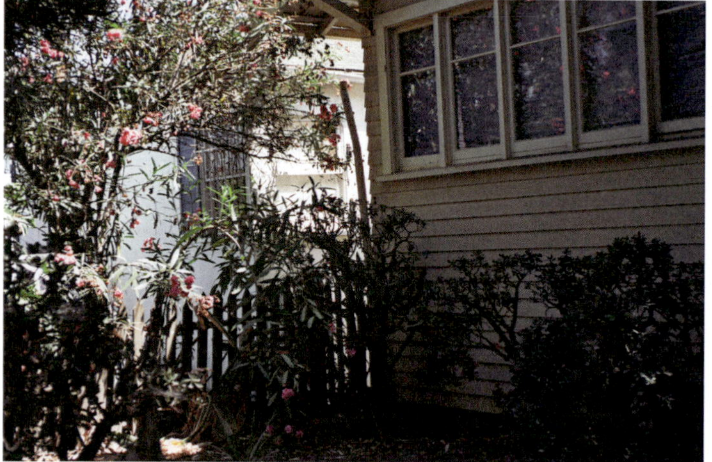
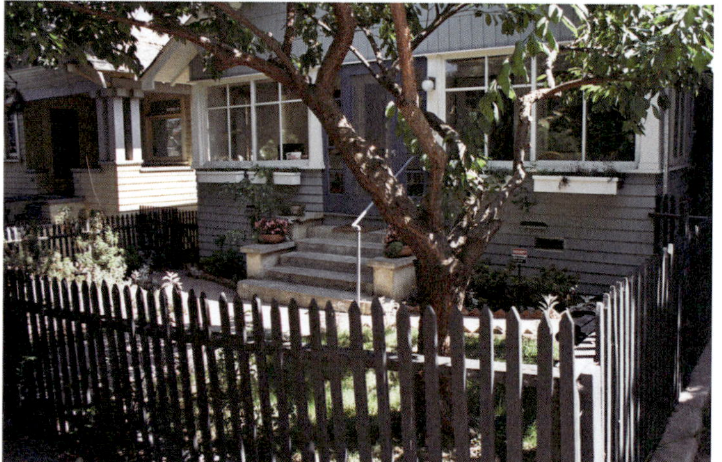
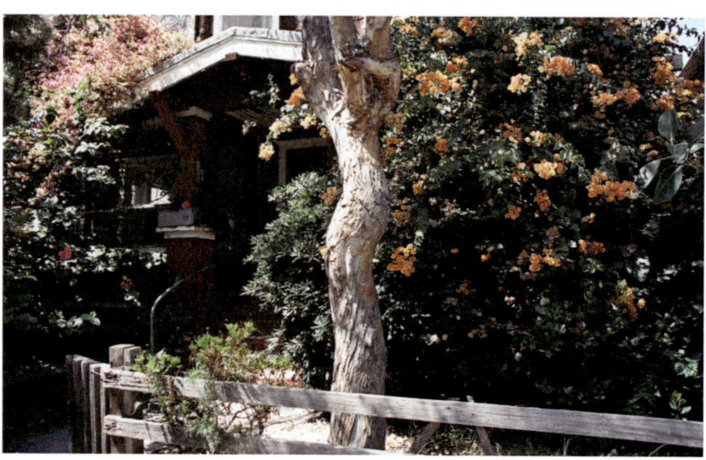
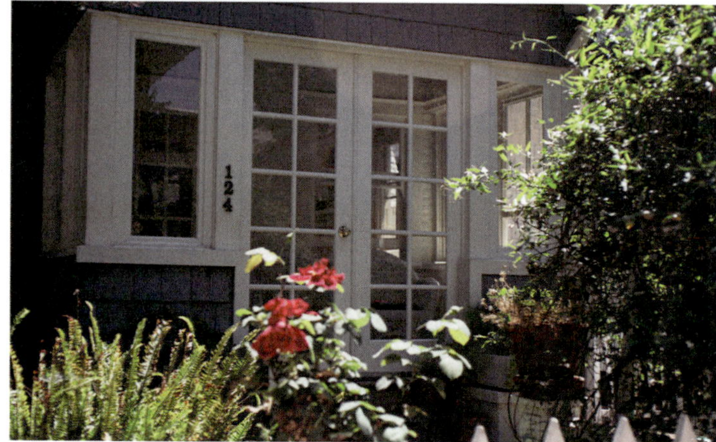

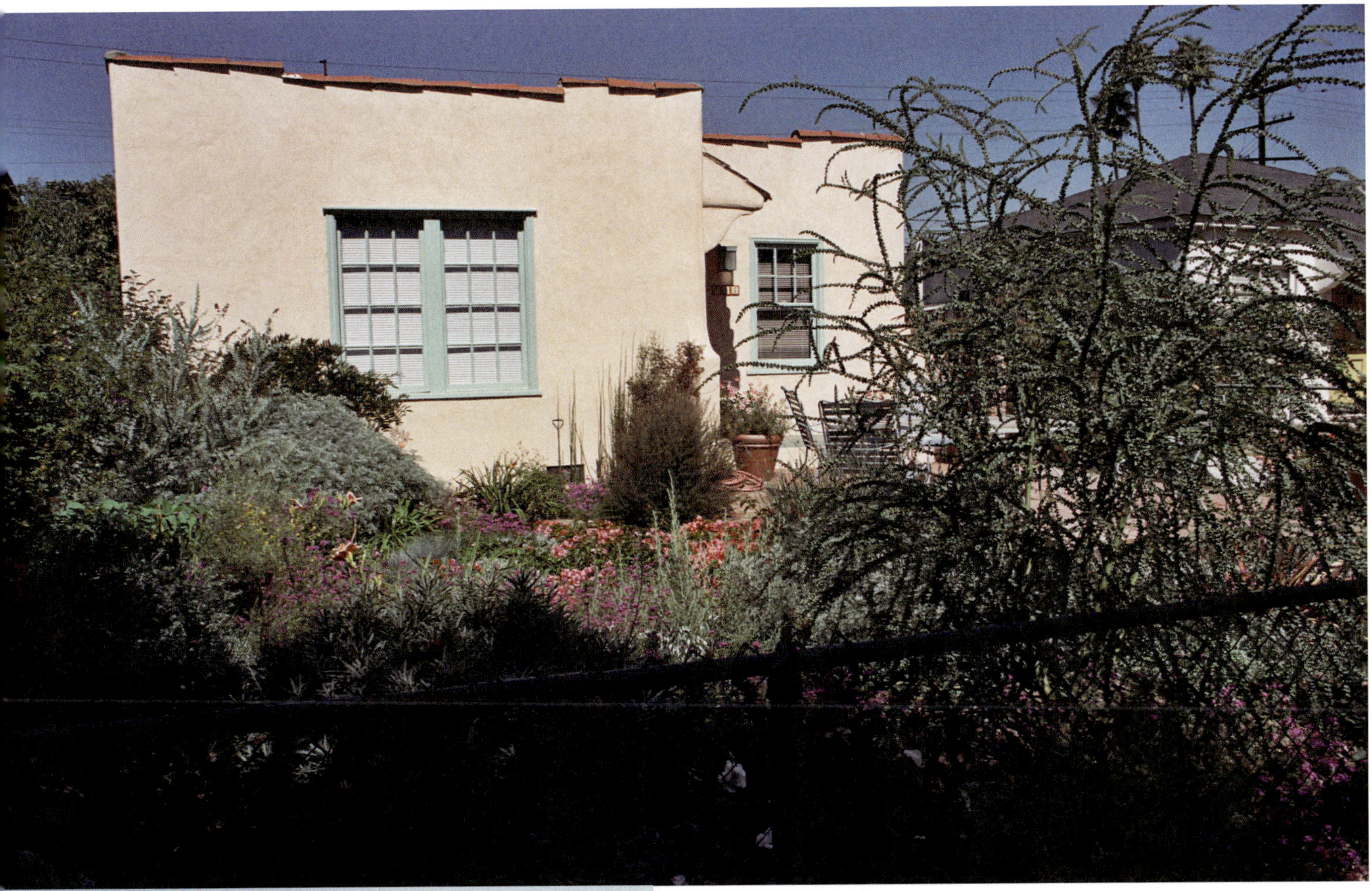

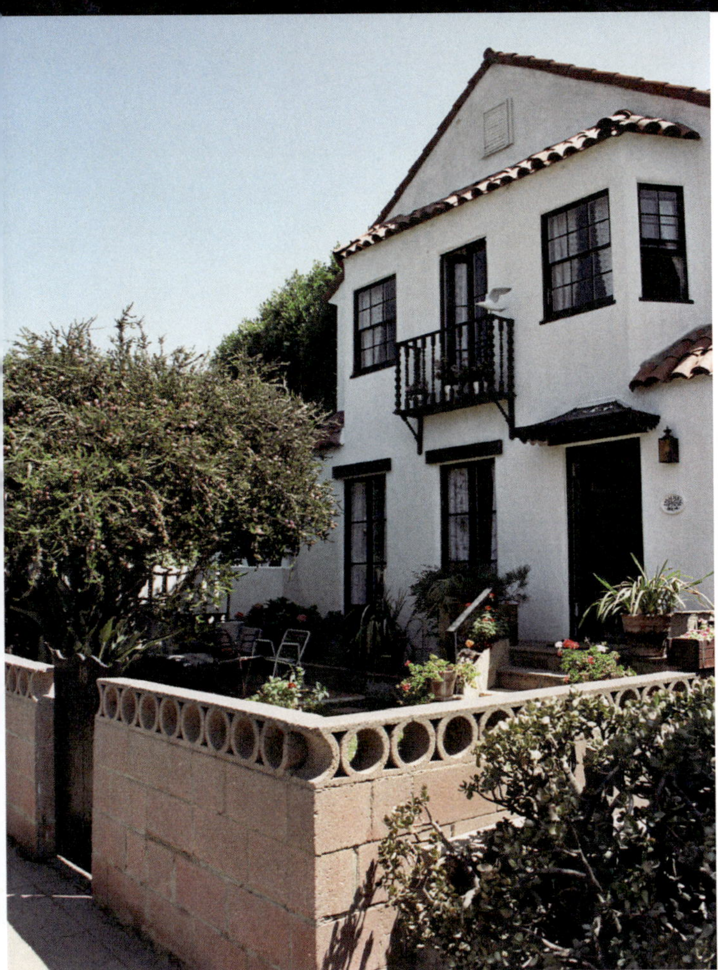

To the Planning Commission: "I would like
to invite yourself and board members to
visit our Walkstreet, and determine what
qualities comprise the "character" of
this neighborhood. I believe you will
see that its character, charm, civility,
indeed its desirability as an Urban
Design is directly a consequence of the
current walkway width, the attendant
fences and gardens. It is the successful
proportion of walk way to waist-high fence
to garden width to house facade, that
marks and creates the unique character
of a walk street. To double the width of
the walkway, to remove all the trees, to
diminish the already minimal front gardens
is to destroy the very "character" you
wish to preserve. —Joseph C. Schogardhod

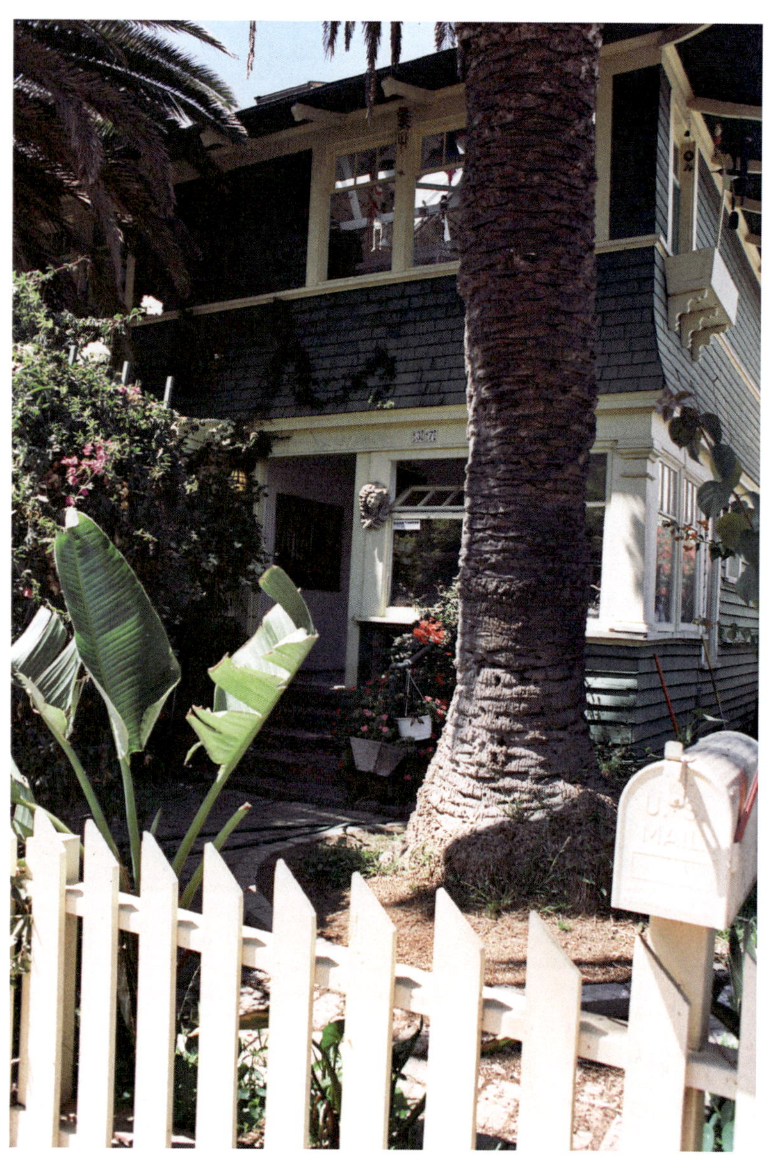

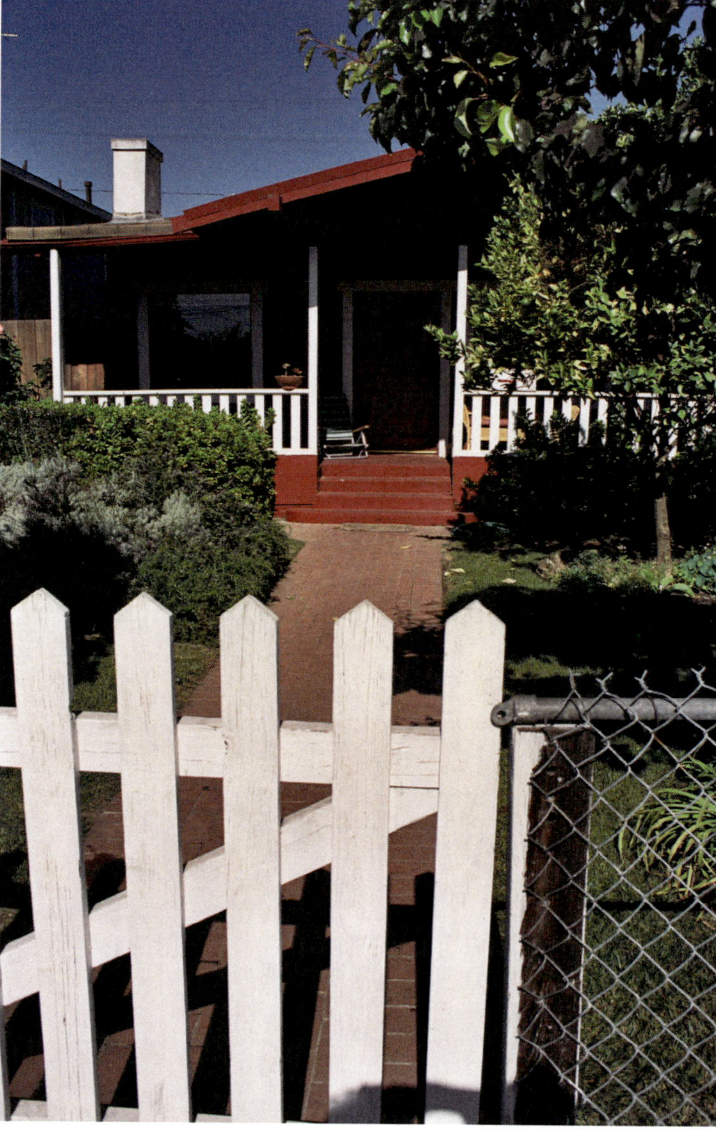

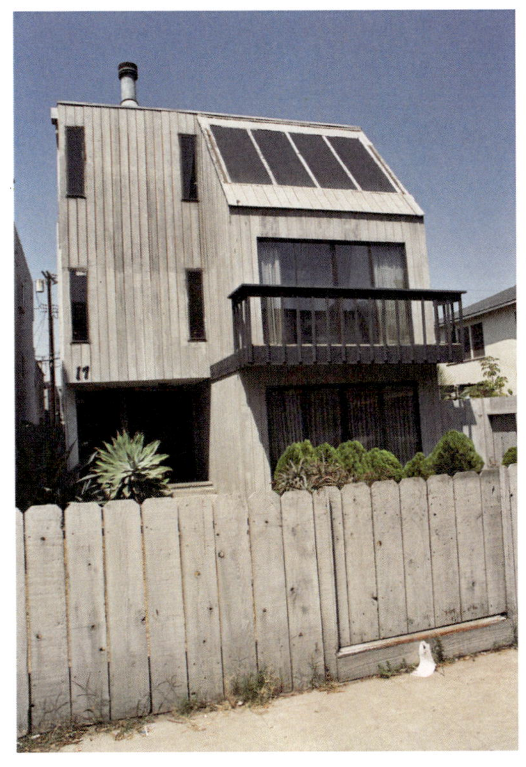

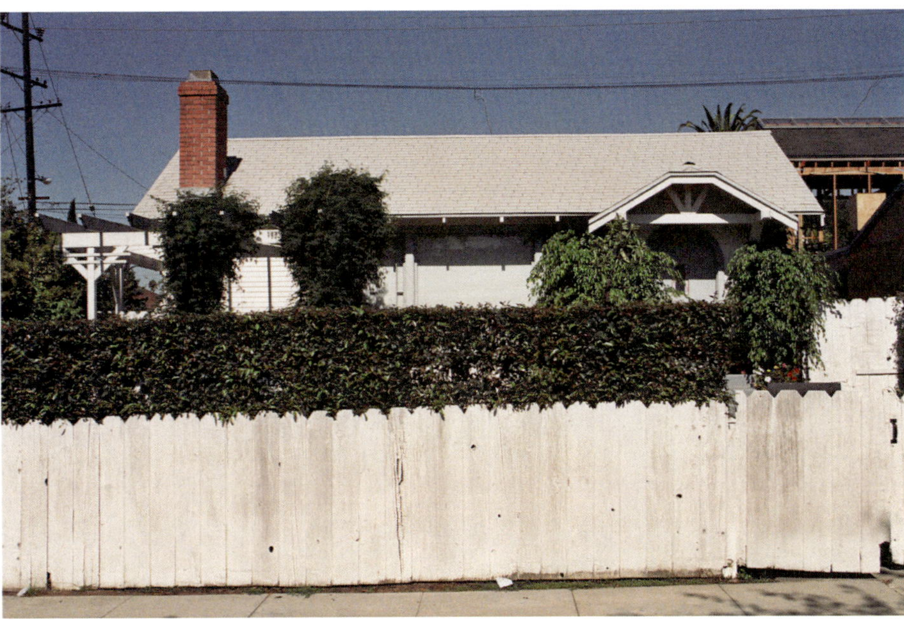

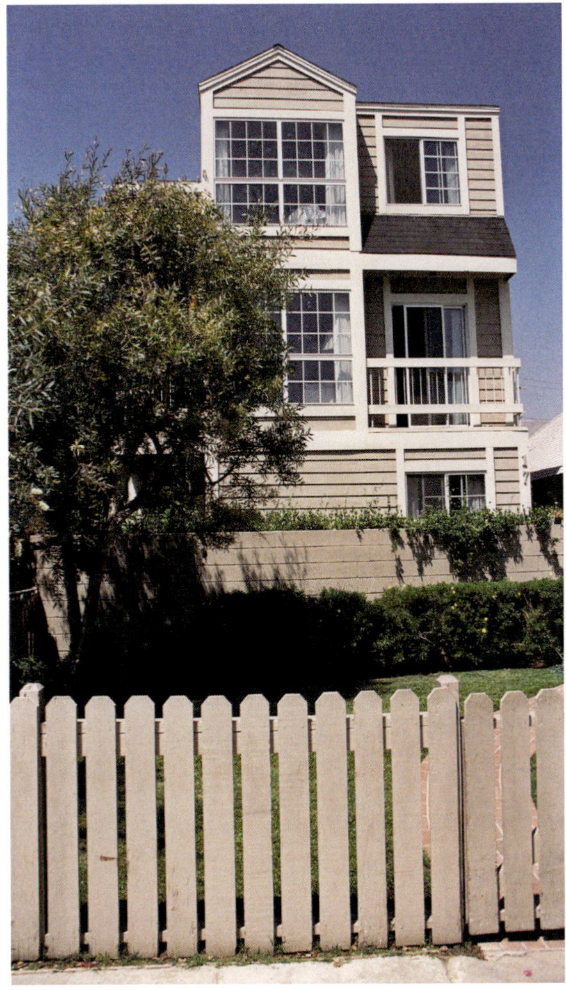

The Walkstreets not only
provide the City with a
historical setting, they
set an example for future
community development. In
our fast paced society,
walkstreet communities
maintain the old standard of
the neighborhood --- a place
where the young and old can
walk, where neighbors can
congregate and share ideas,
where children can play and
safely ride their tricycles.
-Phylis Korn

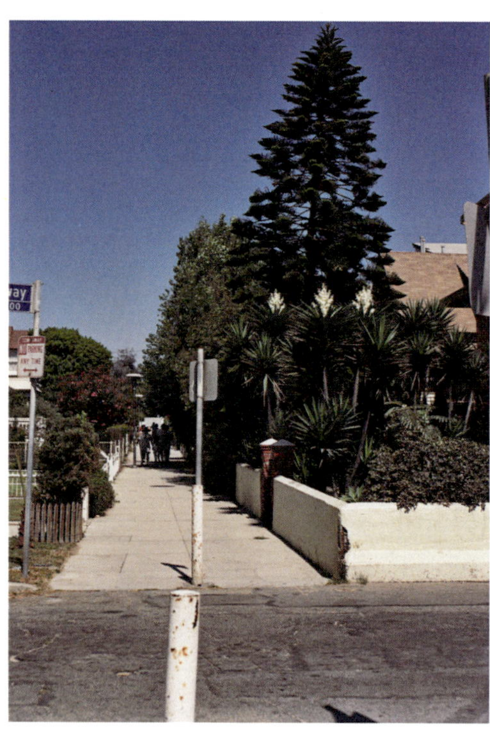 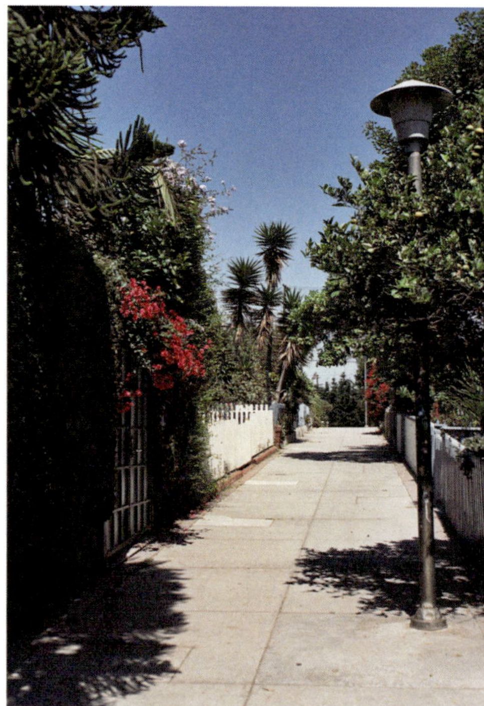 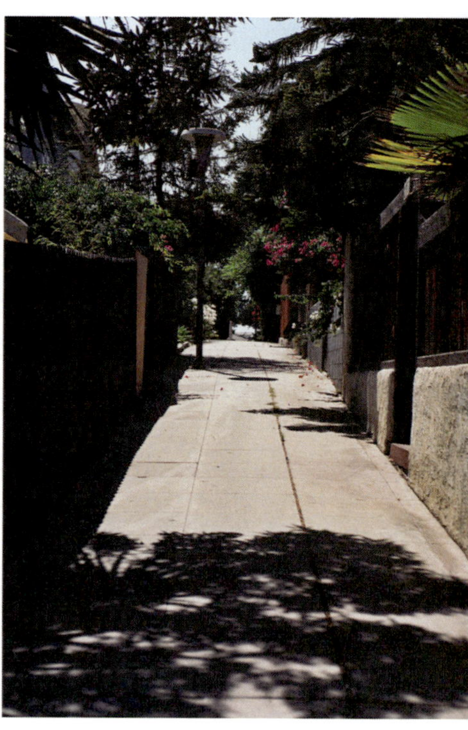

"VISITORS SHOULD BE ACCOMMODATED WITHOUT INAPPROPRIATELY INTERFERING WITH A LOCALITY'S ESSENTIAL FLOW AND FUNCTION BUT AN ESSENTIAL CHARACTERISTIC OF A CITY IS THE EXISTENCE OF A MULTIPLICITY OF USES WHOSE CONTINUATION DEPENDS ON ONE ANOTHER. THIS IMPLIES BALANCE. A BALANCE IN FAVOR OF LOCAL USES AND USERS MAKES THE MOST SENSE."
-ROBERTA BRANDES GRATZ, THE LIVING CITY

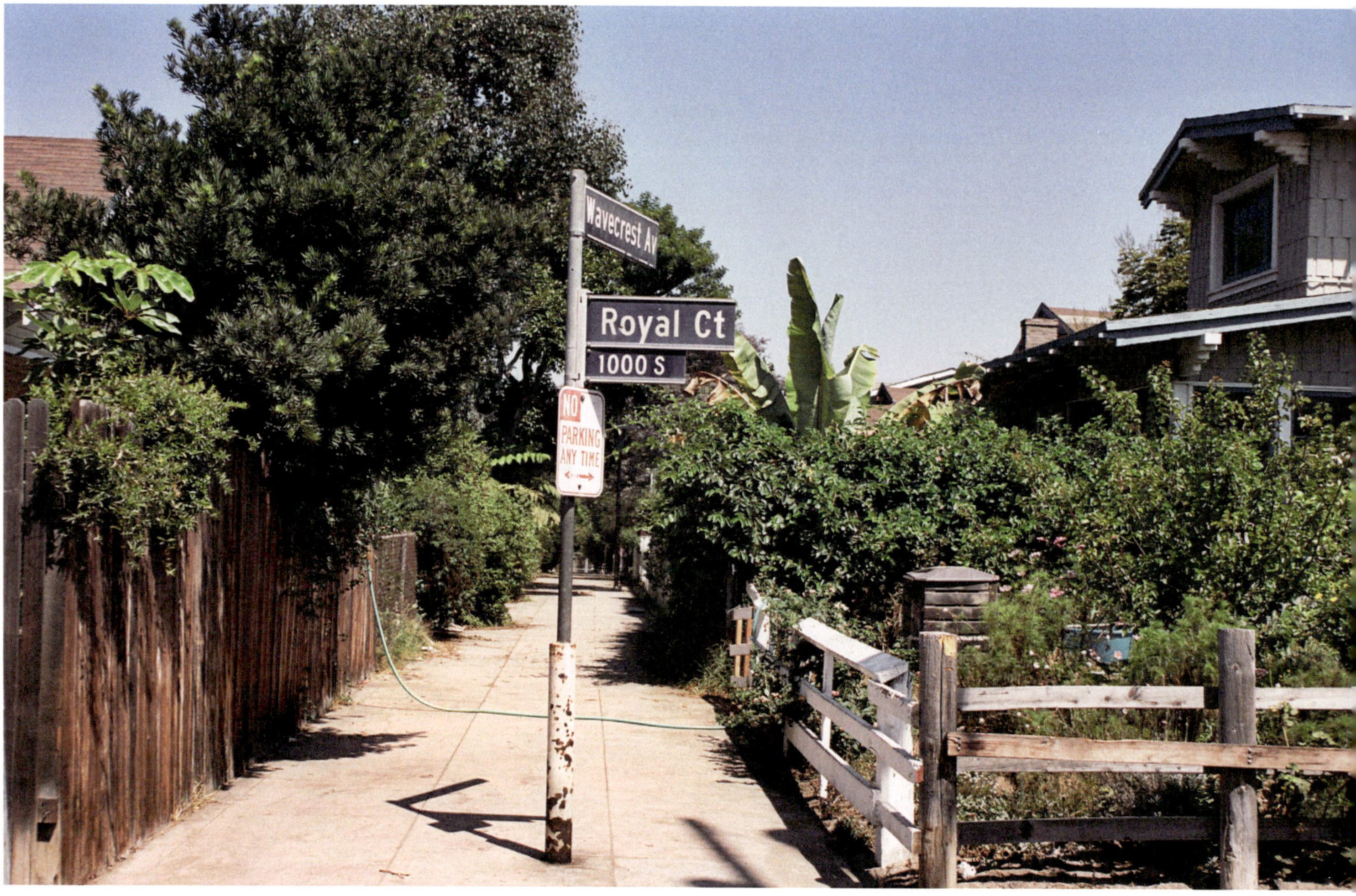

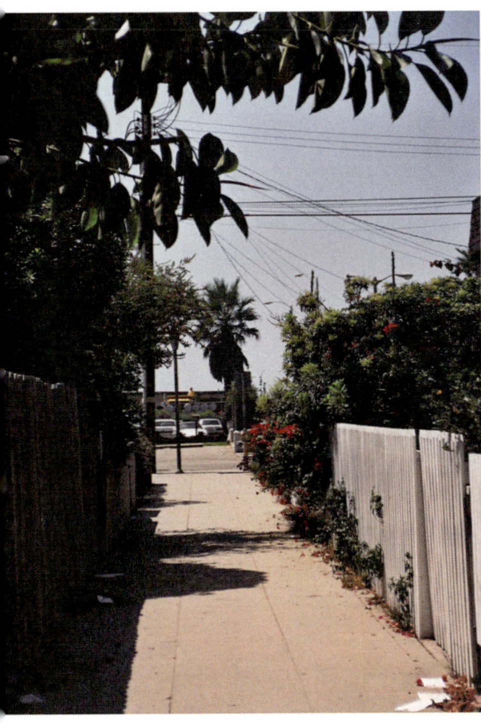 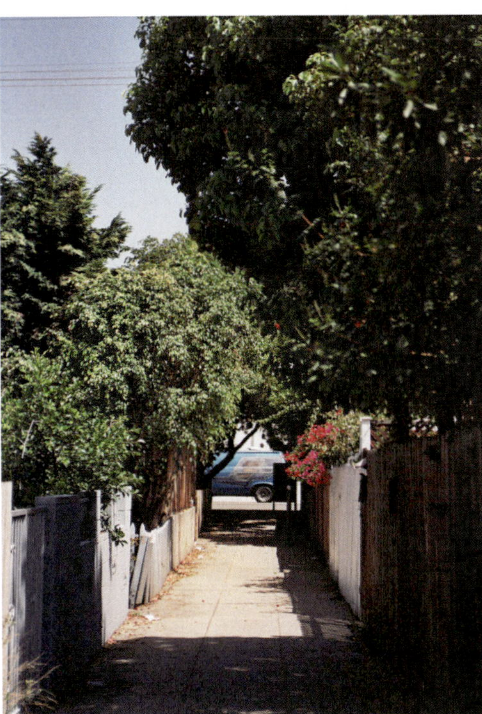 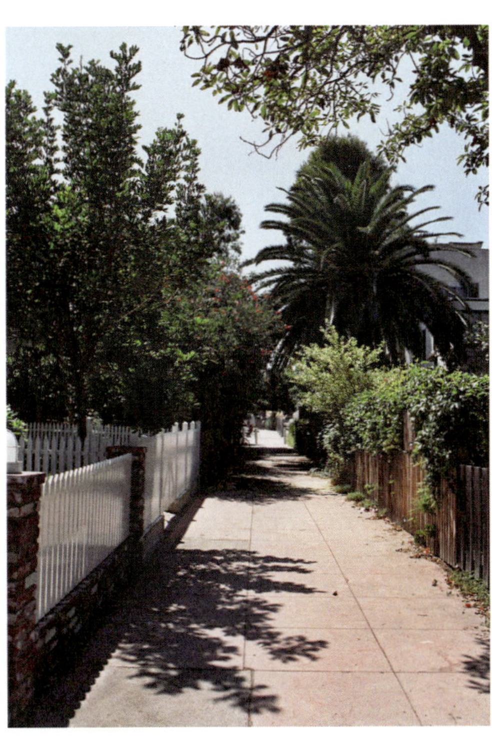

As residents and property owners we believe that Venice is one of the few areas of Los Angeles where people can actually walk and discover what is an interesting, charming and historic part of a city otherwise overrun by cars and freeways. The pedestrian paths and gardens are as much a tourist attraction as are the Ocean Front Walk and the Venice canals. —John Caldwell and Susan Kalinowski

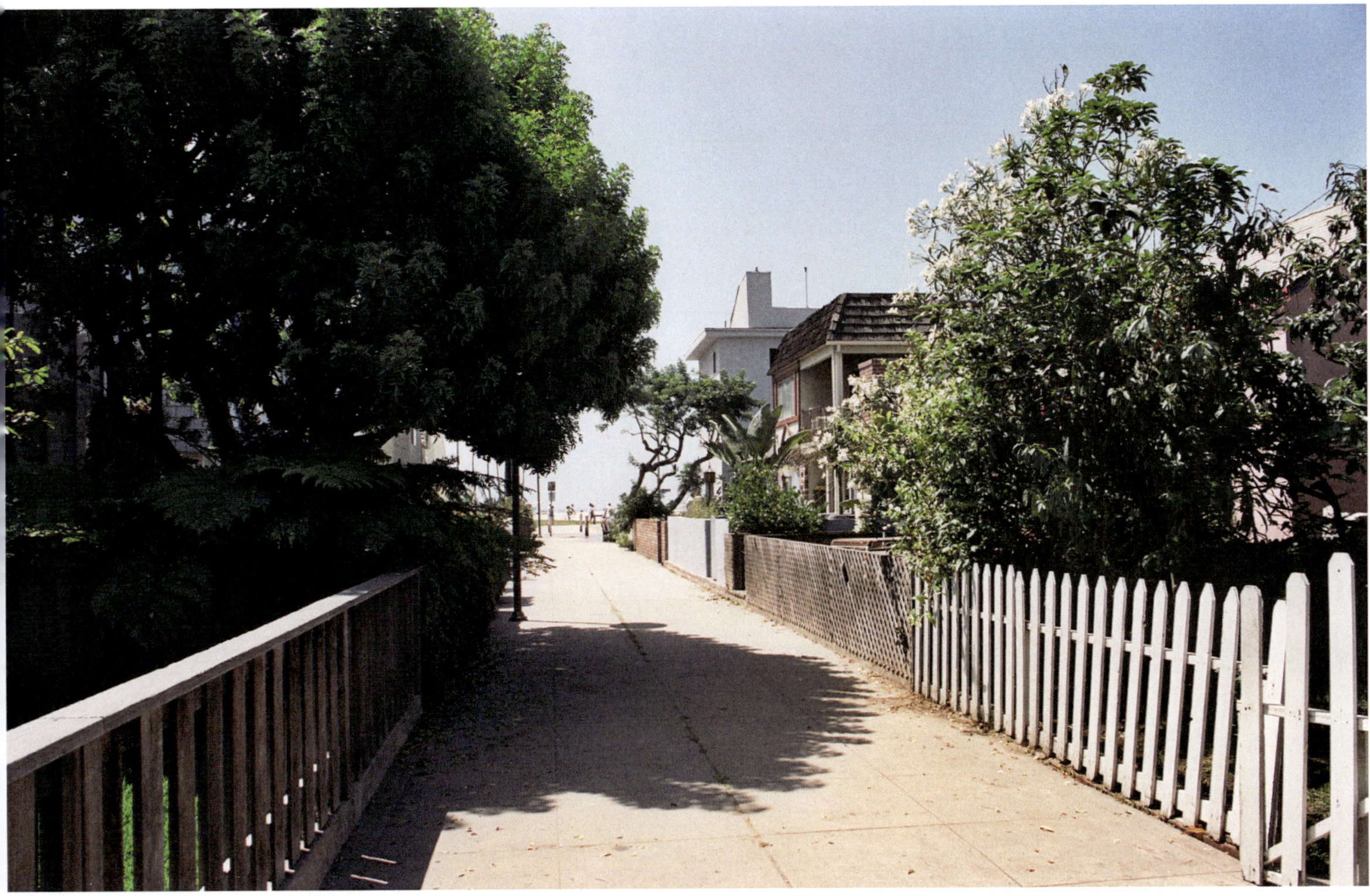

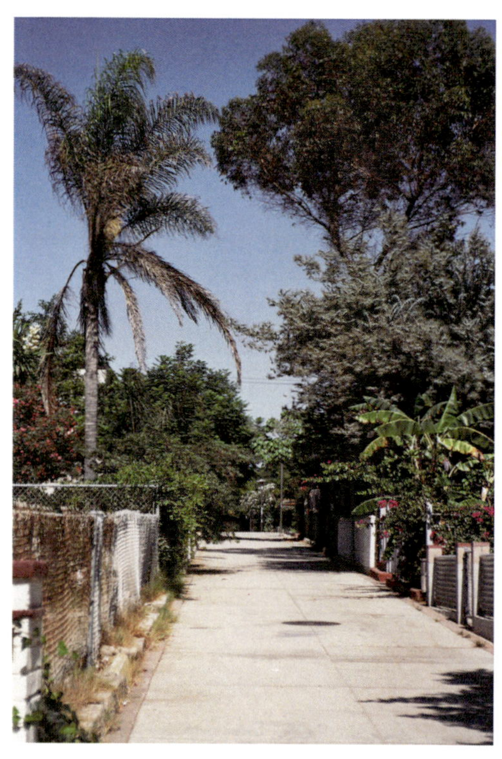
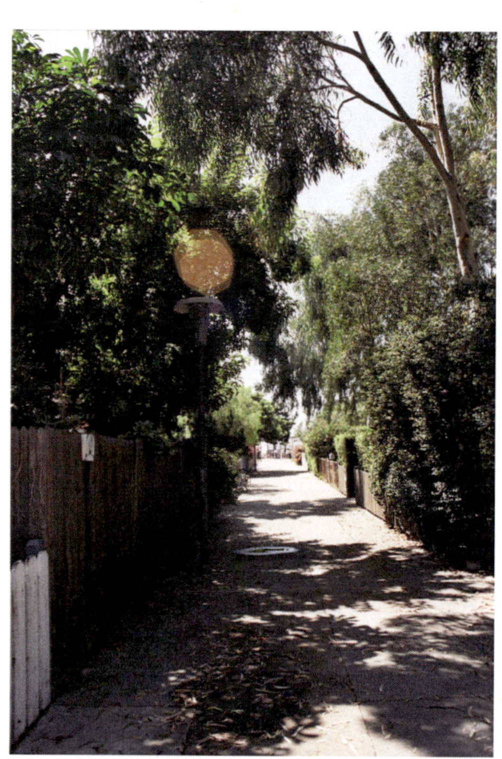
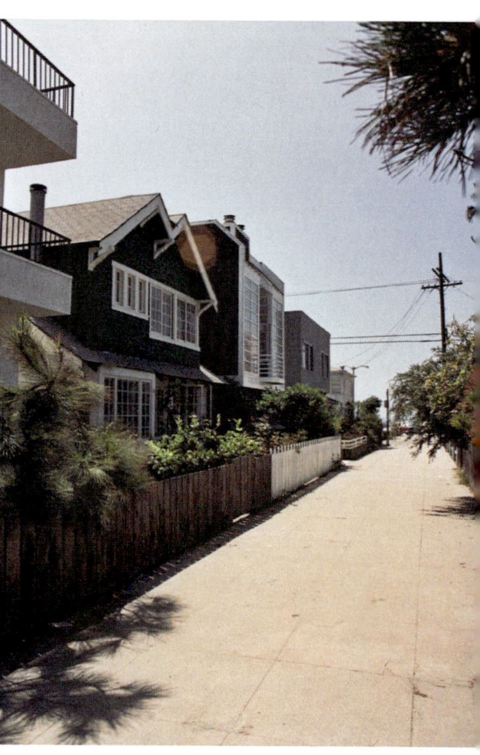

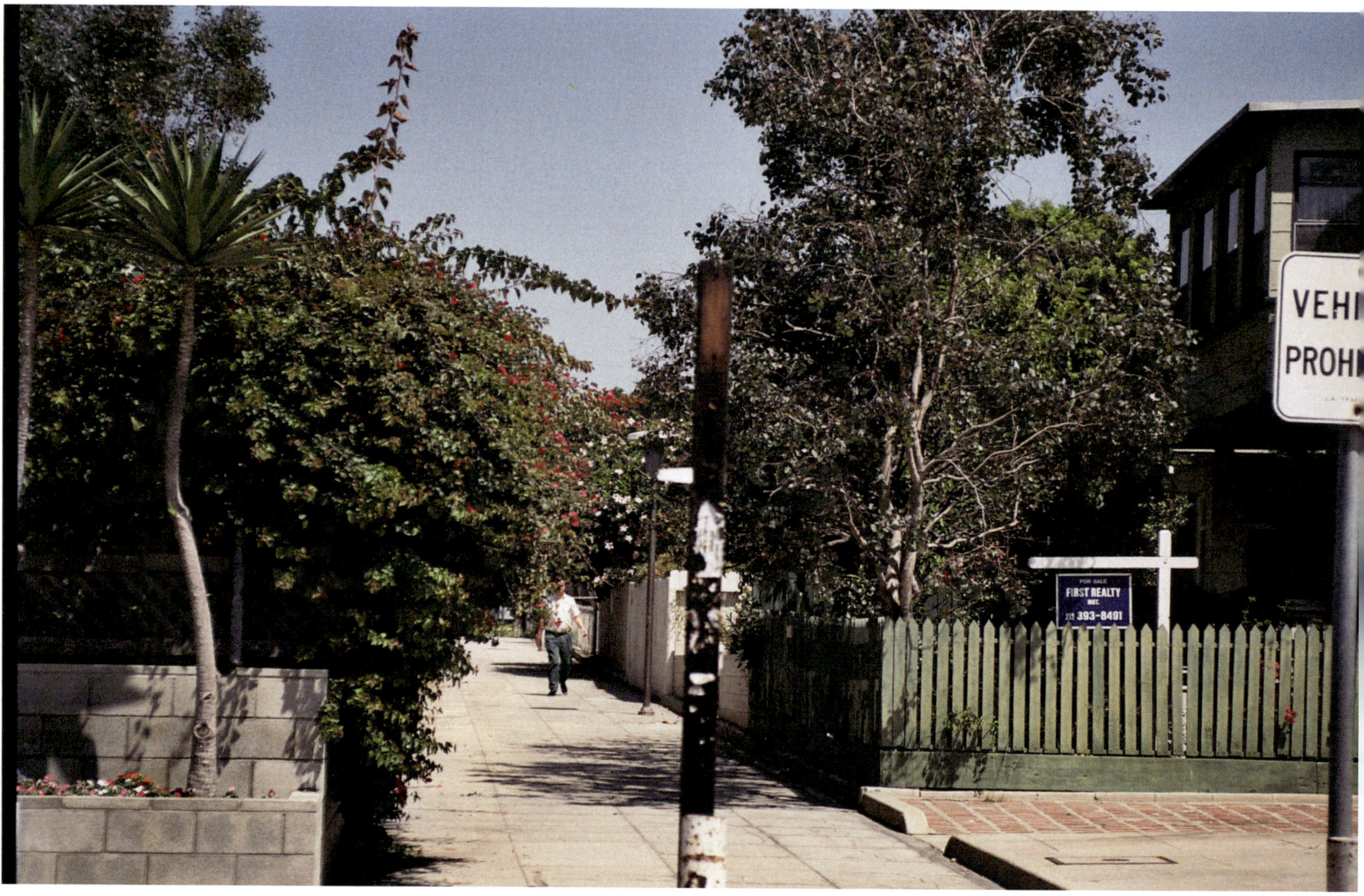

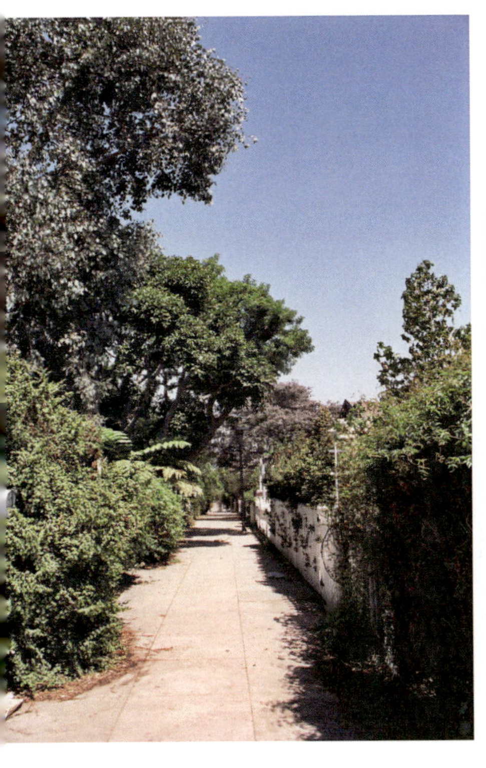
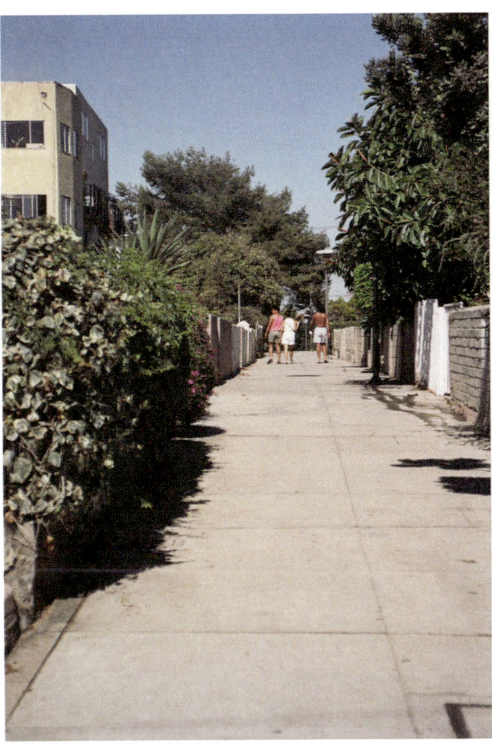
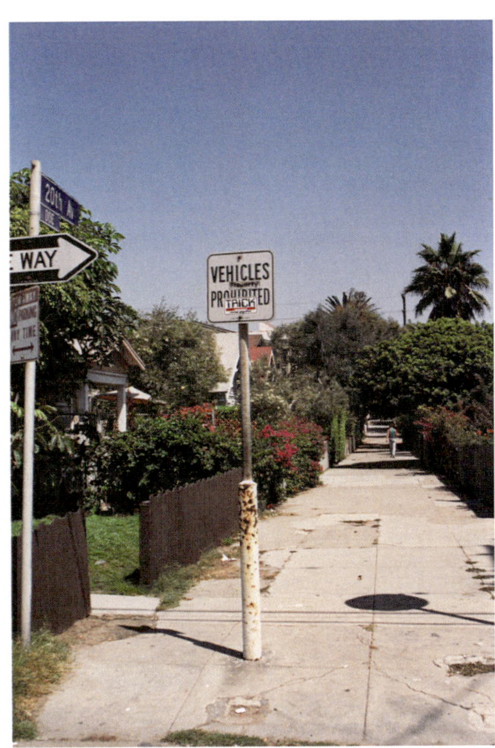
20th
E WAY
VEHICLES
PROHIBITED

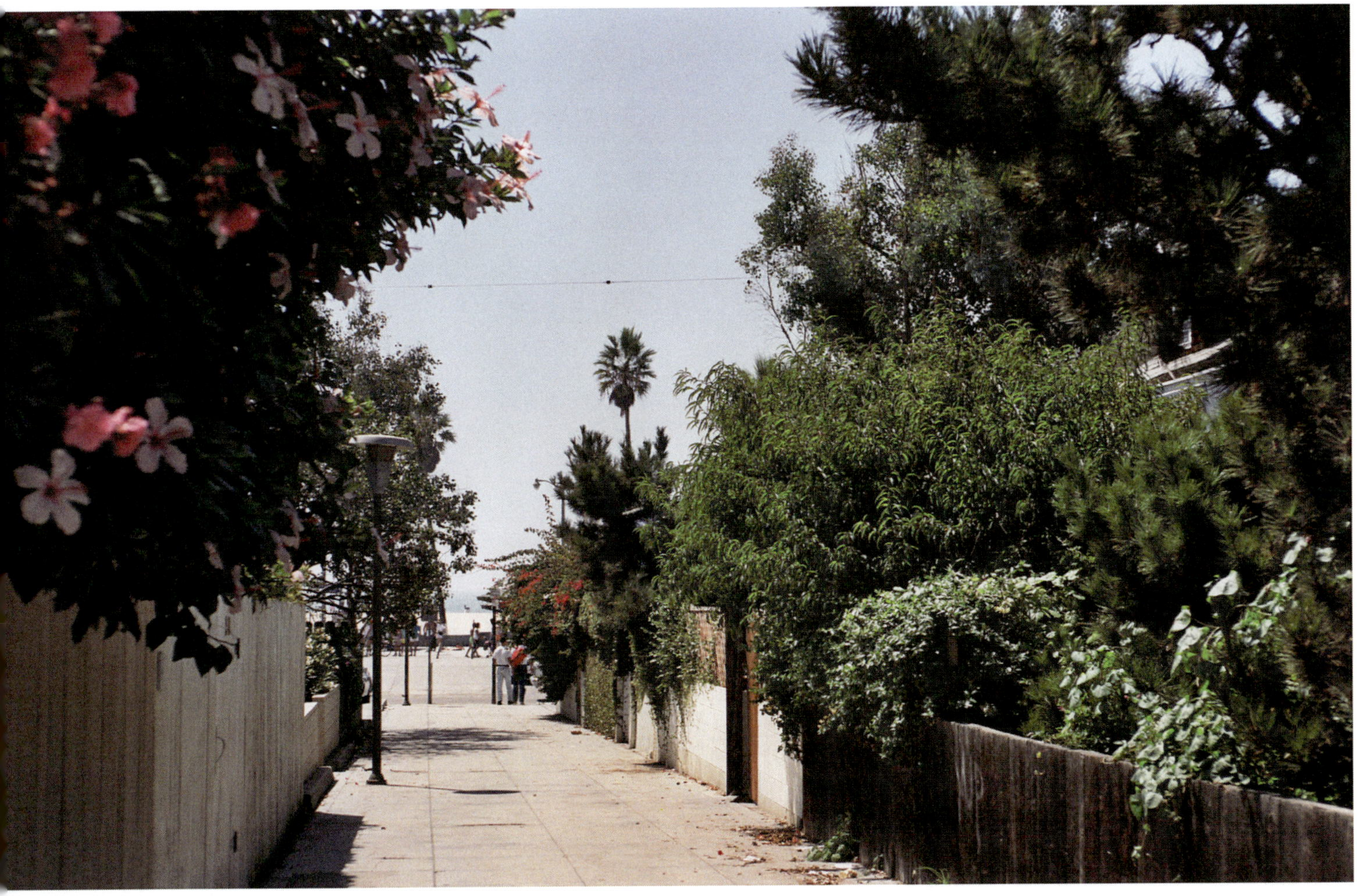

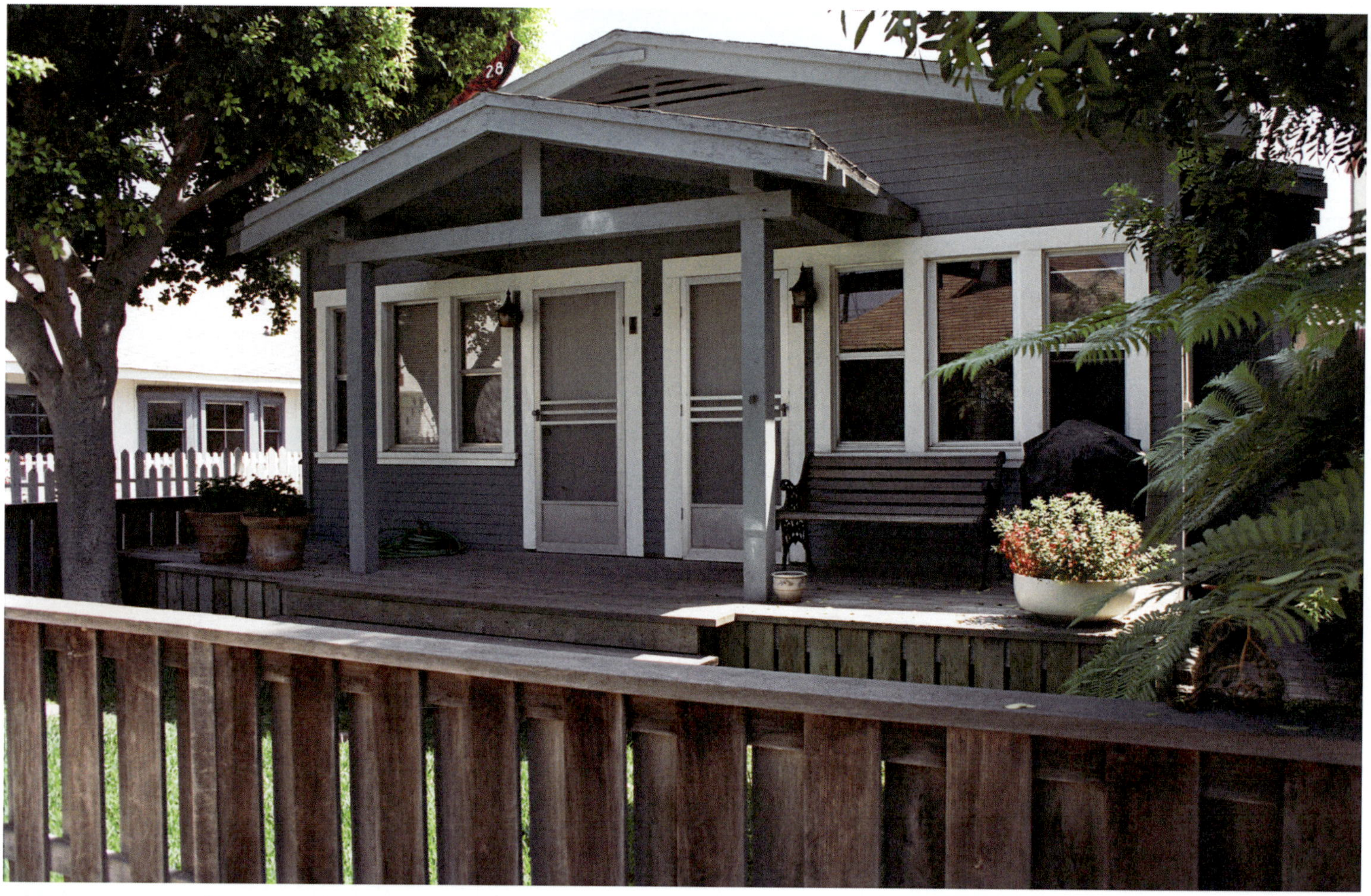

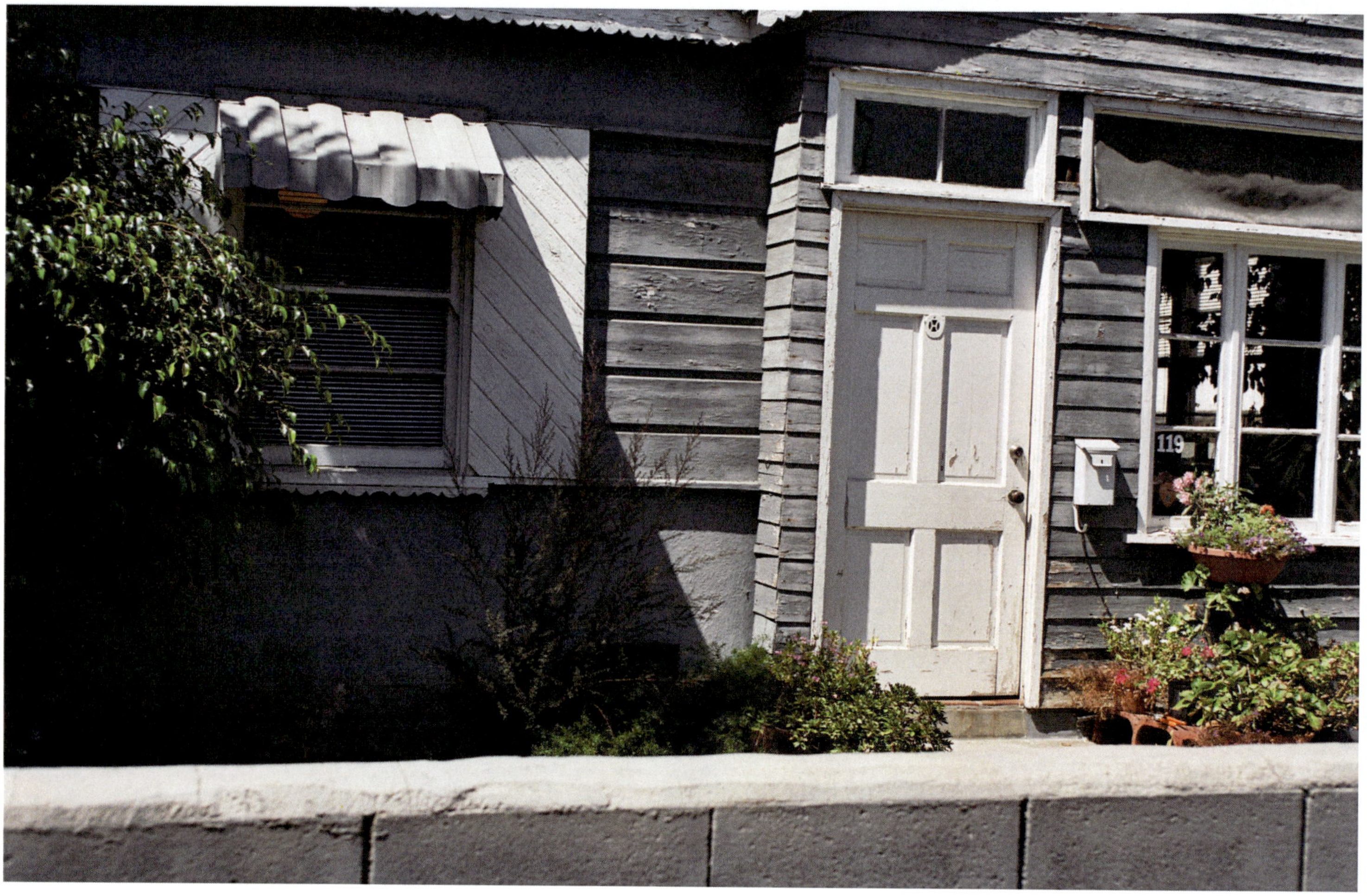

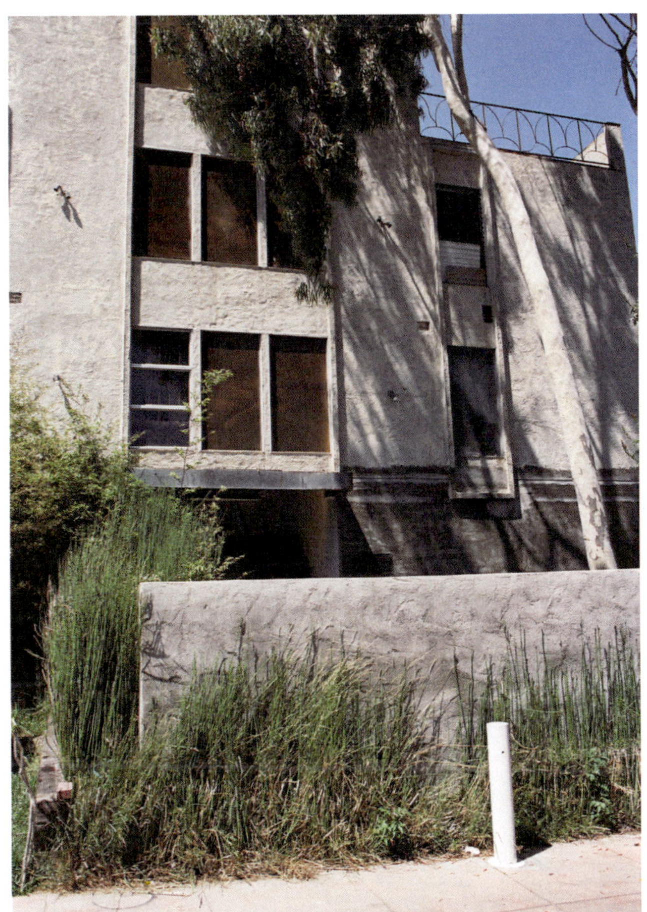

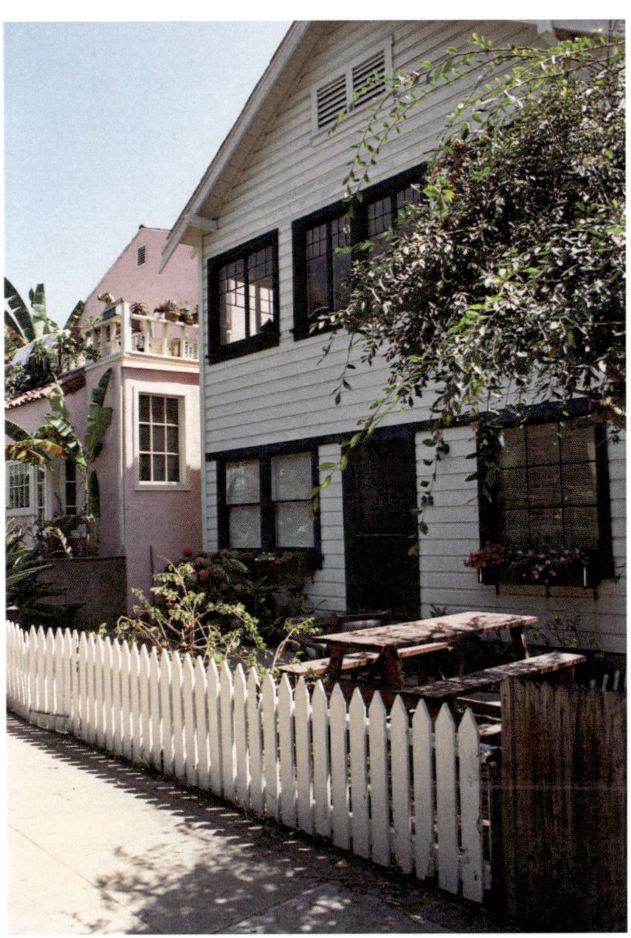

THE RICH STREET LIFE IS NO FRILL. IT IS AN EXPRESSION OF THE MOST ANCIENT FUNCTION OF A CITY -- A PLACE FOR PEOPLE TO COME TOGETHER, ALL KINDS OF PEOPLE, FACE-TO-FACE, AND THERE IS FAR MORE OF THIS CONGRESS HERE THAN IN THE BLAND SHOPPING CENTERS BEING TOUTED AS THE NEW DOWNTOWN. -WILLIAM H. WHYTE, NEW YORK MAGAZINE, JULY 1974

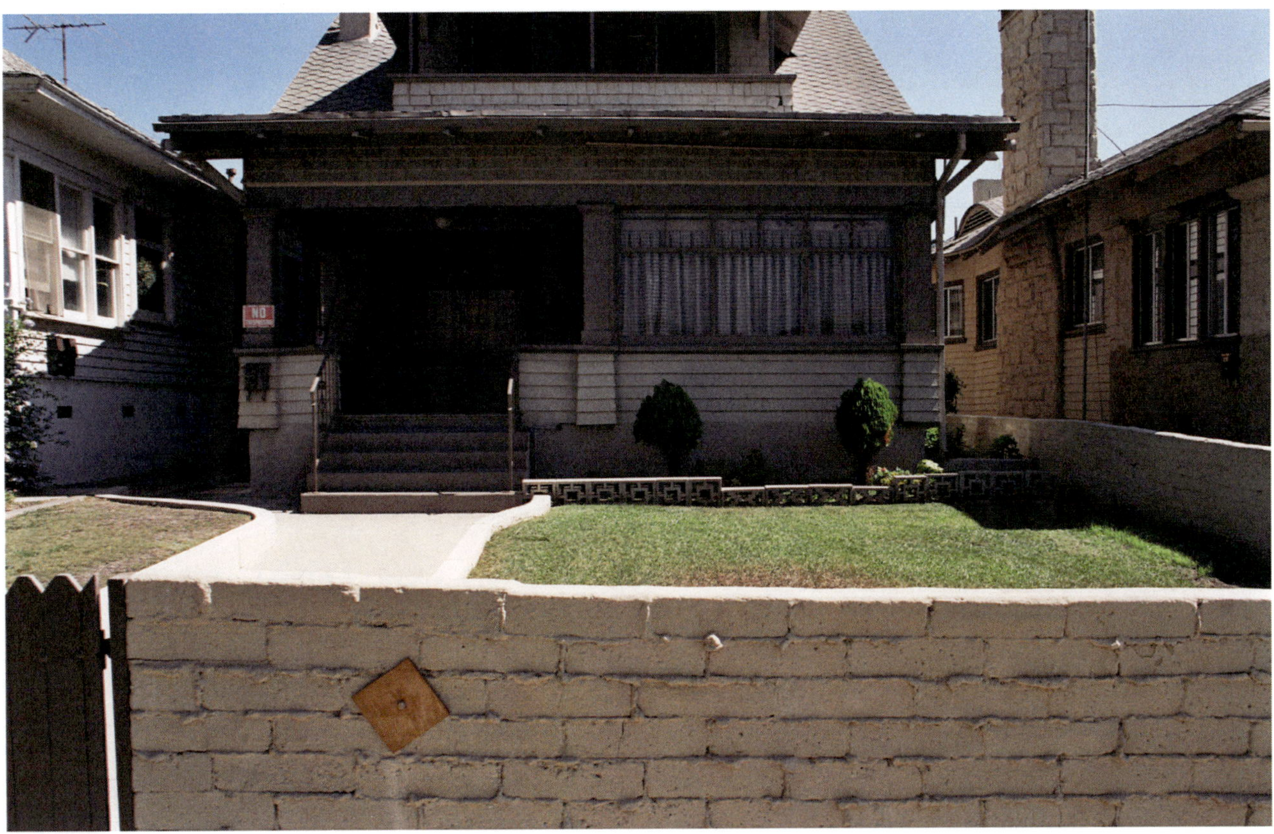

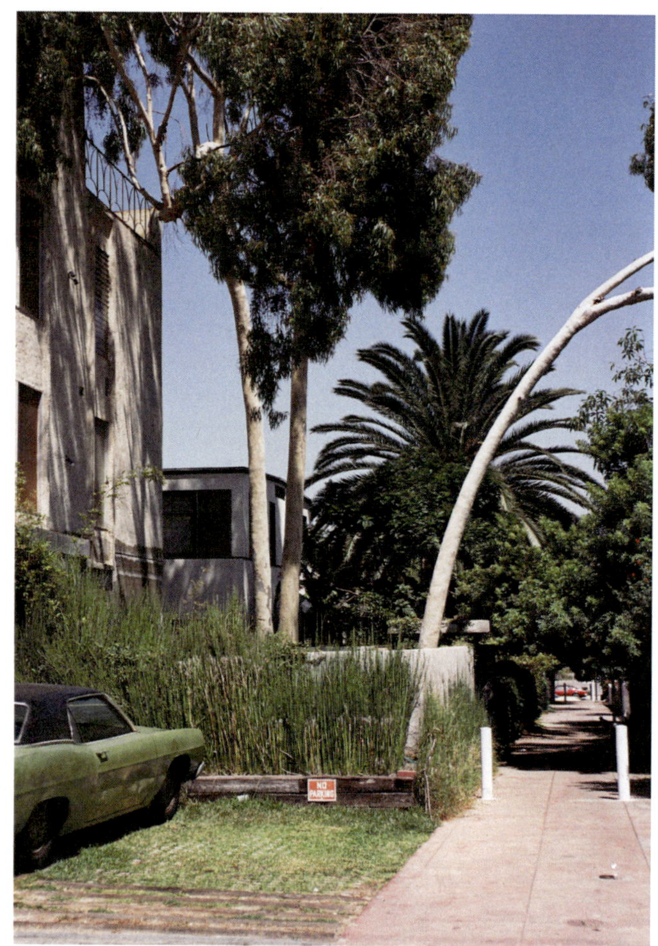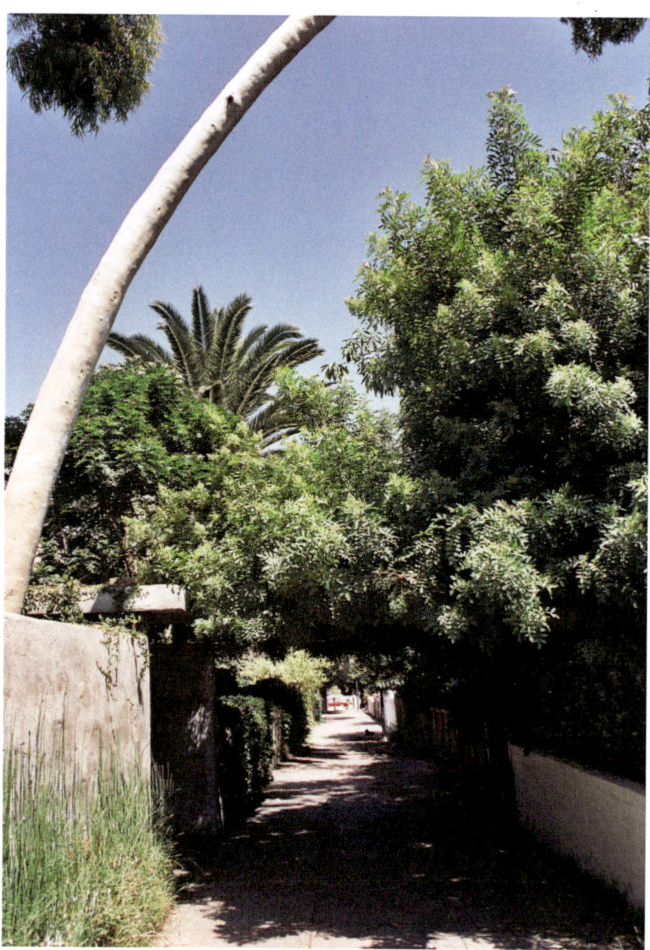

STREETS LINK ALL THE MIXED FUNCTIONS OF A CITY. THE FIRST FUNDAMENTAL MISSTEP A SUBURBAN MALL DOES WHEN SUPERIMPOSED ON AN URBAN DOWNTOWN IS ELIMINATE THE STREET. -WILLIAM H. WHYTE, NEW YORK MAGAZINE, JULY 1974

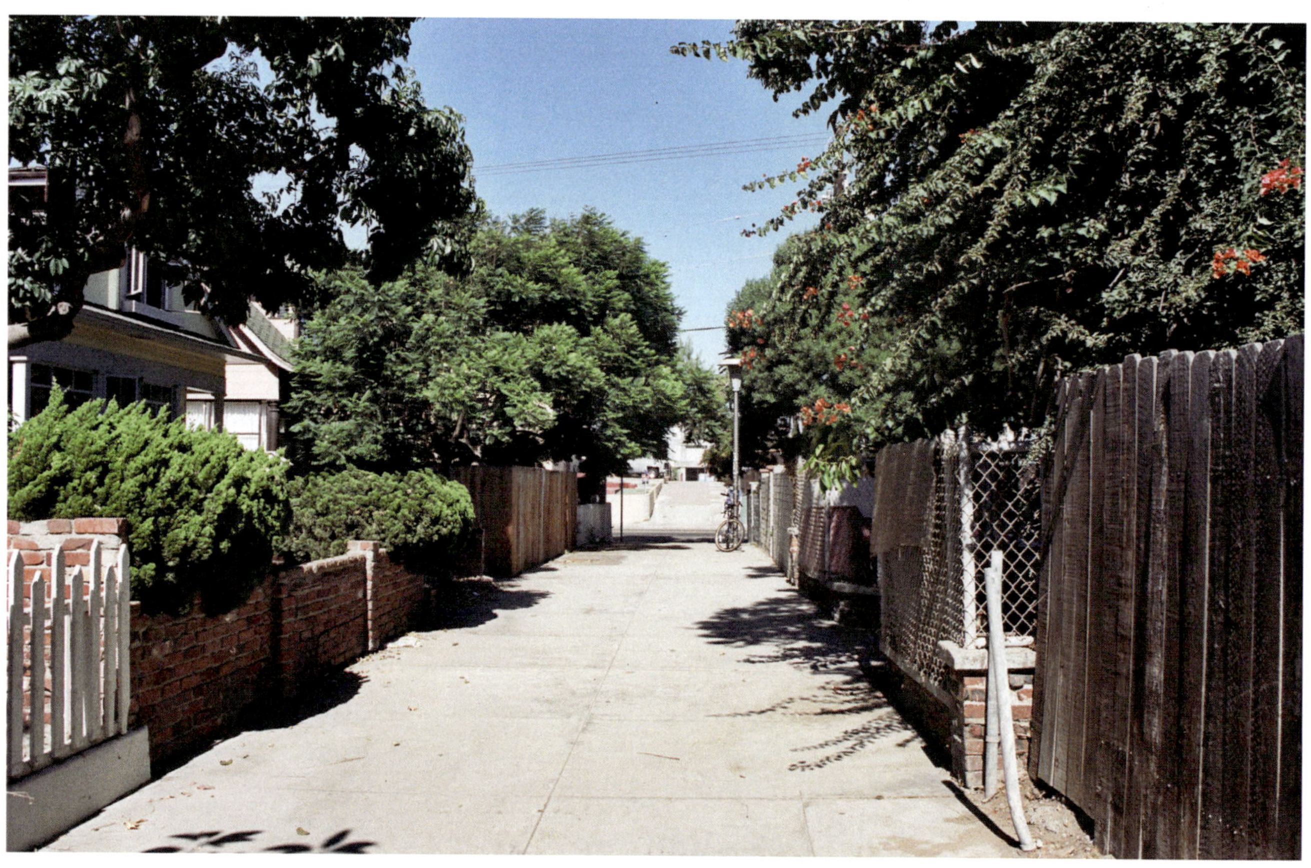

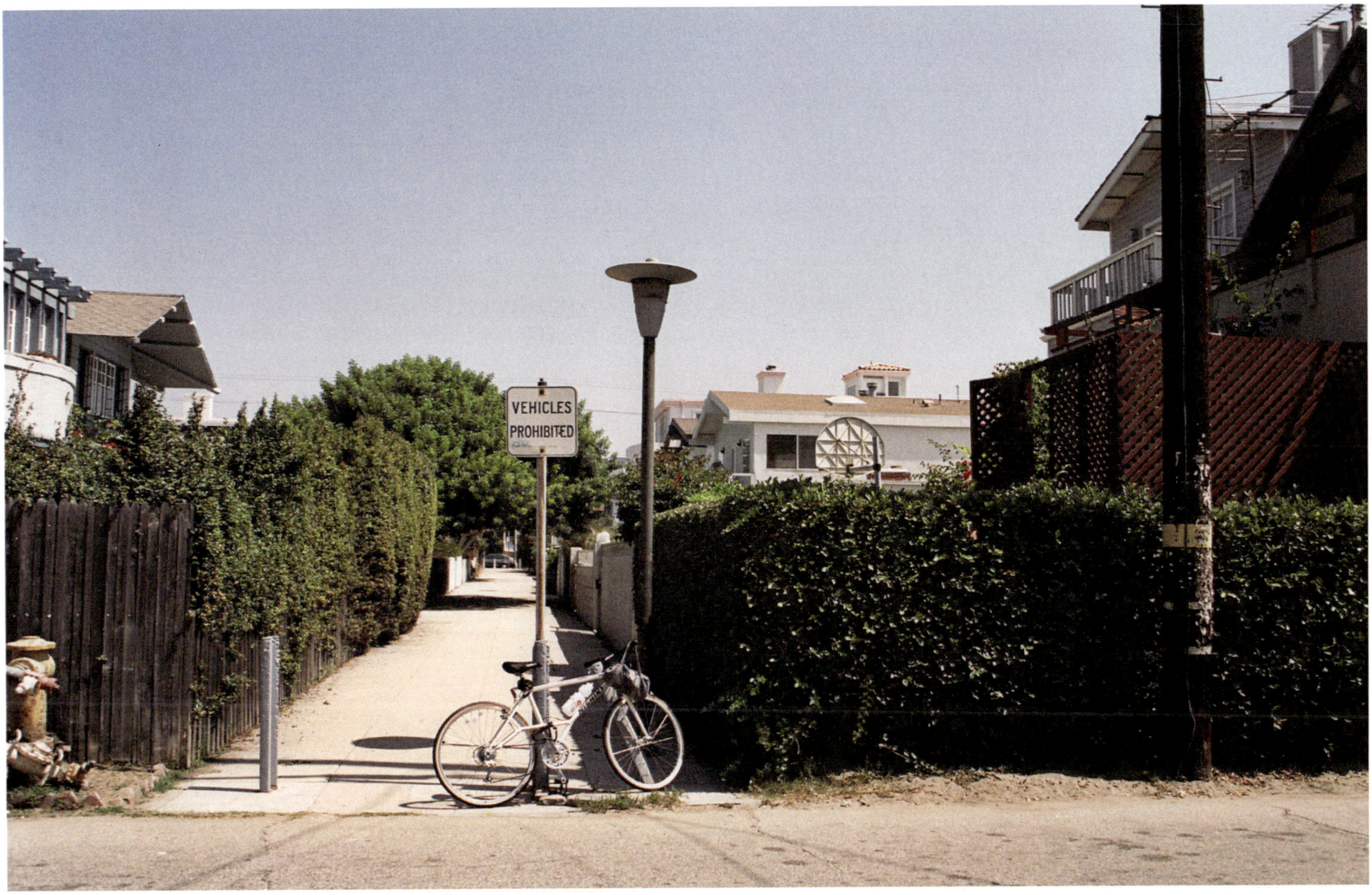

VEHICLES
PROHIBITED

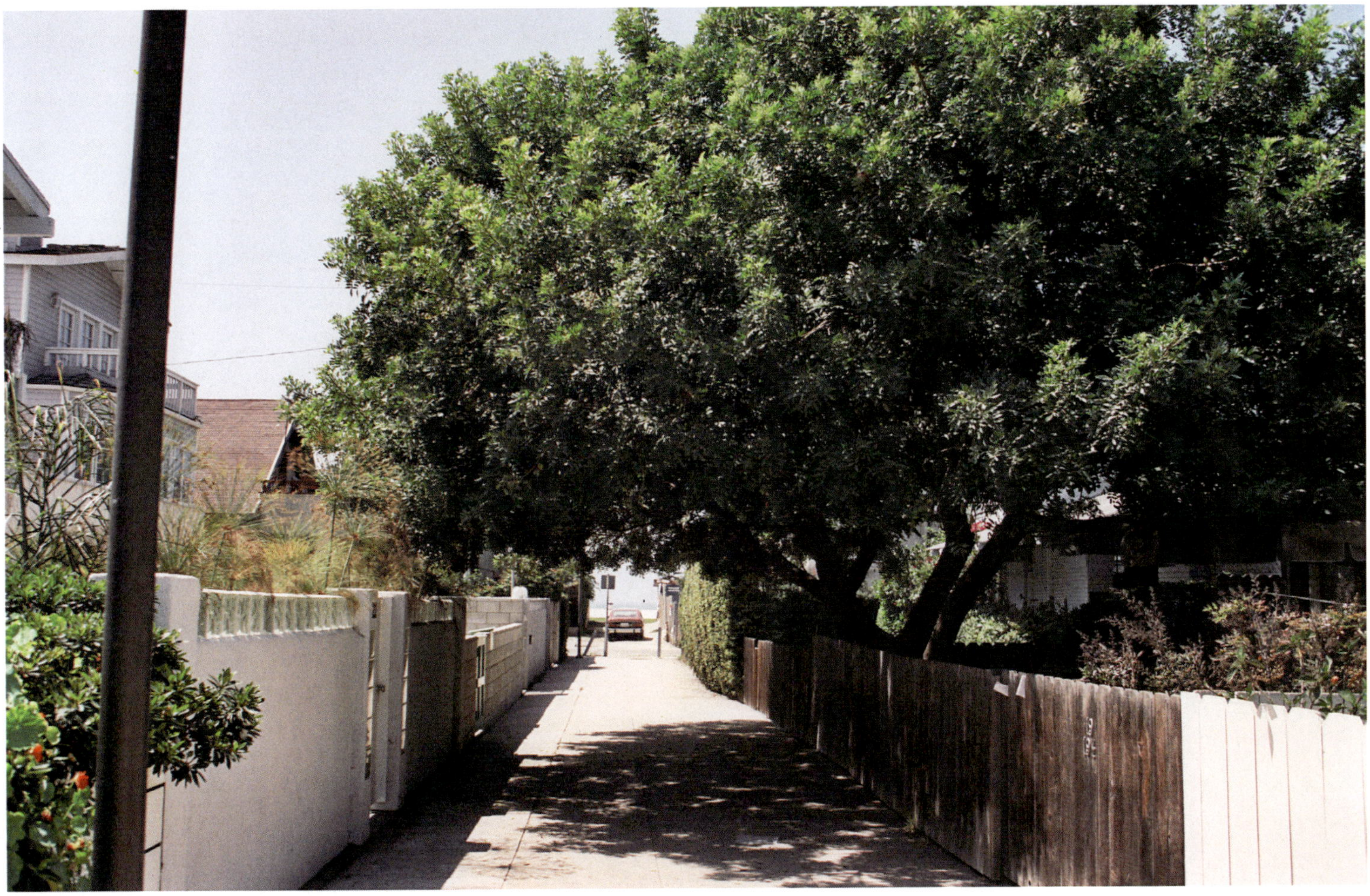

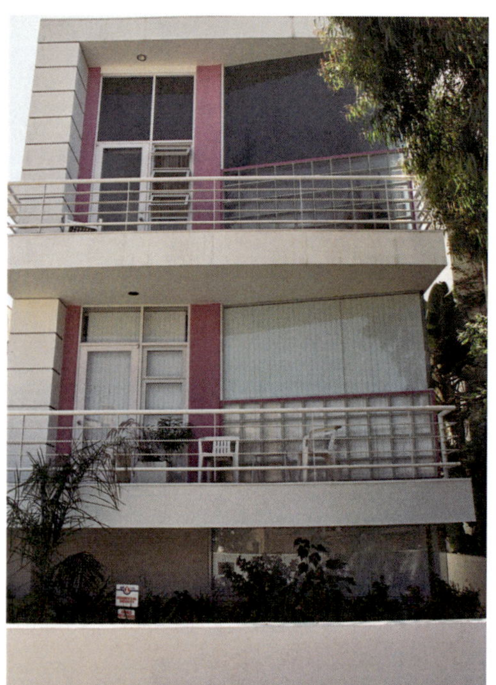 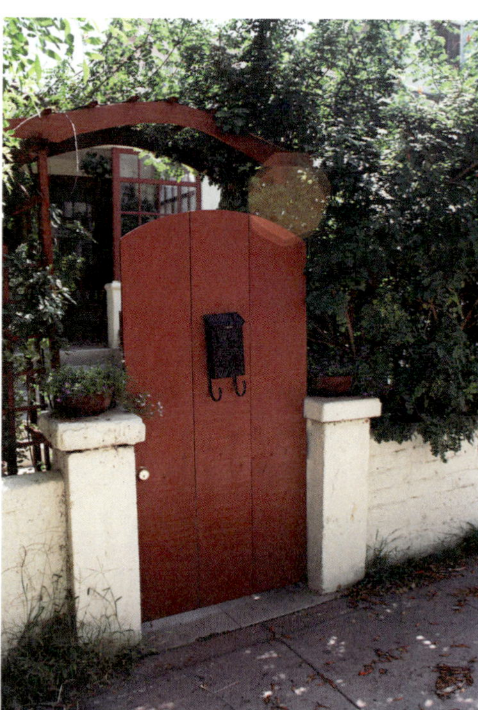 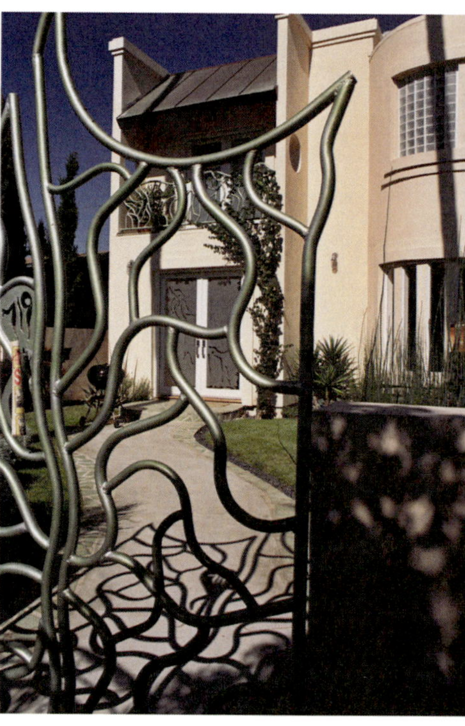

The Venice Walkstreets have retained the qualities of their original unique design for nearly a century. Like the beaches, the canals, and the marina, the walkstreets are part of the ambiance of the locale for thousands of visitors annually. The walk streets are a resource to the entire community. They are certainly a passage if not a stop on many tourist visits to the area. In a life dominated by the automobile, they create a scaled environment found nowhere else in Los Angeles, and, like the canals, offer a serene car free zone or island unachievable anywhere else – certainly at this density. In addition, they provide for residents, a sense of neighborhood unique to urban areas. They possess a quality termed "intervisibility" by city planners which refers to the aspect of their design which enables the public to look in and enjoy the neighborhood gardens and patios and the neighbors to look out and derive a sense of community.
—The Walkstreet Preservation Committee Report 11/5/92

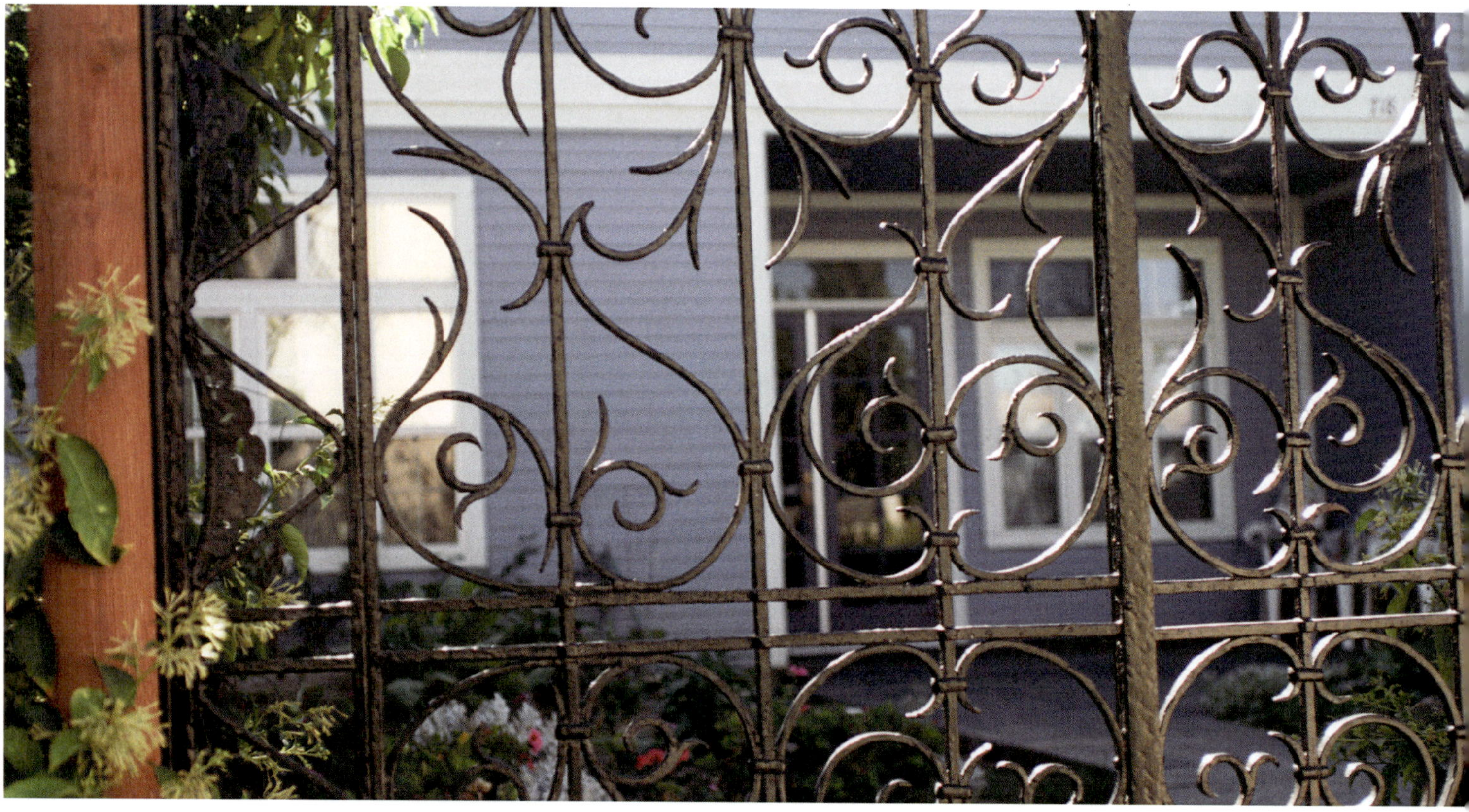

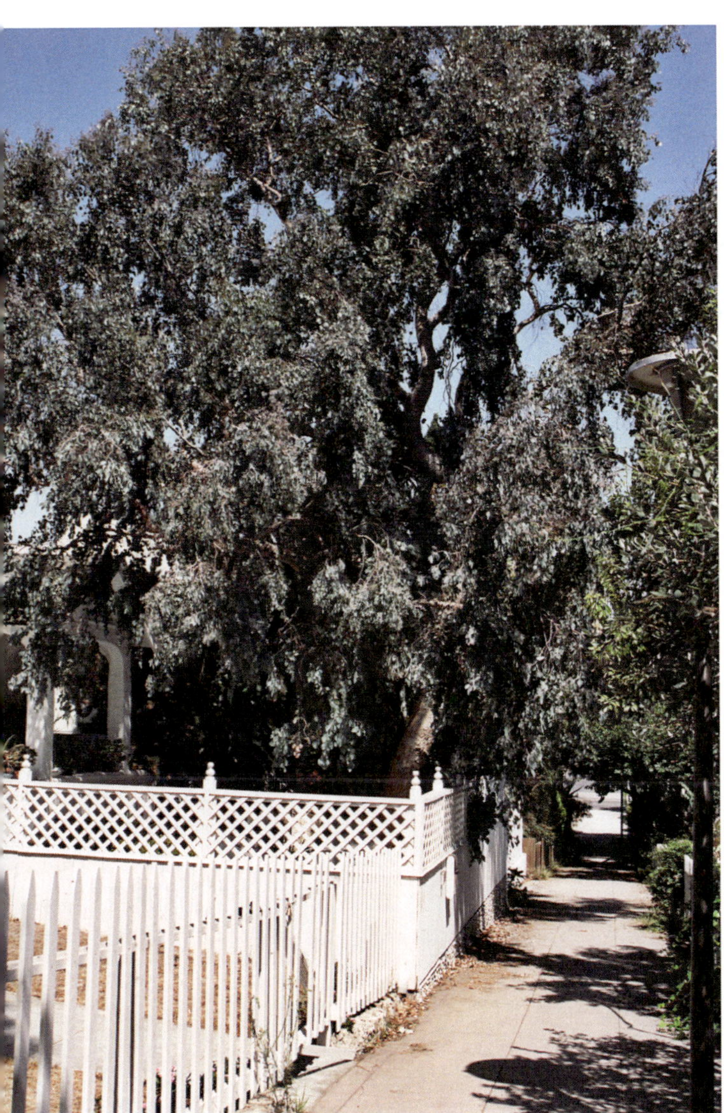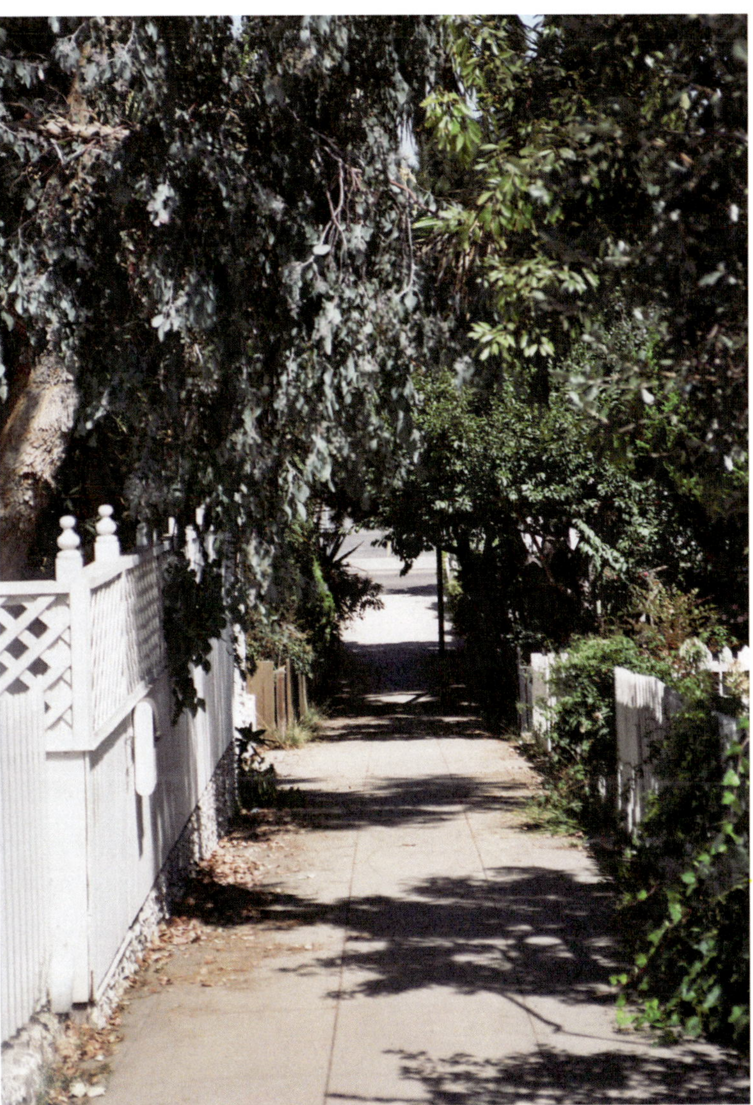

Unlike an historic or architecturally significant structure, affective elements such as space, light and the interplay of zones of human movement v. landscaped areas are often not noticed until they are destroyed. Our walkways work "invisibly" to "engineer" a pleasurable walking pace which enables conversation and an insightful observation of the incredibly varied, often eccentric variety of patio/garden design and residential architecture. The garden/patios between the fences and the buildings provide an important transitional zone between the busy public pathways and private dwellings. These garden/patios are enjoyed by both the public and the residents and contribute much to the charm and property values of these small parcels of land. —Betsy Goldman, President, Venice Historical Society

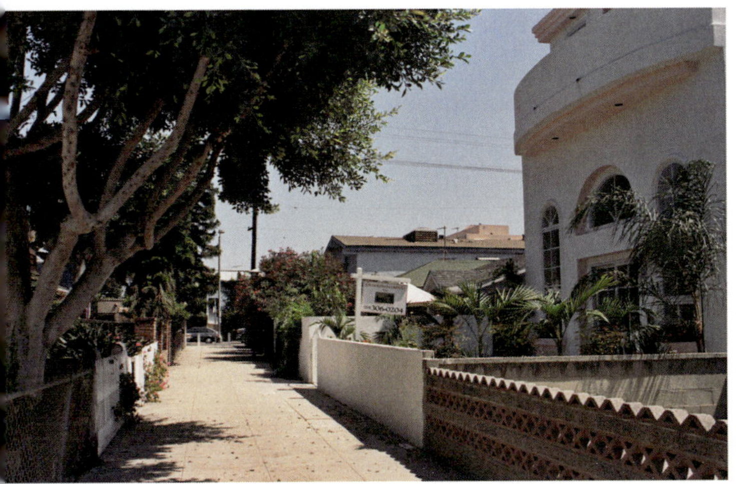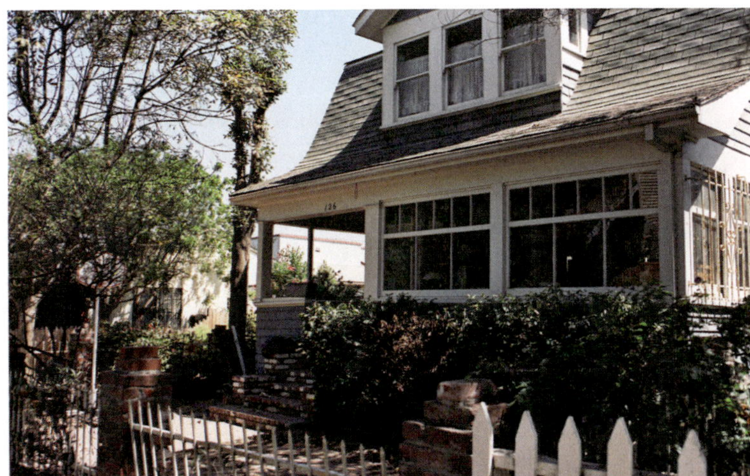

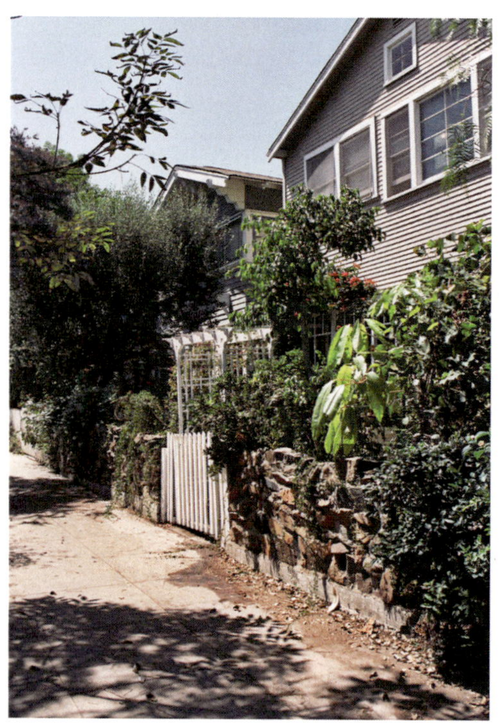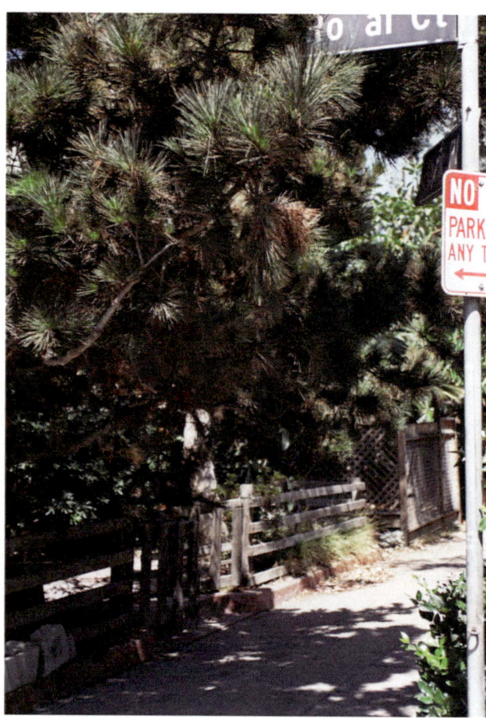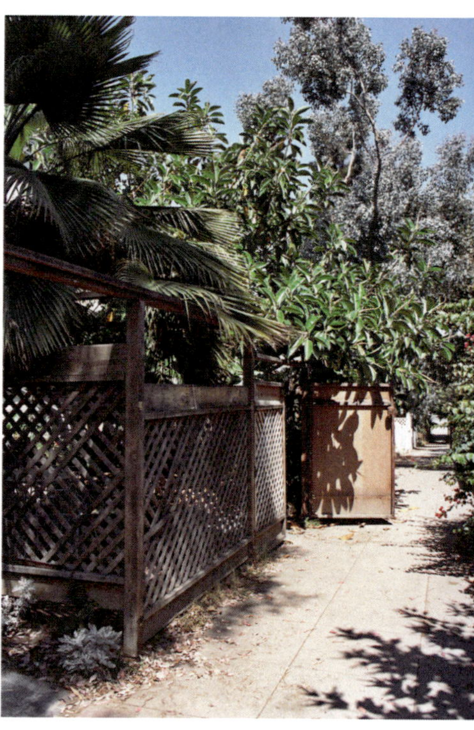

As a longtime resident (1915) of Venice and still a property owner,
I feel the walkways are a unique part of the charm of Venice and
should be retained. —Lila E. Shanley

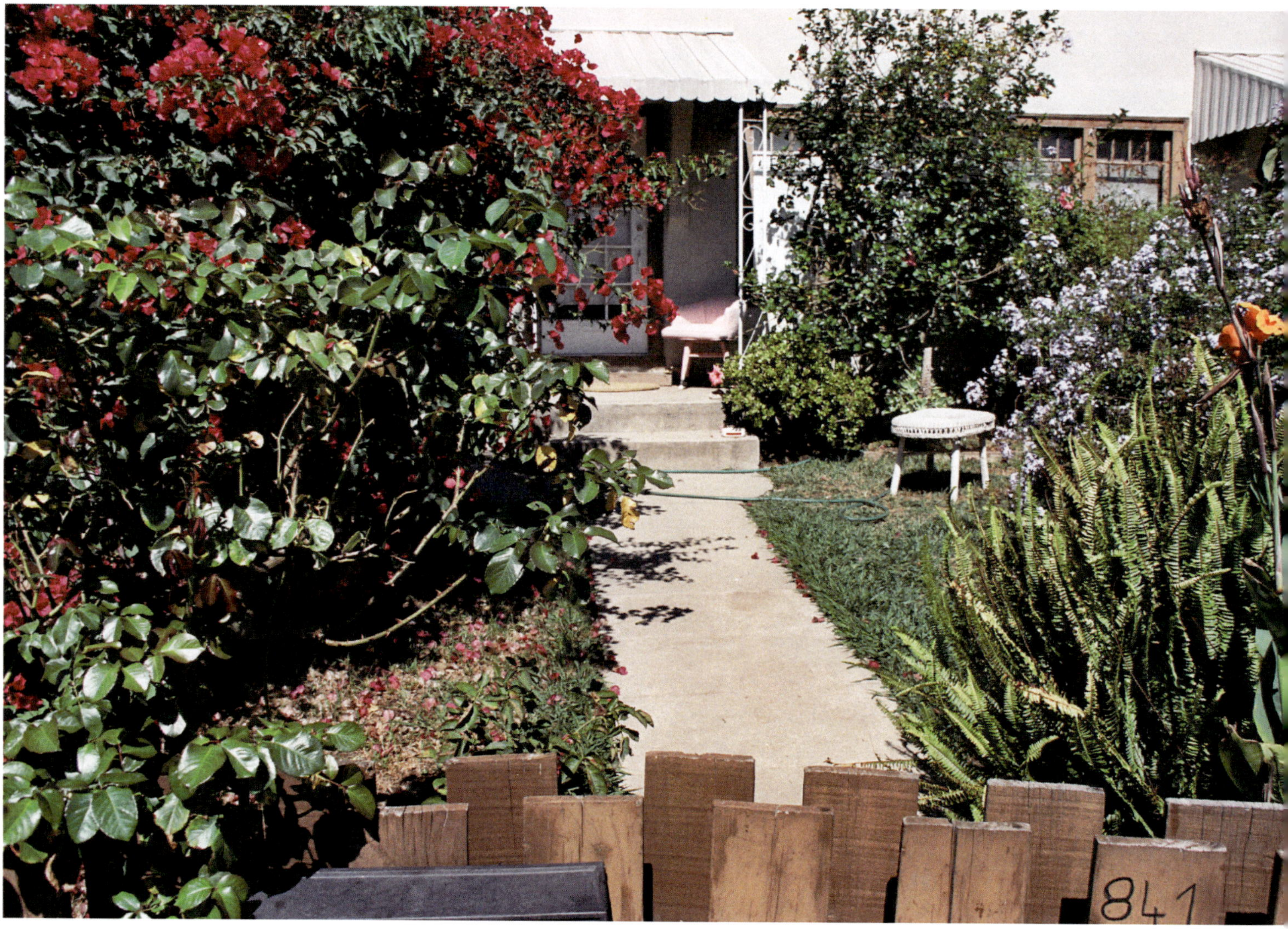

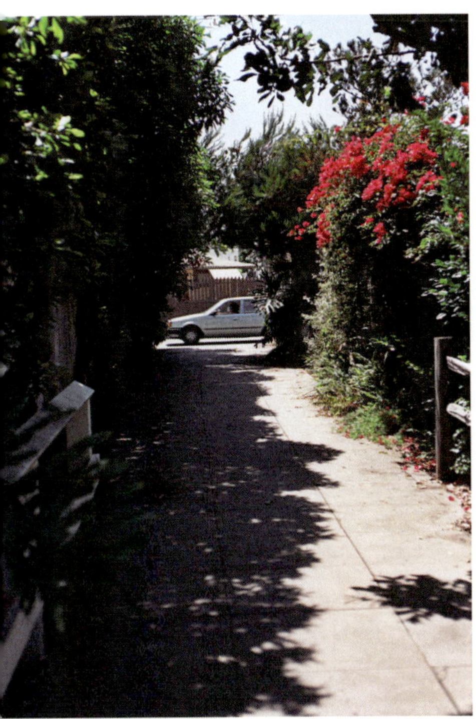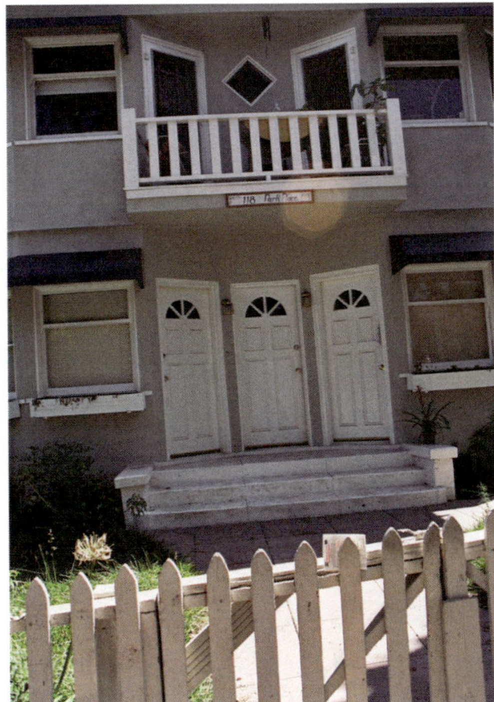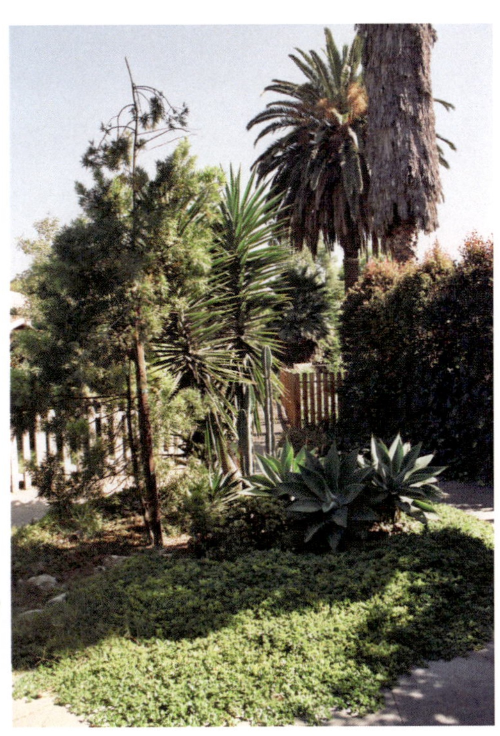

I live on Thornton Avenue and experience the charm of a walkway every day. I am horrified at the possibility that this unique area might be destroyed. —Helen Alland

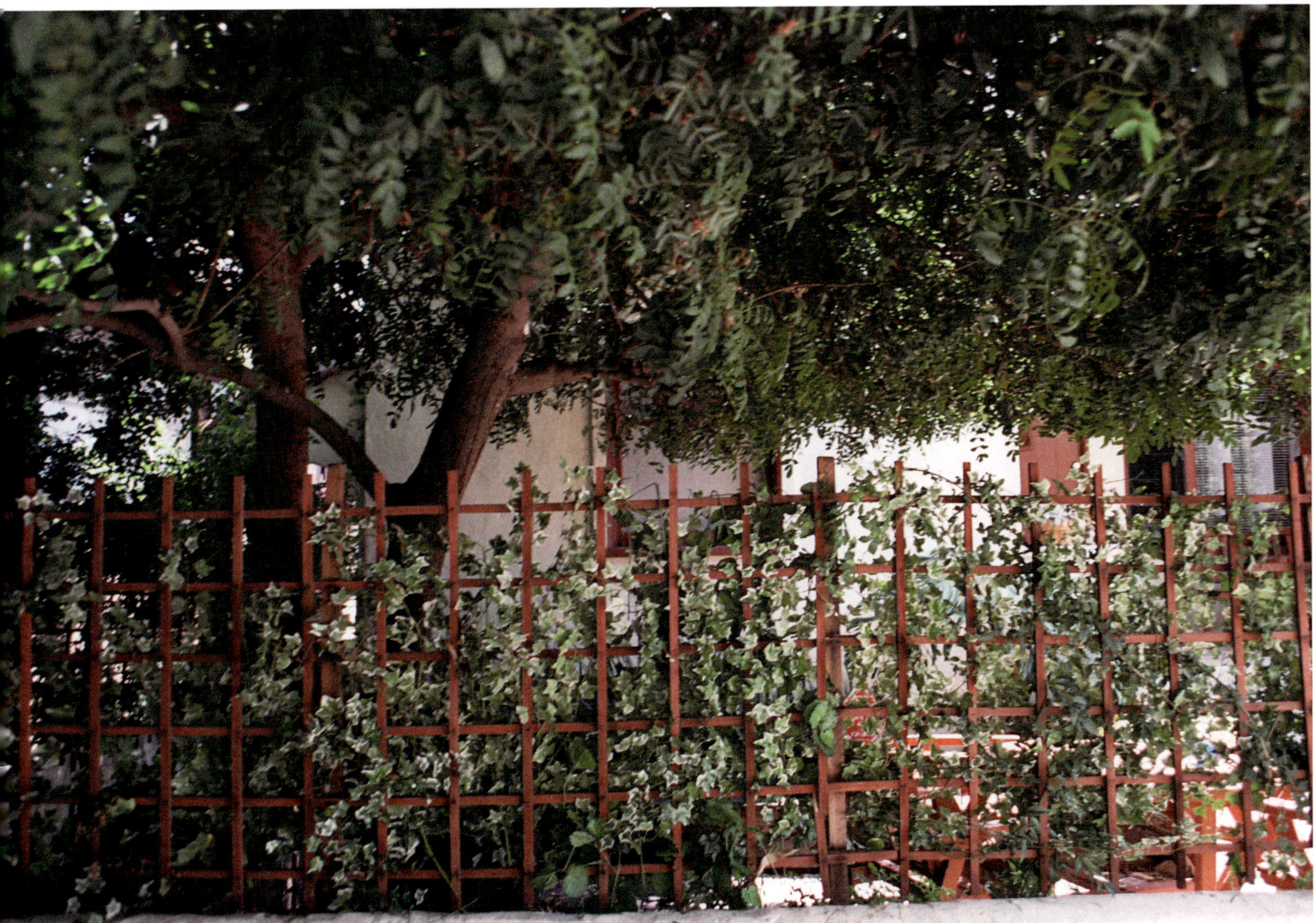

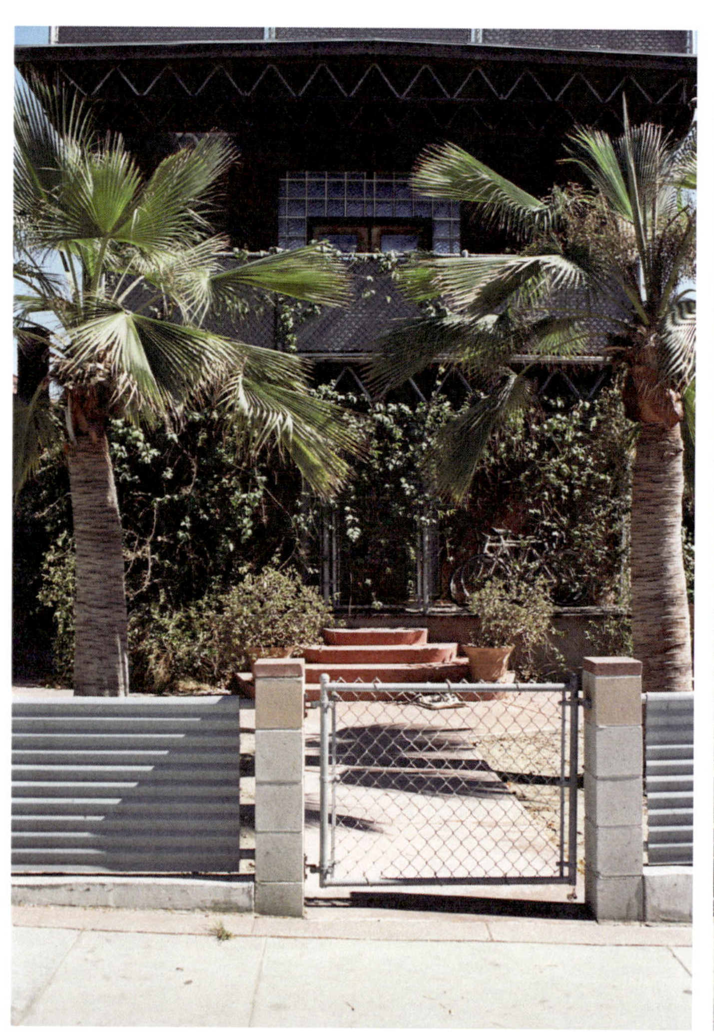
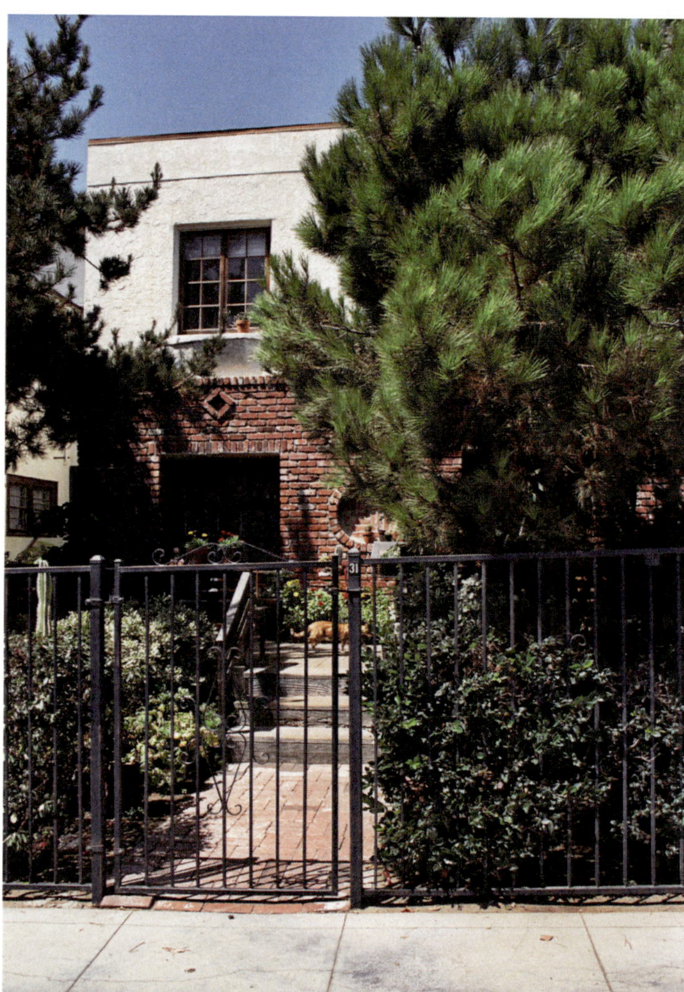

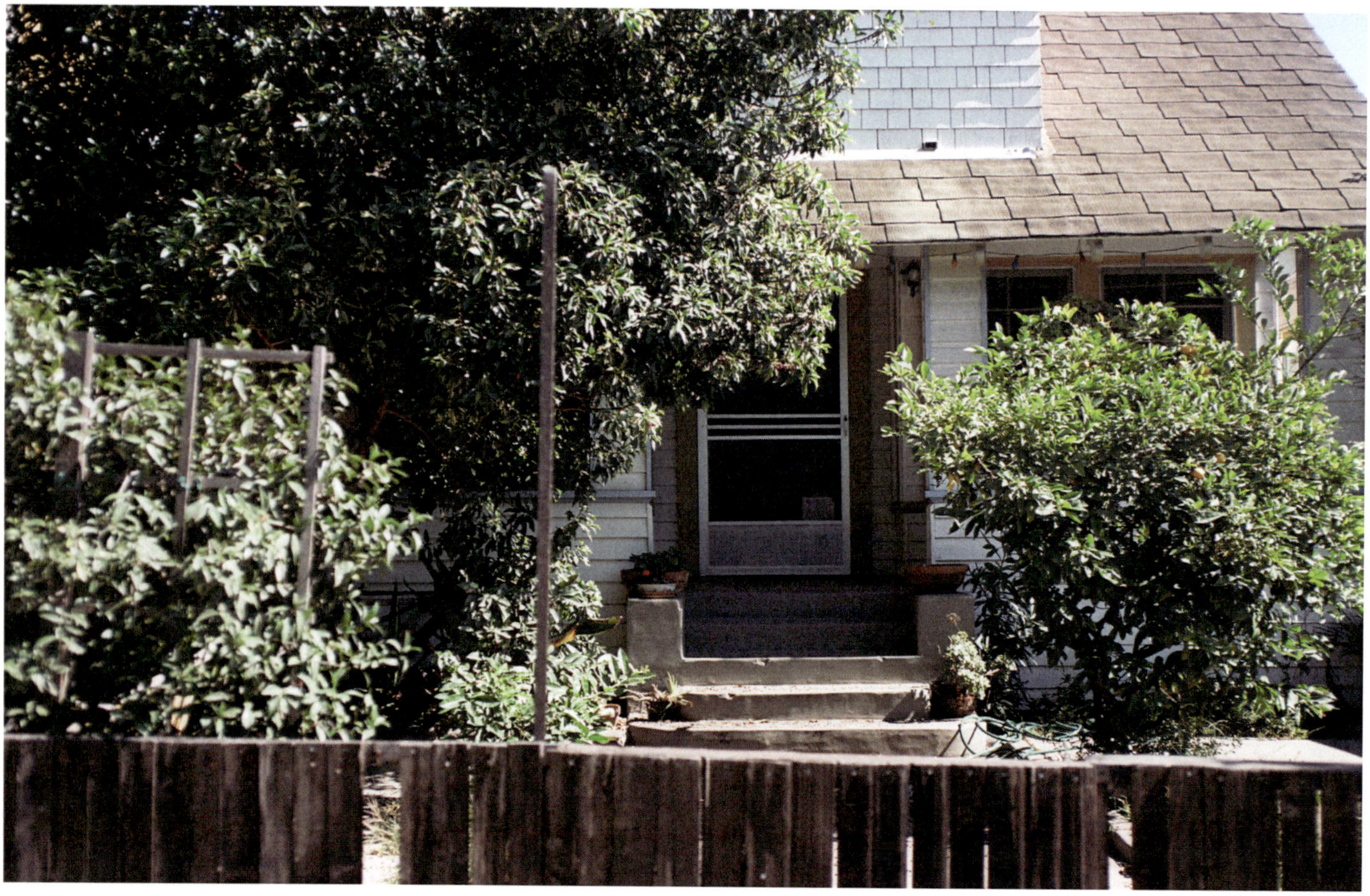

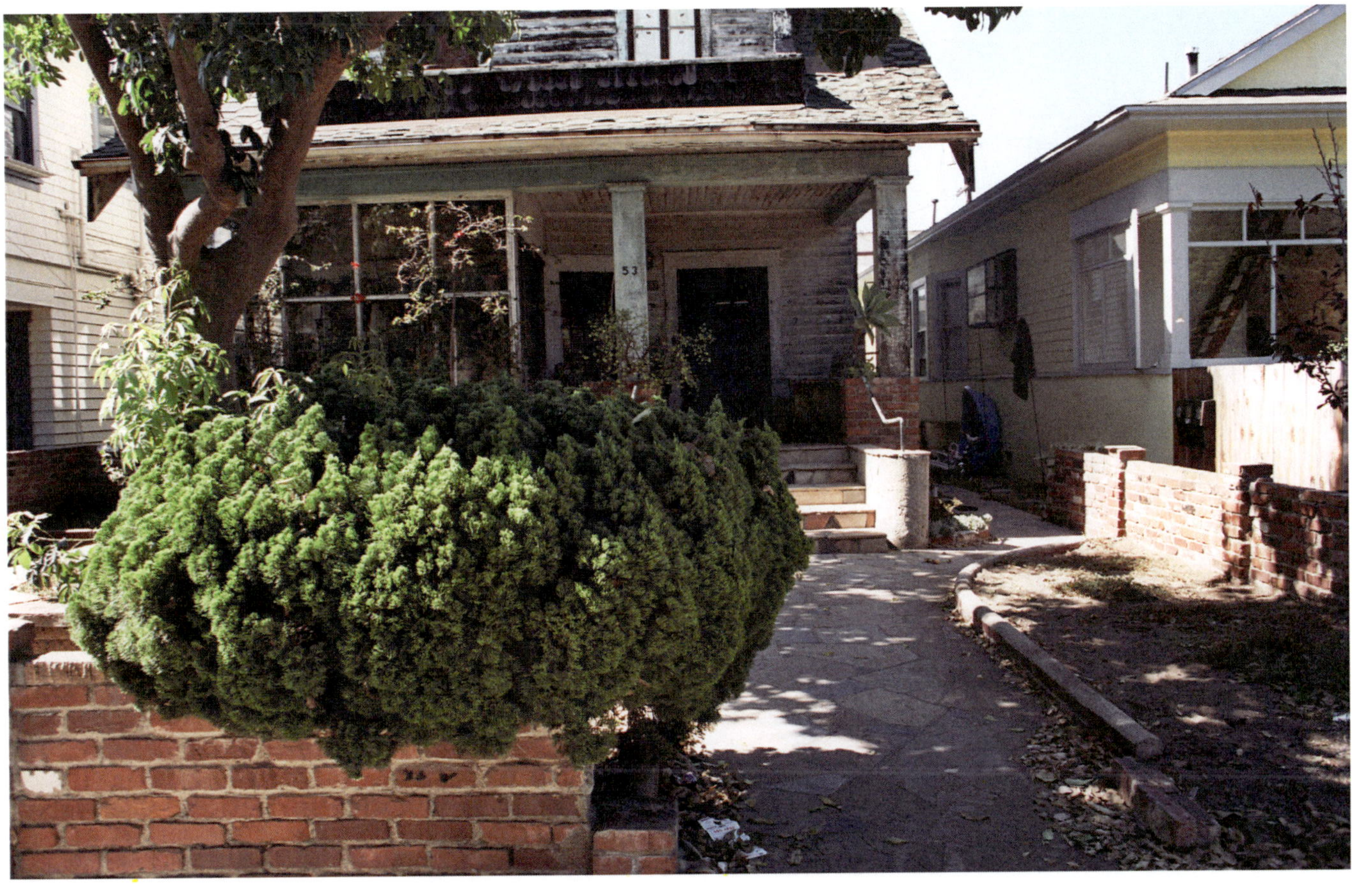

The walk streets are an essential and unique urban element of the
Venice community. Converting them into streets would be an aberration.
Widening them would be an insensitive act, the benefits of which (better
fire protection access), would be far outweighed by the loss of scale
and intimacy. —Albert Elzas, President, Ozone Properties

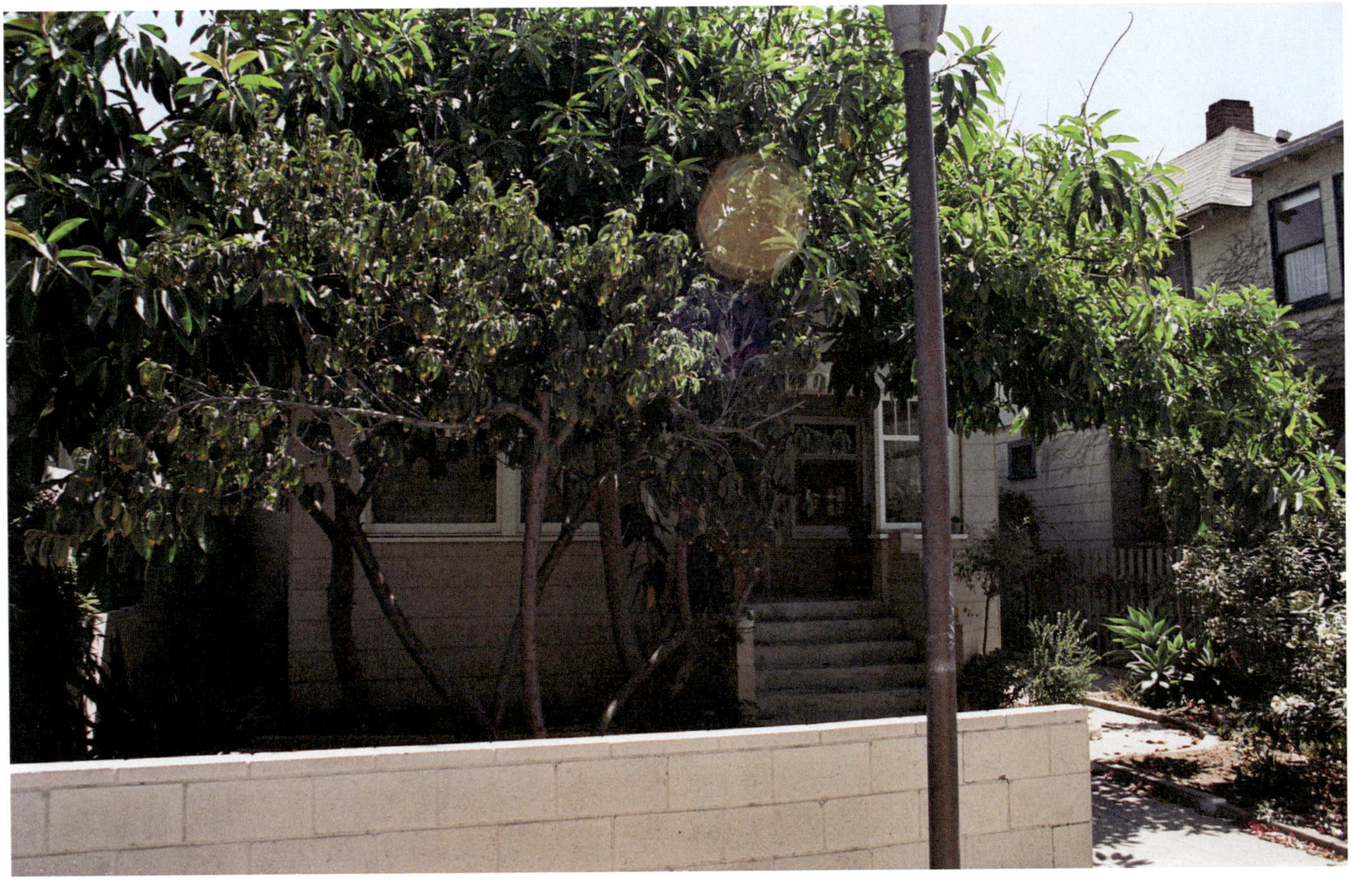

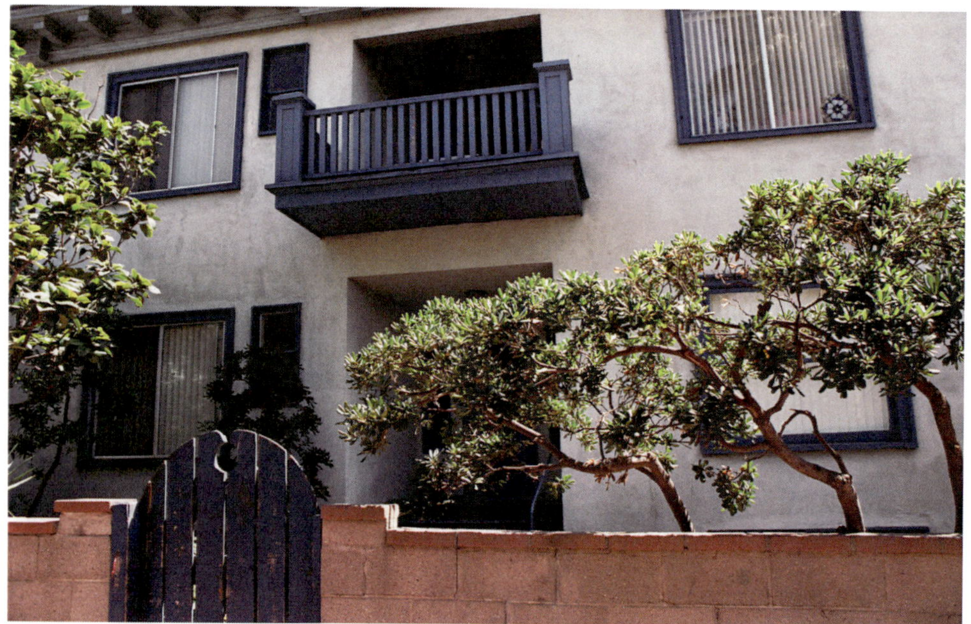

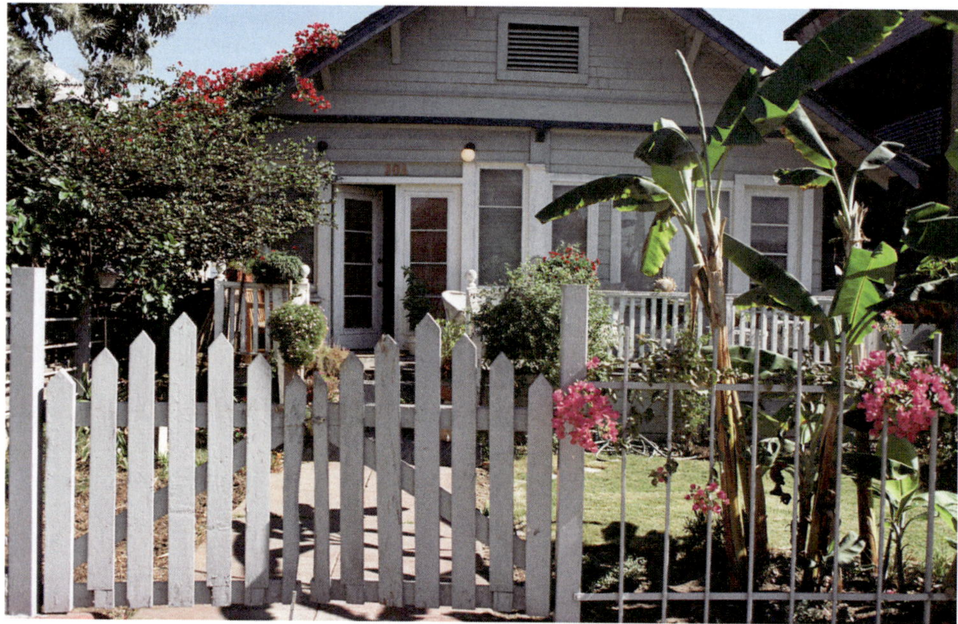

Over a hundred trees,
vegetable gardens,
herb gardens would
be destroyed.
A public nuisance
would be created.
Existing alleyways
are sufficient for
emergency vehicles.
Put energy into
enforcement of
parking restrictions
in alleyways, not
into adding
cement to walkways.
—Sidney Copilow

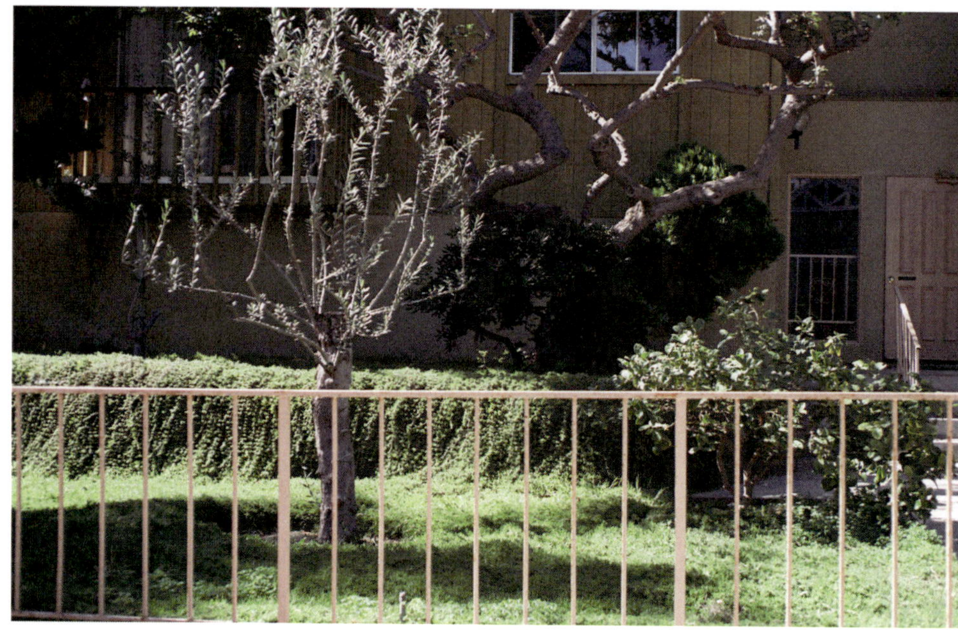

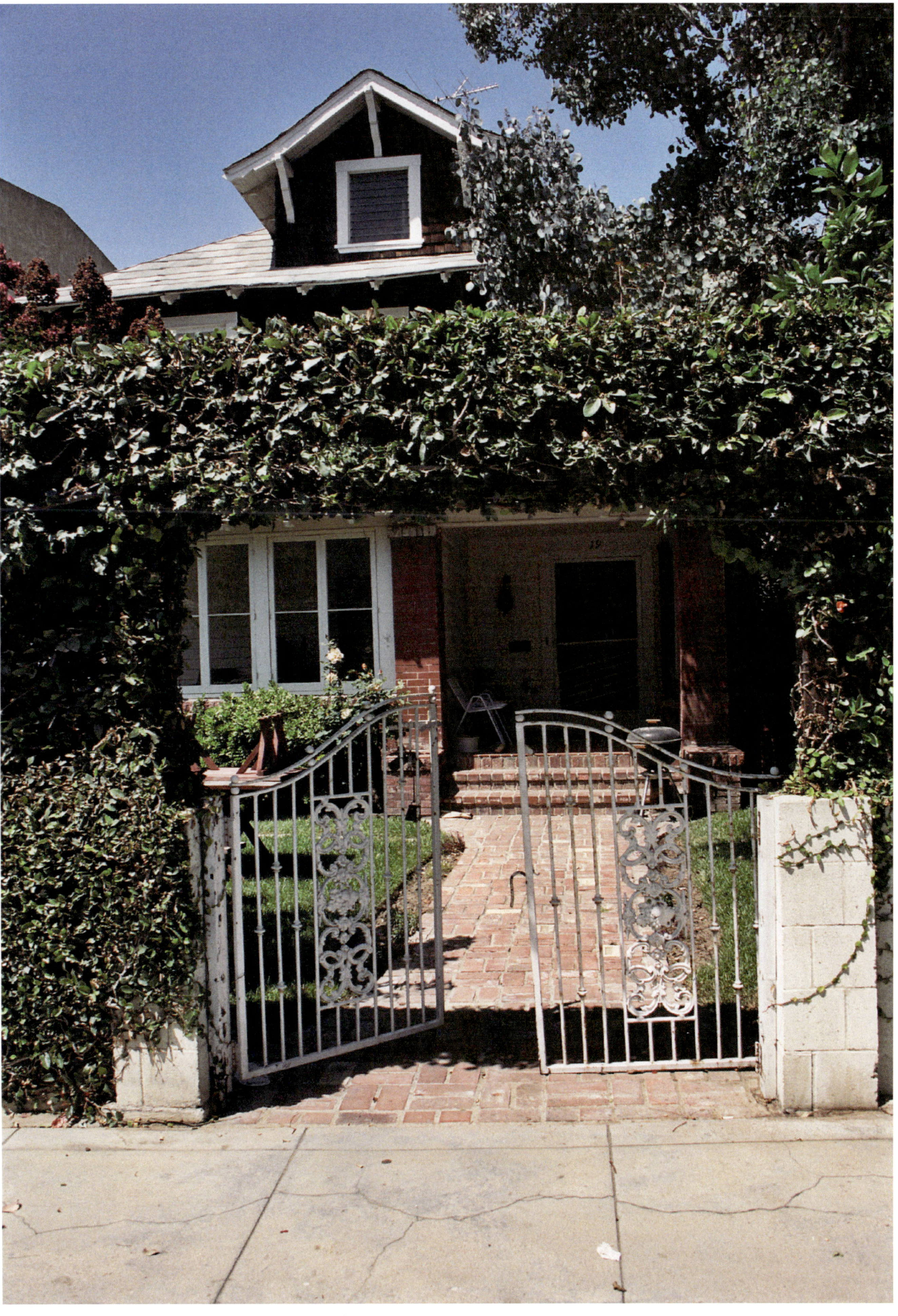

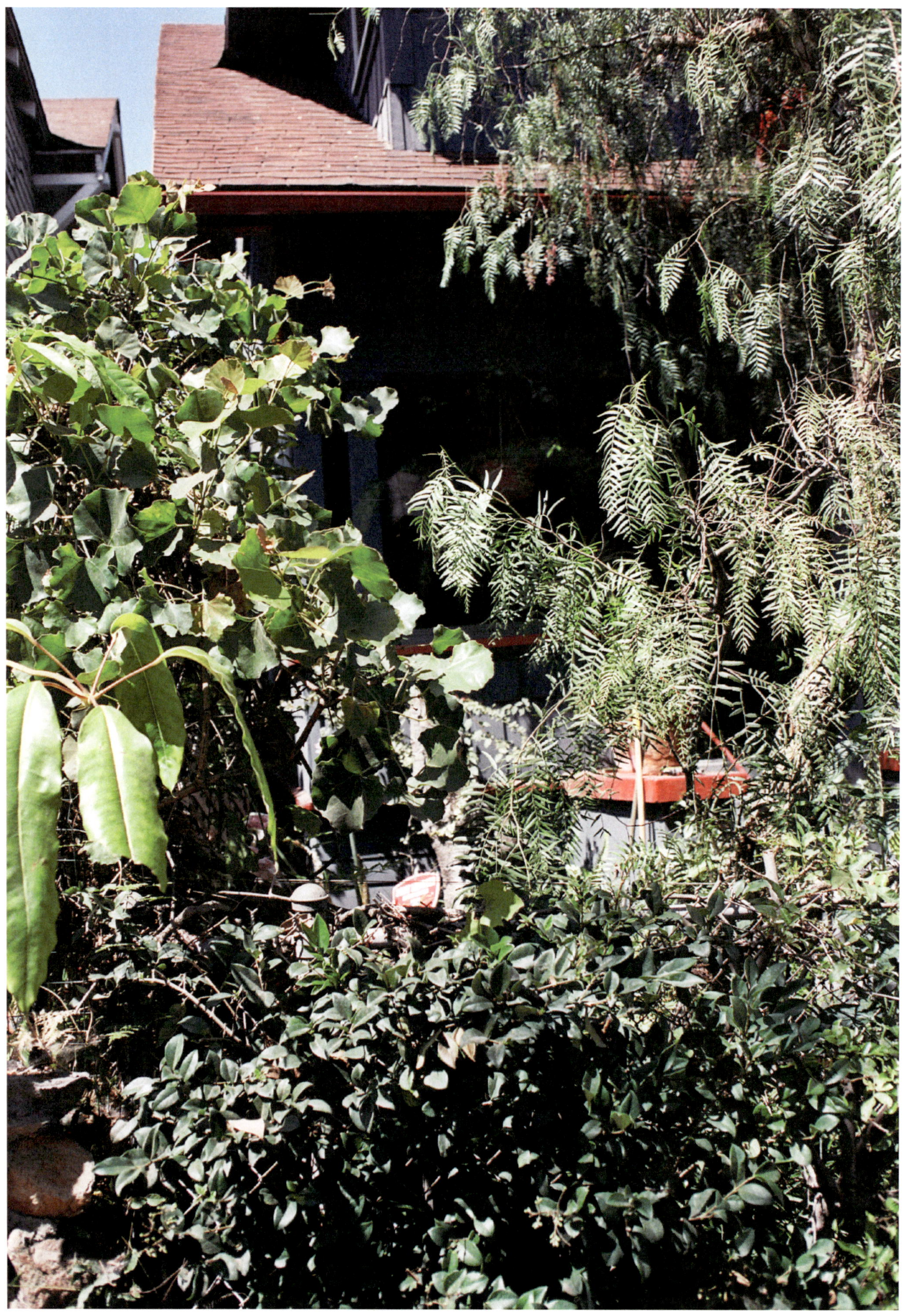

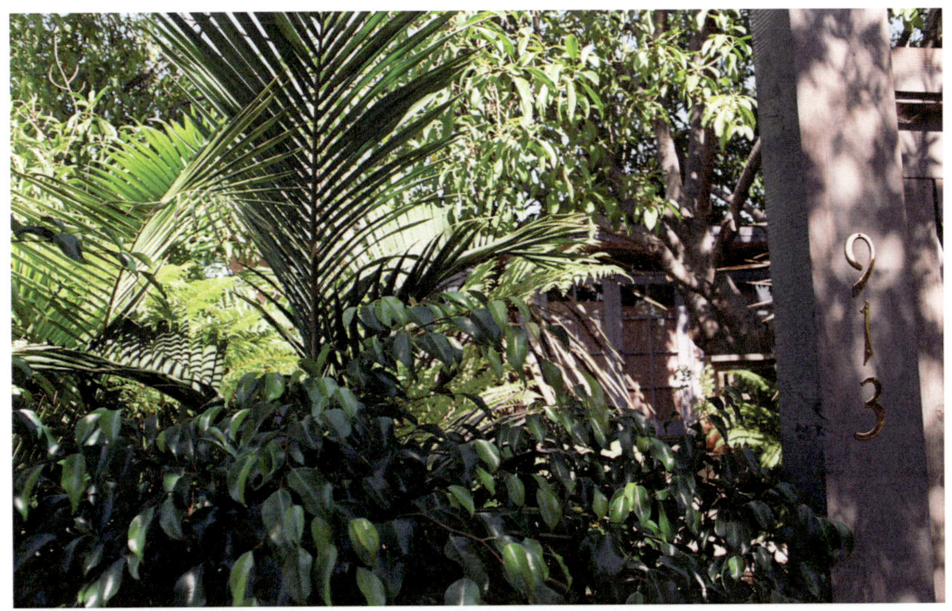

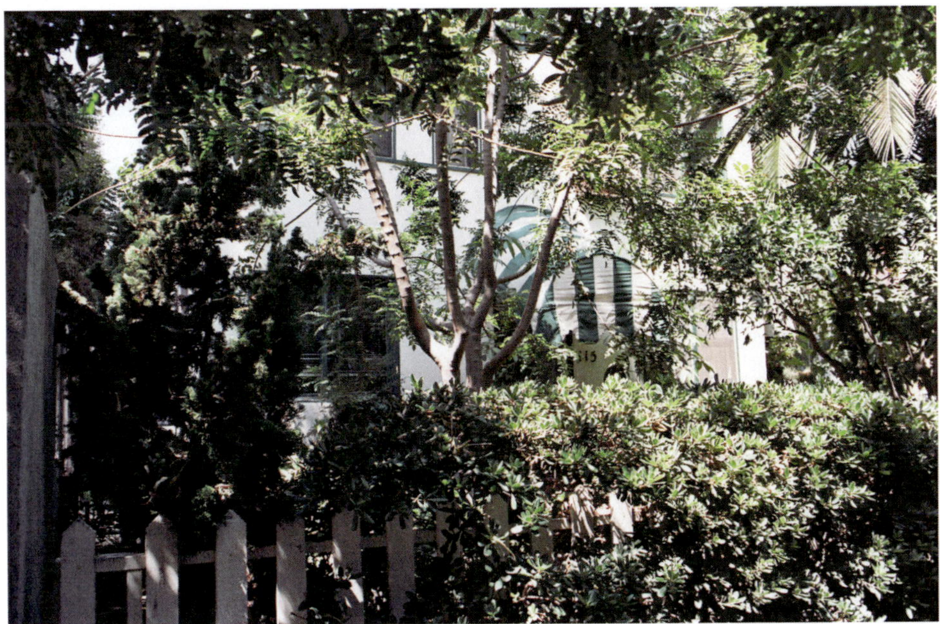

My family has lived
in Venice for the
last thirteen years.
The walk streets, to
us, have come to be
the most important
piece of landscape
architecture in
our lives. In
a city in which
peace and quiet are
ever more difficult
commodities to come
by, the walks in
Venice provide a
much needed buffer
between sanity
and continued
development of our
beach community.
Let us avoid, at
almost any cost, the
destruction of this
tranquil zone within
our neighborhood.
-Stan Swerling

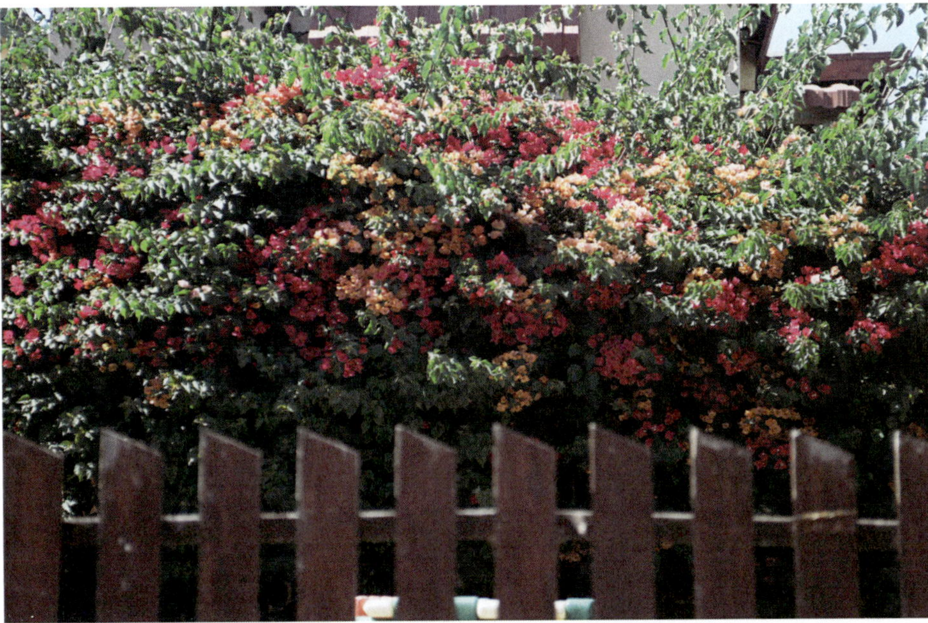

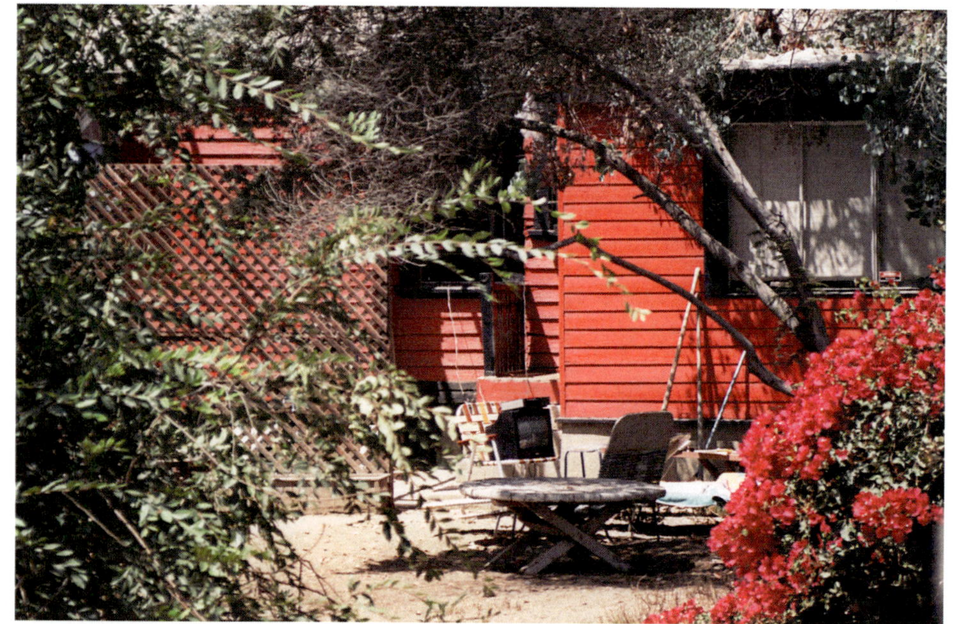

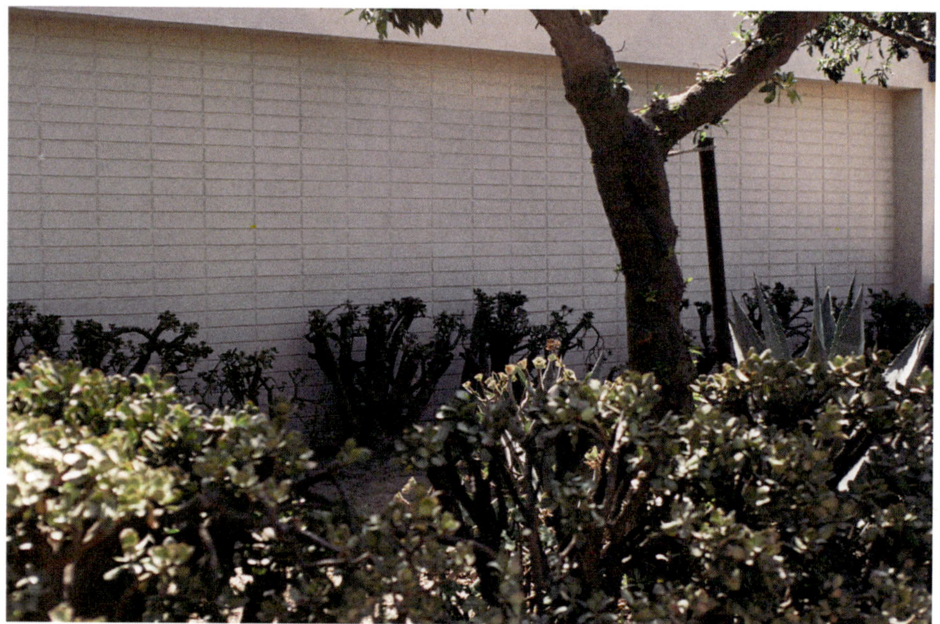

To demolish the walk
streets would destroy
the rural—like atmosphere
and beauty residents as
well as city dwellers
(who frequent these
areas on Week ends
and holidays) enjoy.
Allowing vehicles the
use of the above mentioned
streets would pollute the
air, add noise and create
congestion.
—Sara Bil Lee Skidelsky

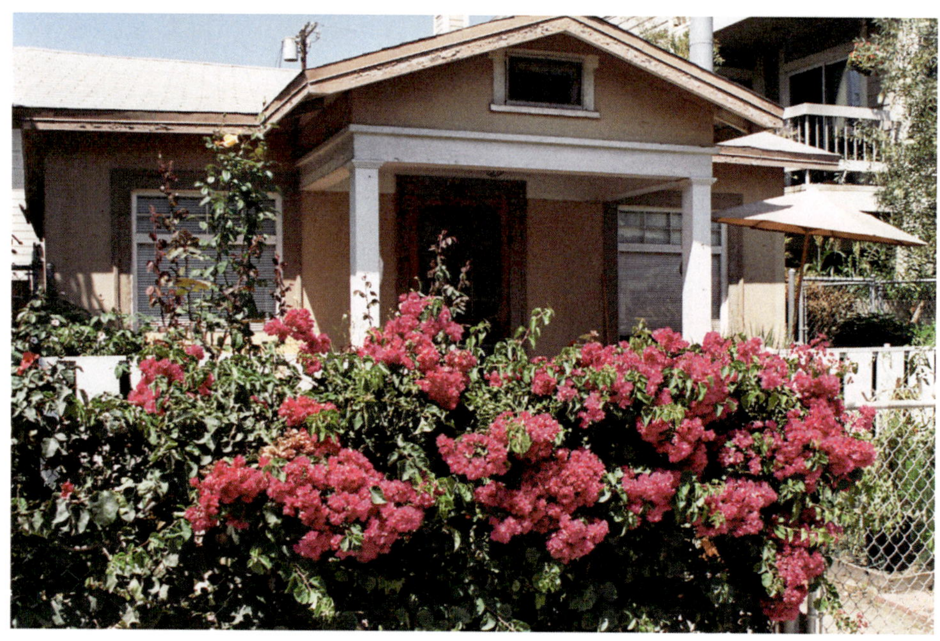

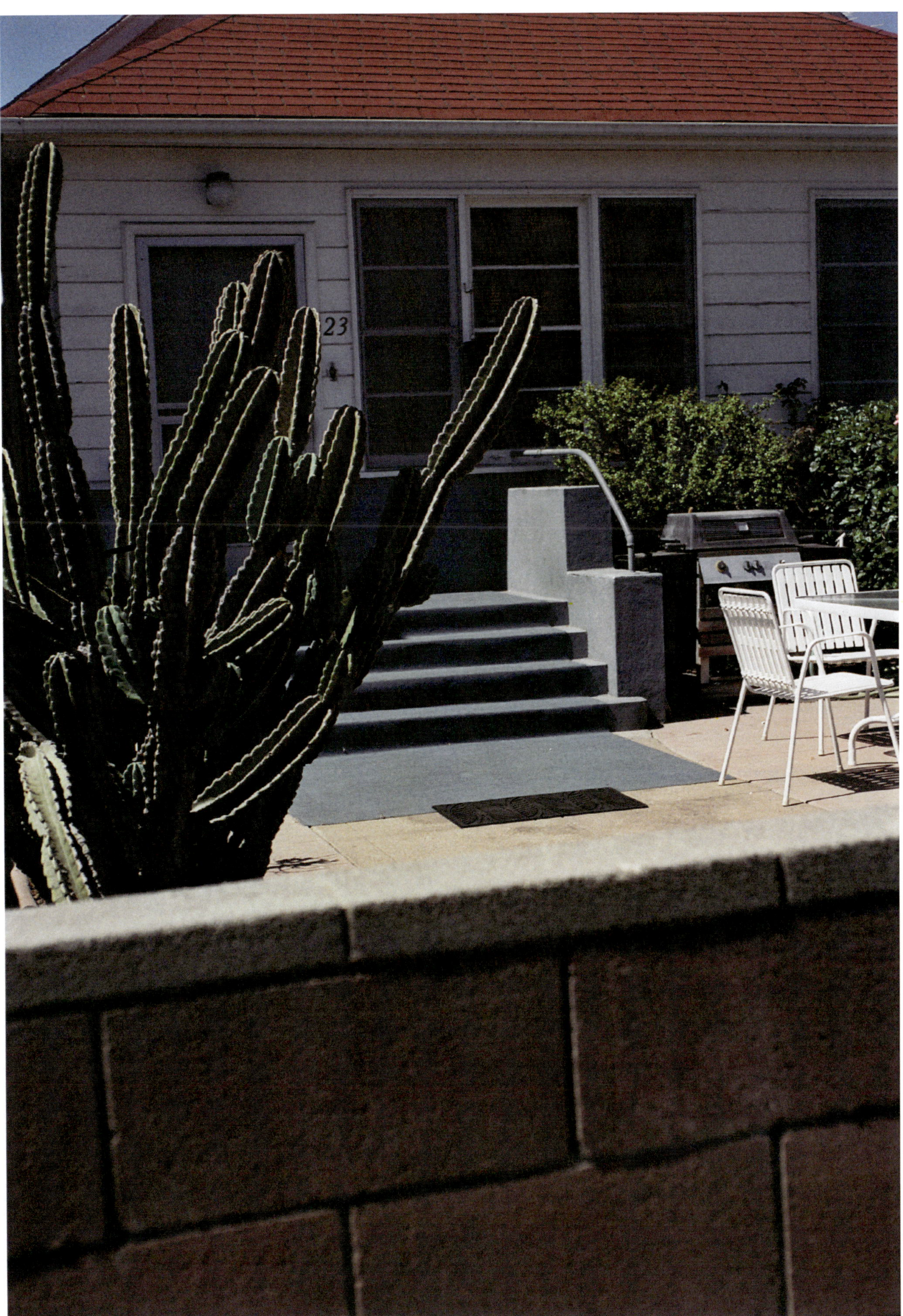

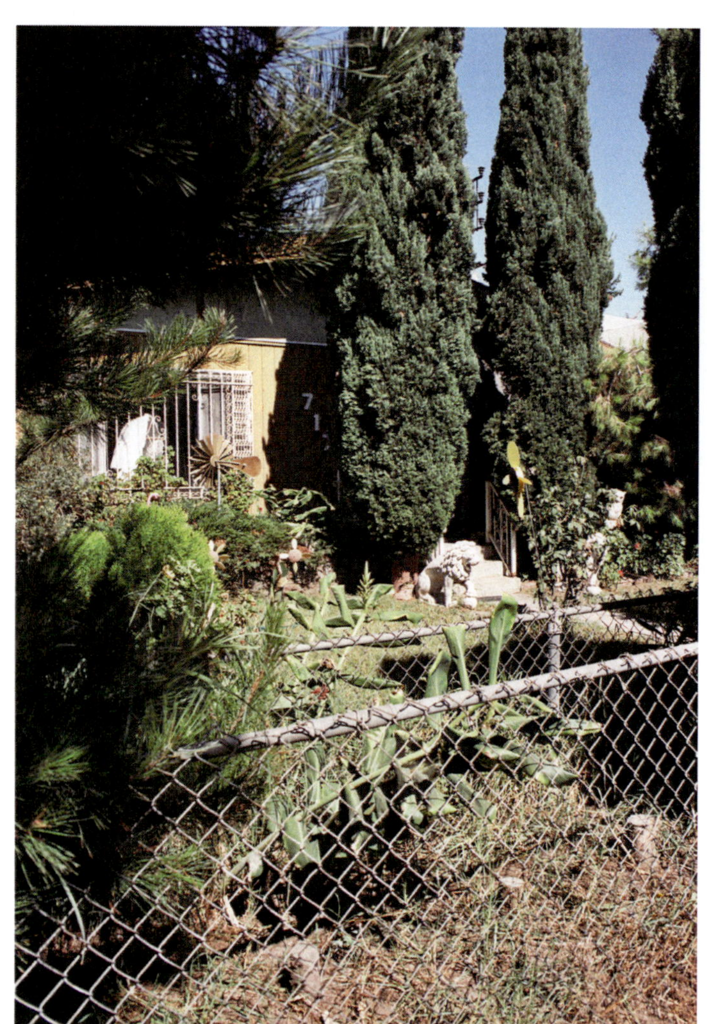
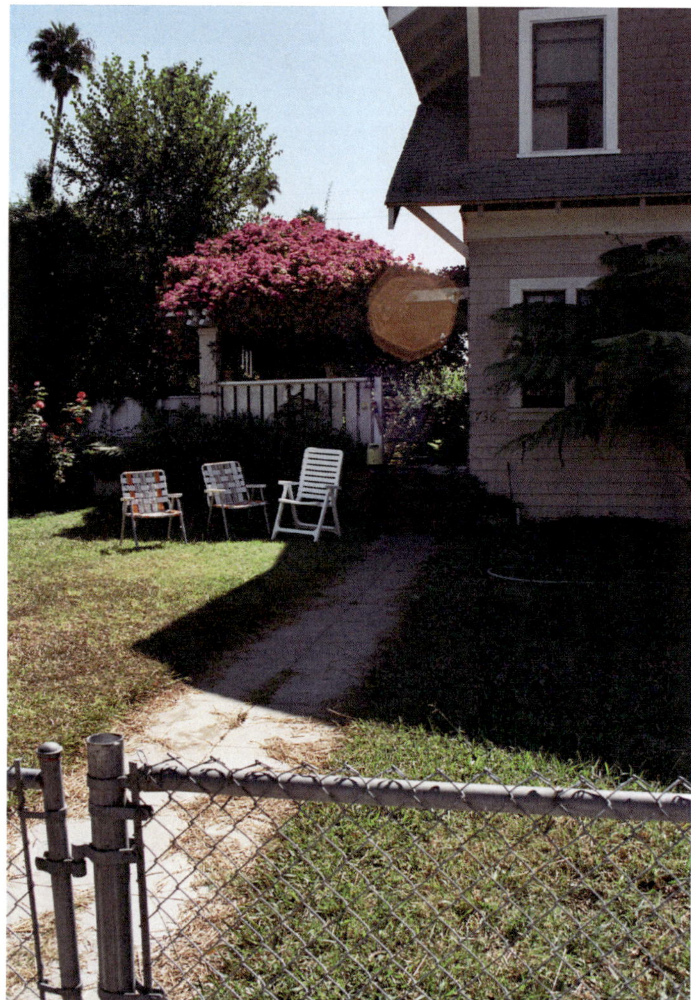

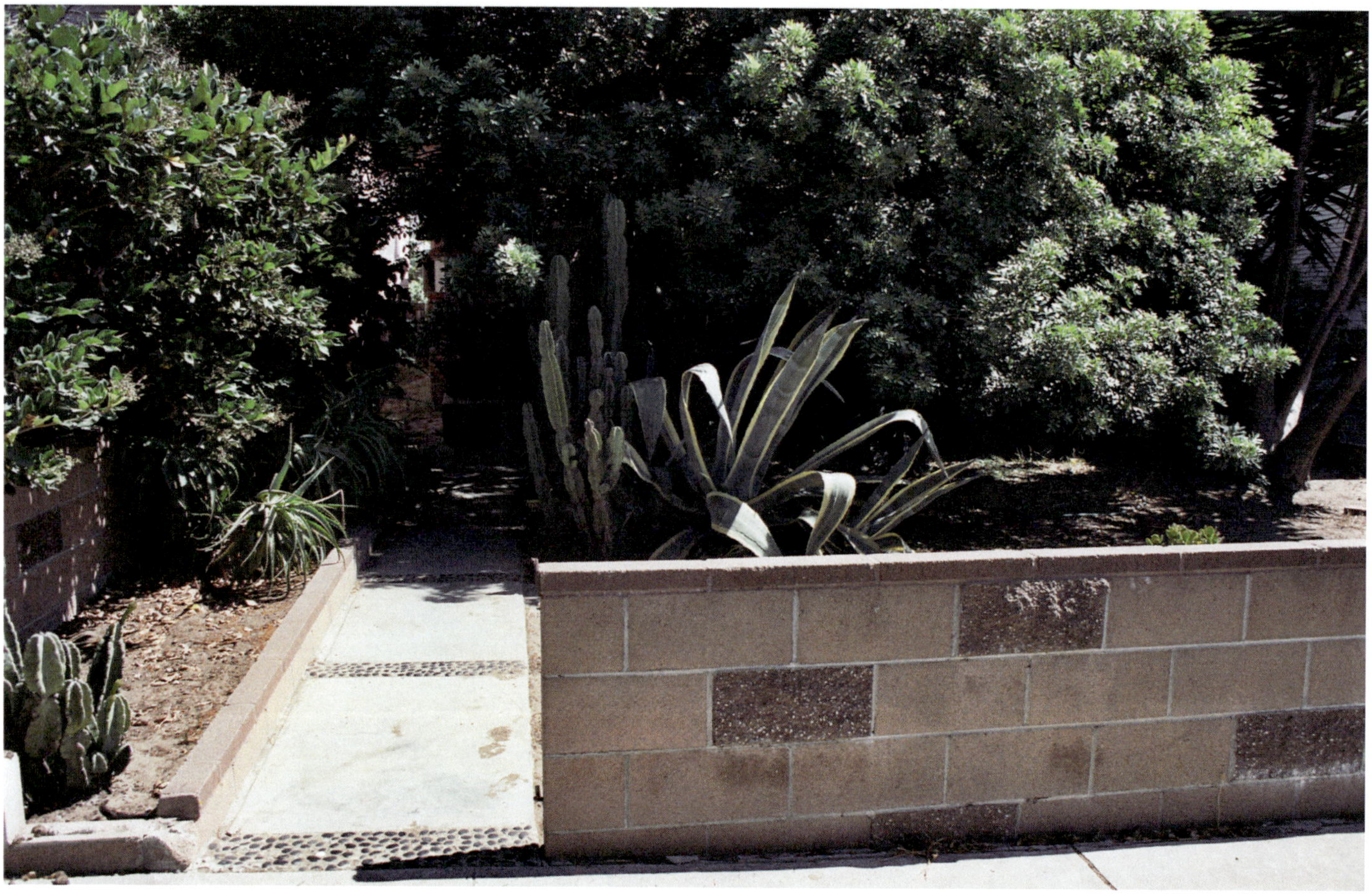

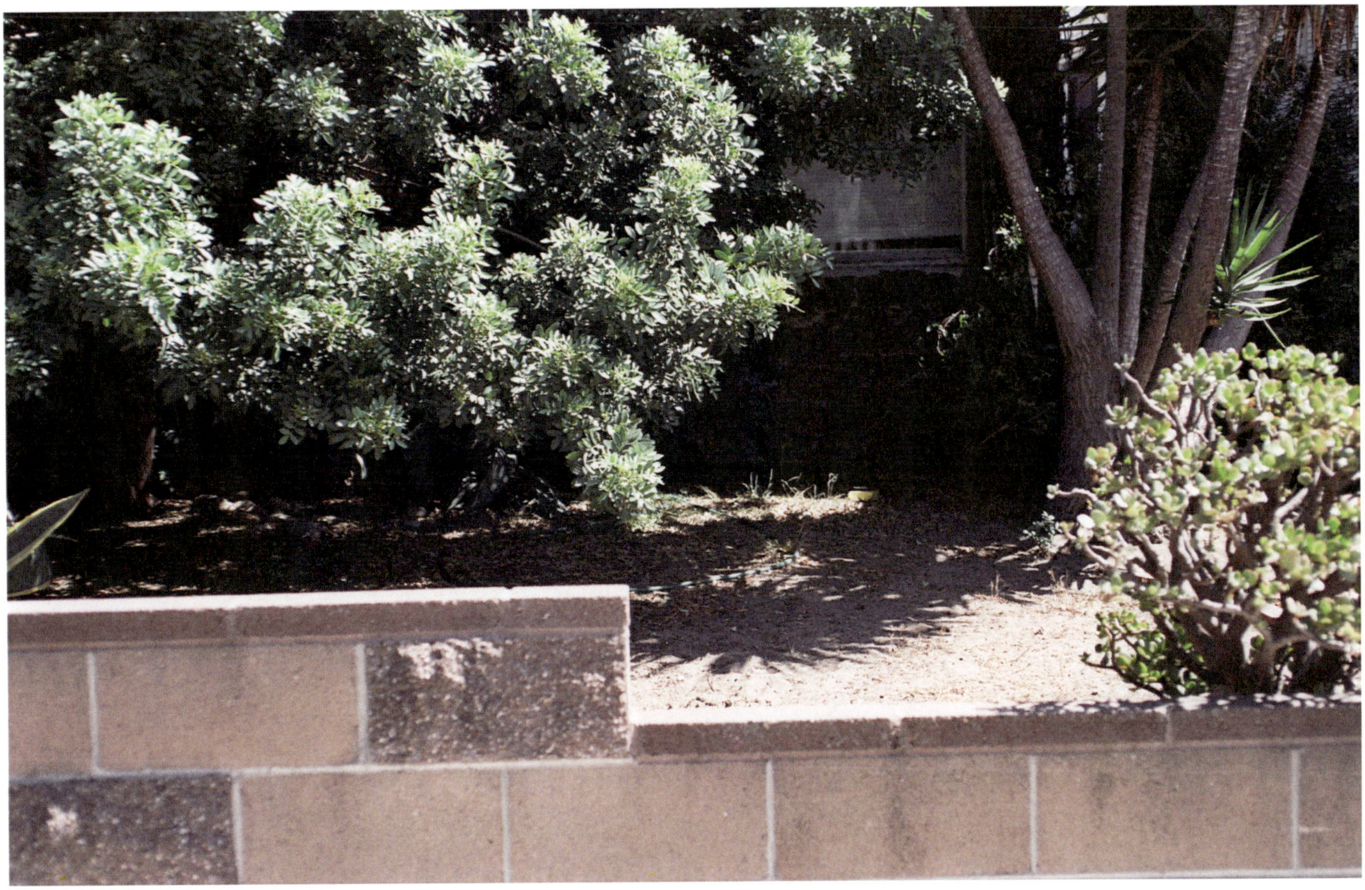

When we discovered the walk streets in the Milwood area, we were
immediately charmed. Much of the charm is due to the narrow
walkways, and we feel strongly that broadening them would destroy
the character of the neighborhood. —Marilyn Levy

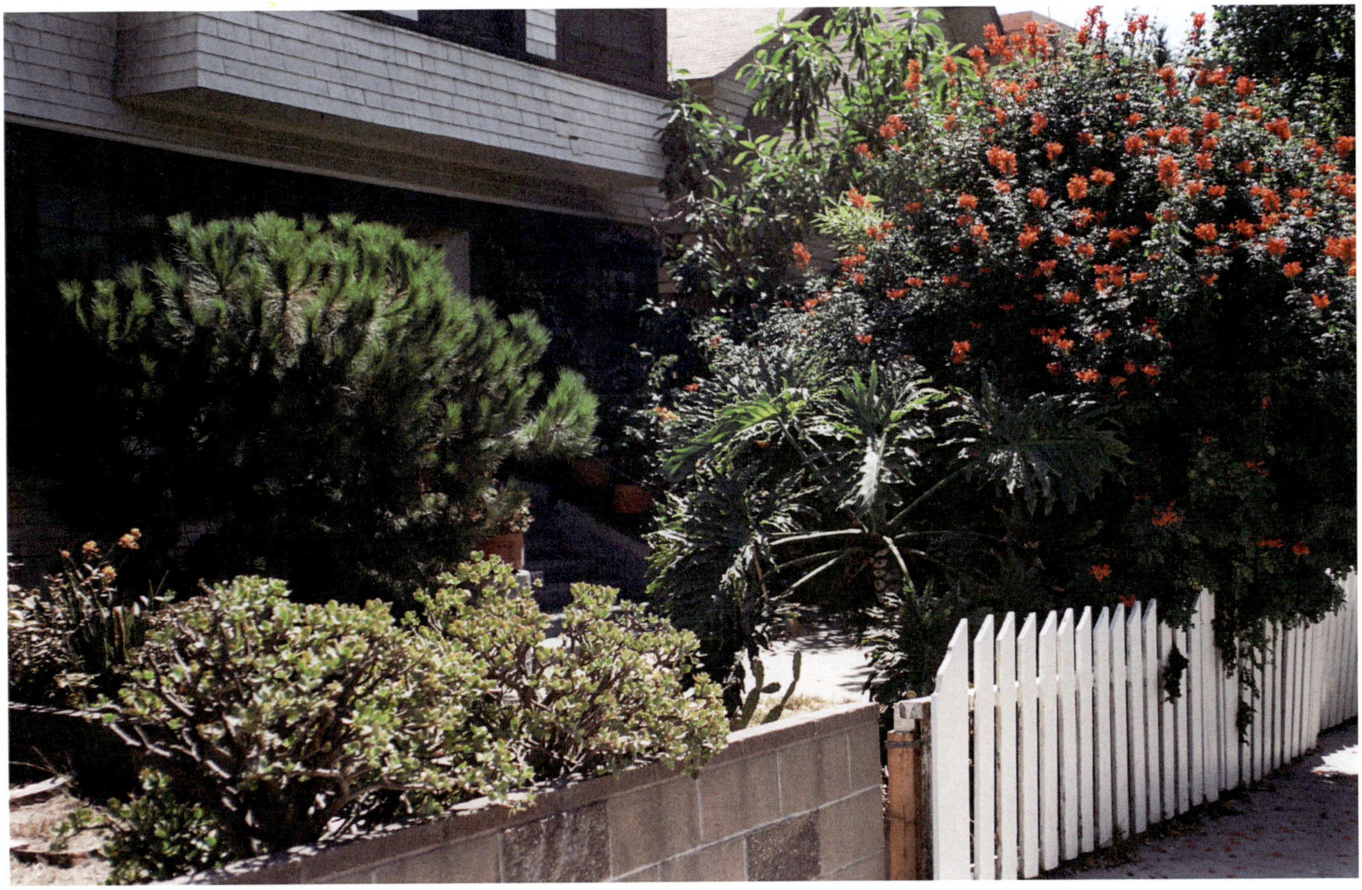

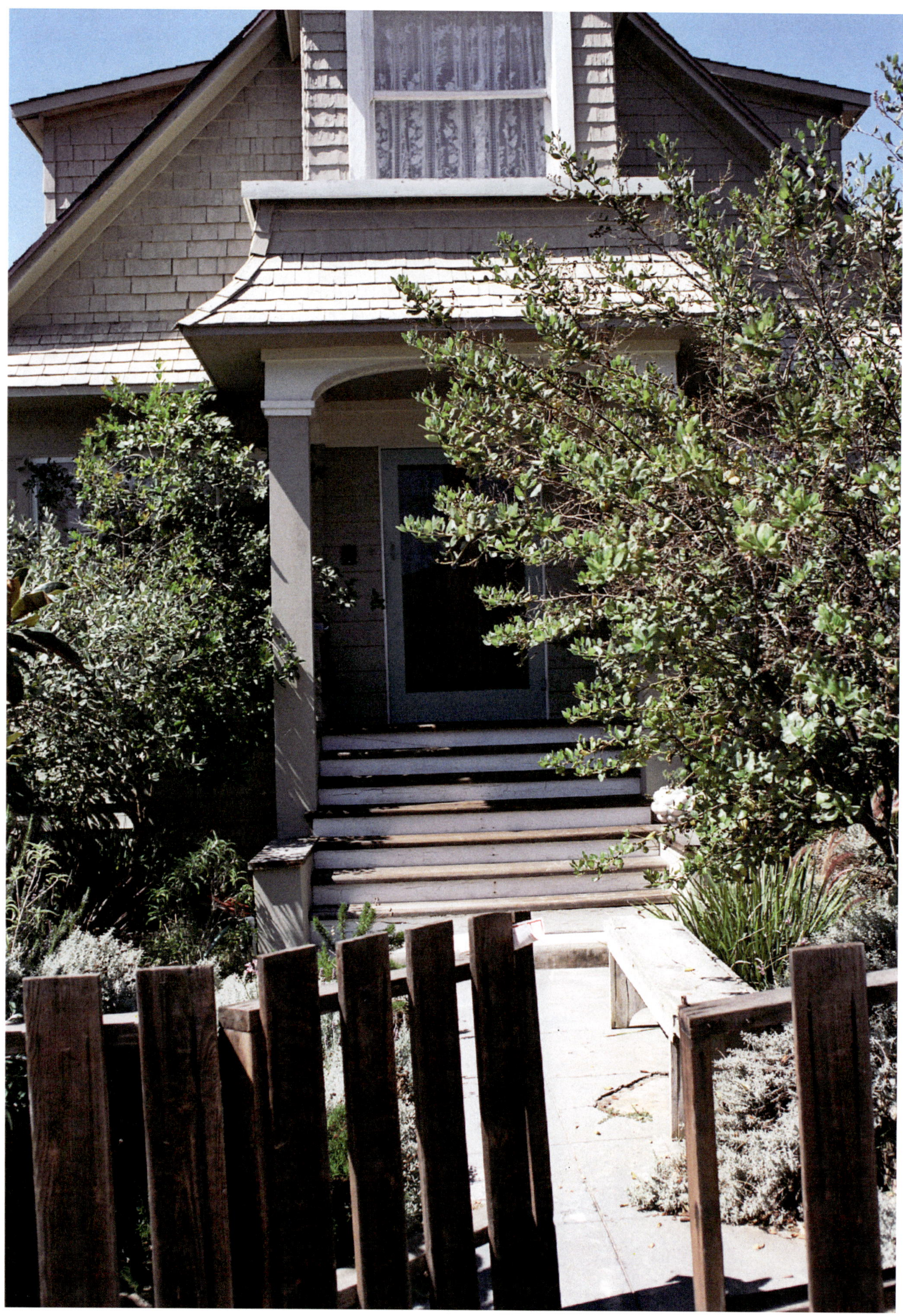

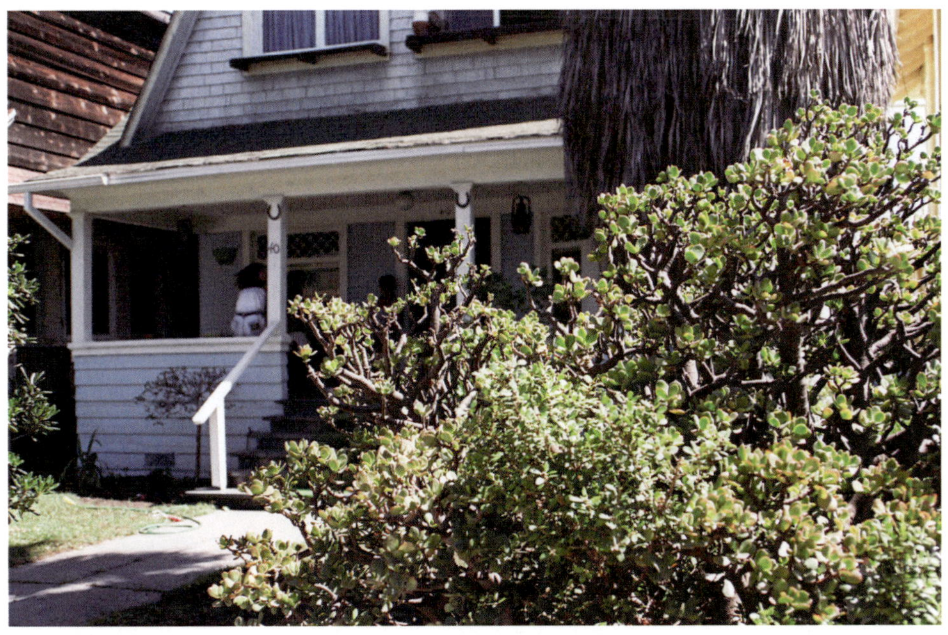

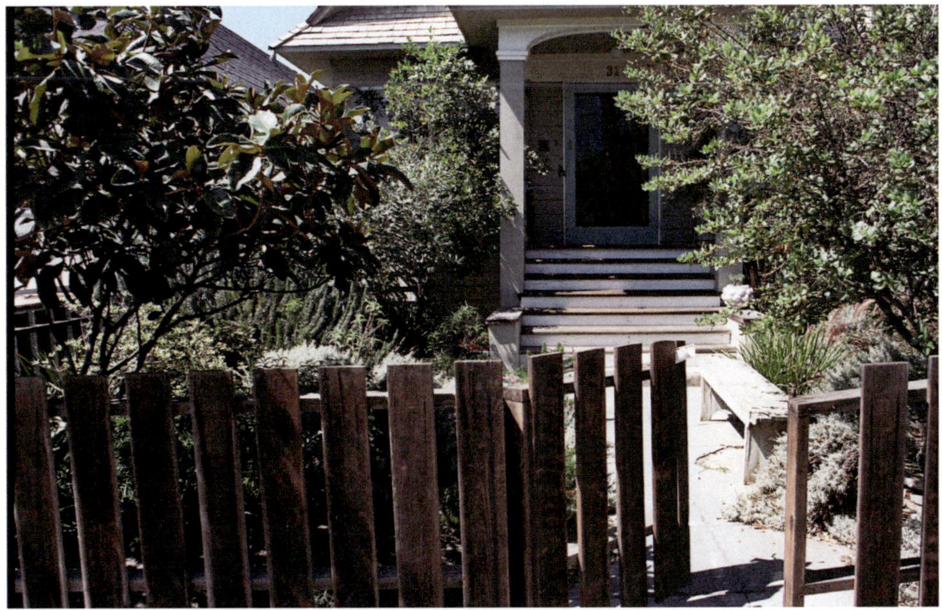

Jane Jacobs, in her classic treatise of city planning, "The Death and Life of Great American Cities", notes the importance of this type of design for neighborhood safety, both for the visiting public and residents. Venice residents experience this delicate balance of their front yards and patios offering neighborhood charm to visitors while these yards simultaneously provide a buffer zone for their own privacy"
—Walk Street Preservation Committee.

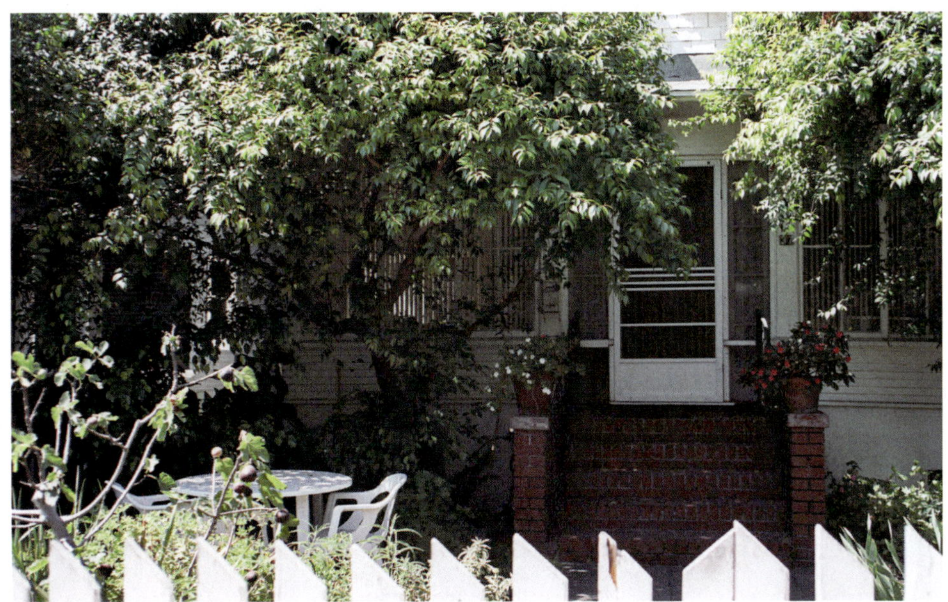

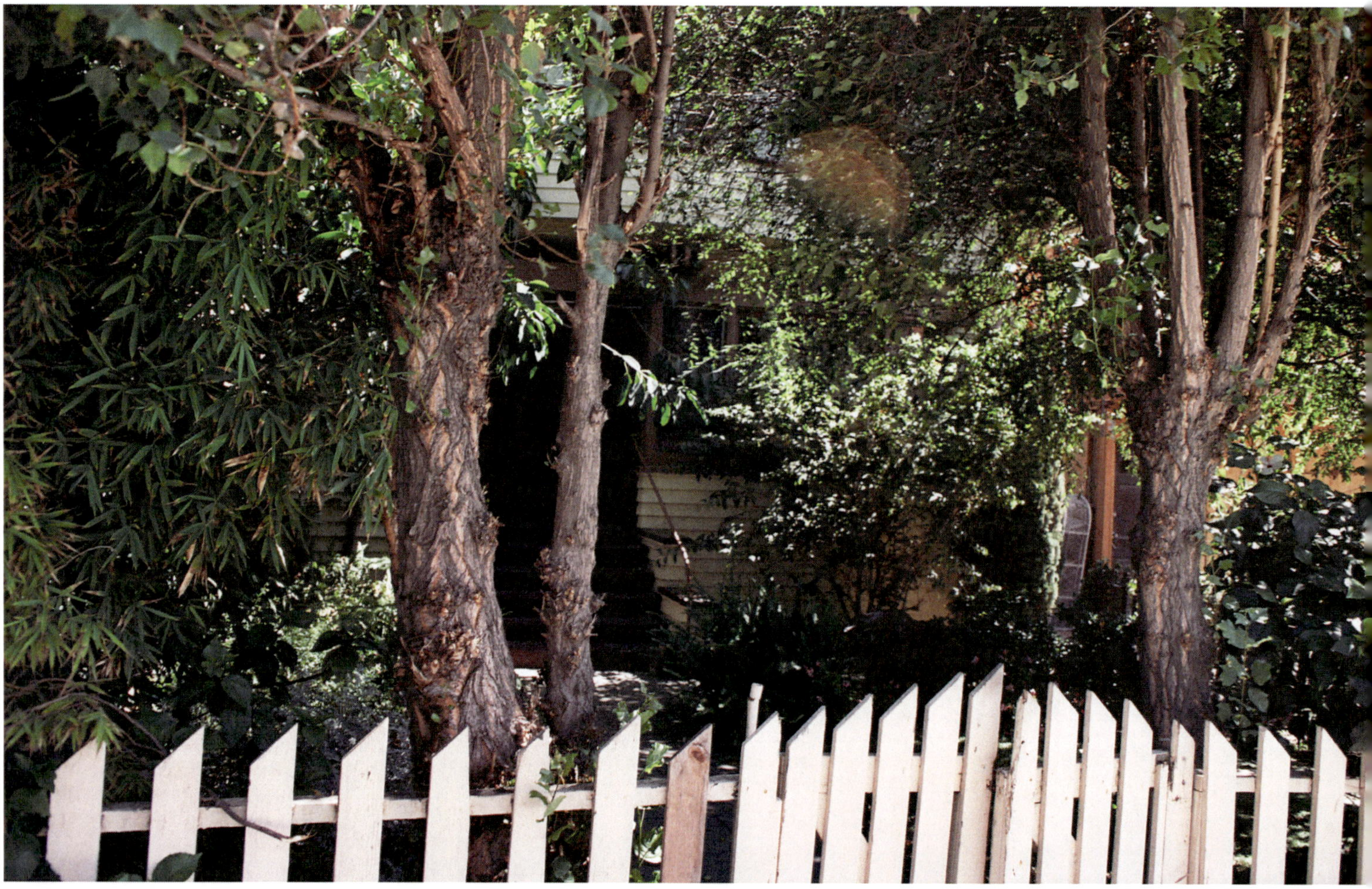

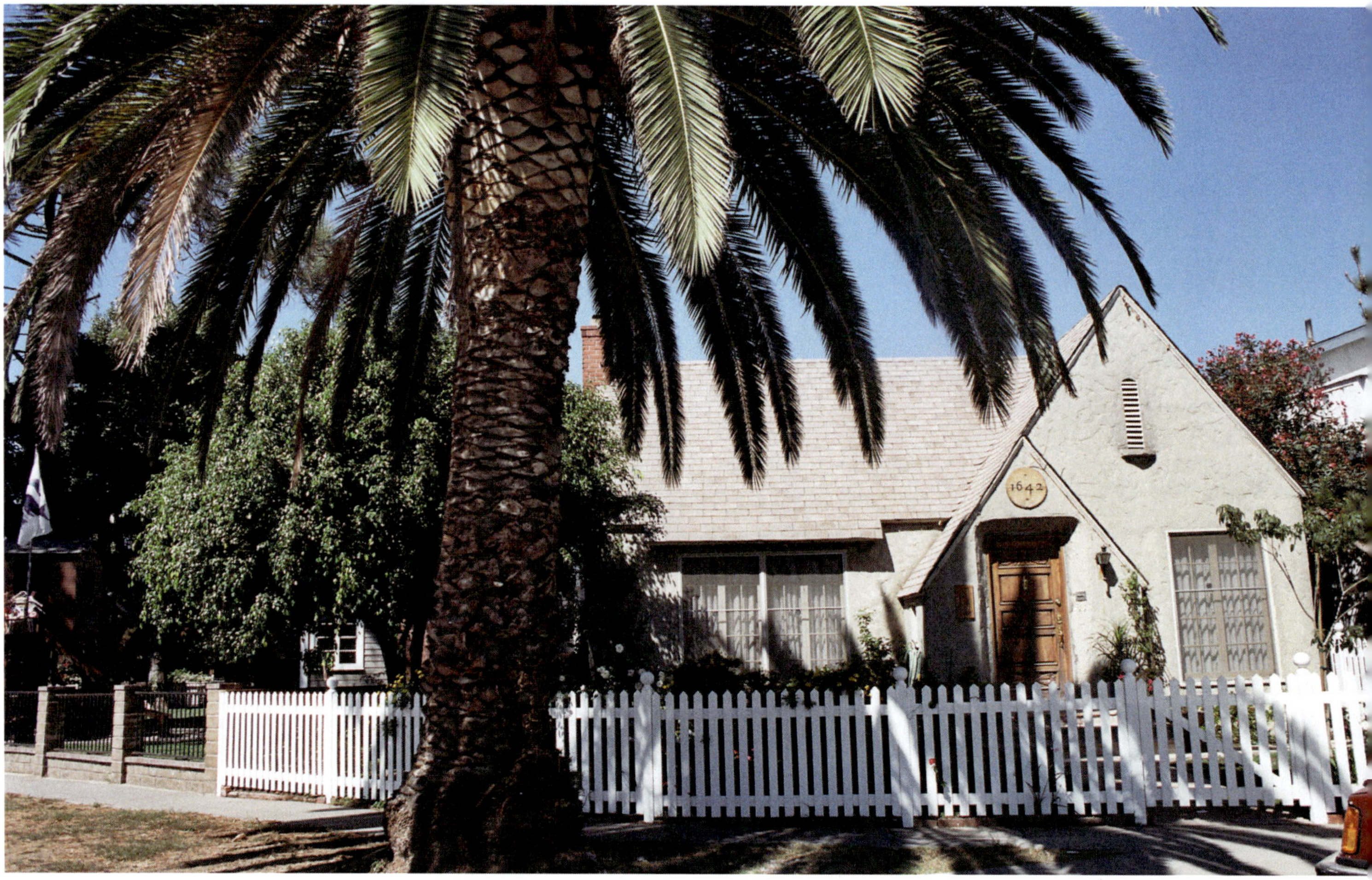

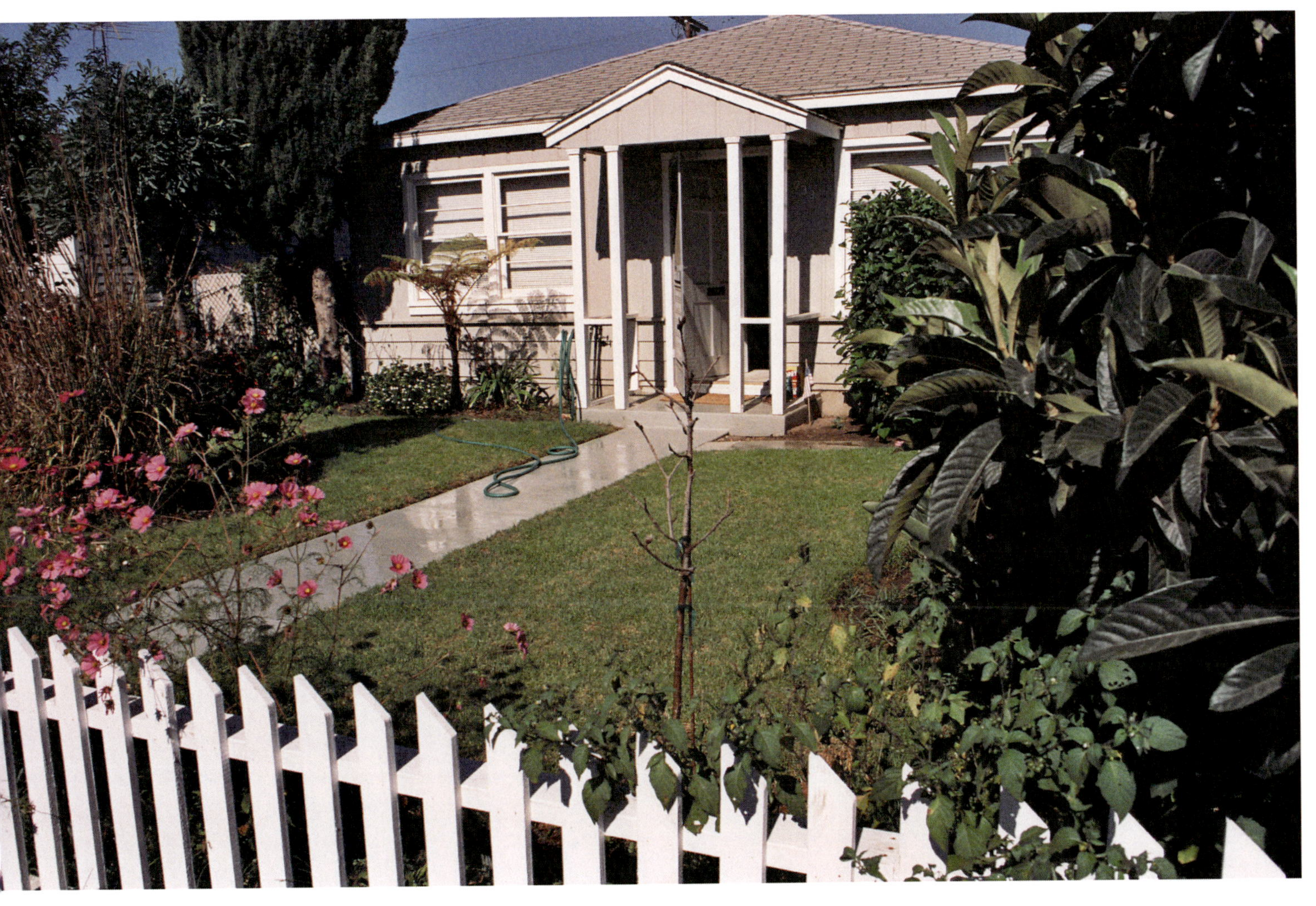

As a walkstreet resident I can attest that these unique walkways provide an intimate respite from the typically impersonal, car-oriented living arrangements that reign supreme in Los Angeles. First and foremost, the walkstreets provide an aesthetic delight in a city of residential eyesores. Most walkstreets have beautiful and variant yards adorning charming character-filled houses or apartments. The absence of cars gives the area an almost garden-like quality. When I sit outside I marvel at how distant I feel from the nearby streets crowded with cars. Having lived in other neighborhoods on the Westside, I appreciate the beauty of the walkstreet neighborhoods. Widening these walkstreets by 10, 15 or even 20 feet will permanently alter and scar this aesthetic oasis. The removal of trees and yards and the wider expanses of concrete will cause the walkstreets to begin to resemble the car-strewn alleys that back most of the buildings in this neighborhood. Widening will rob this residential setting of its uniqueness. —Jens Koepke

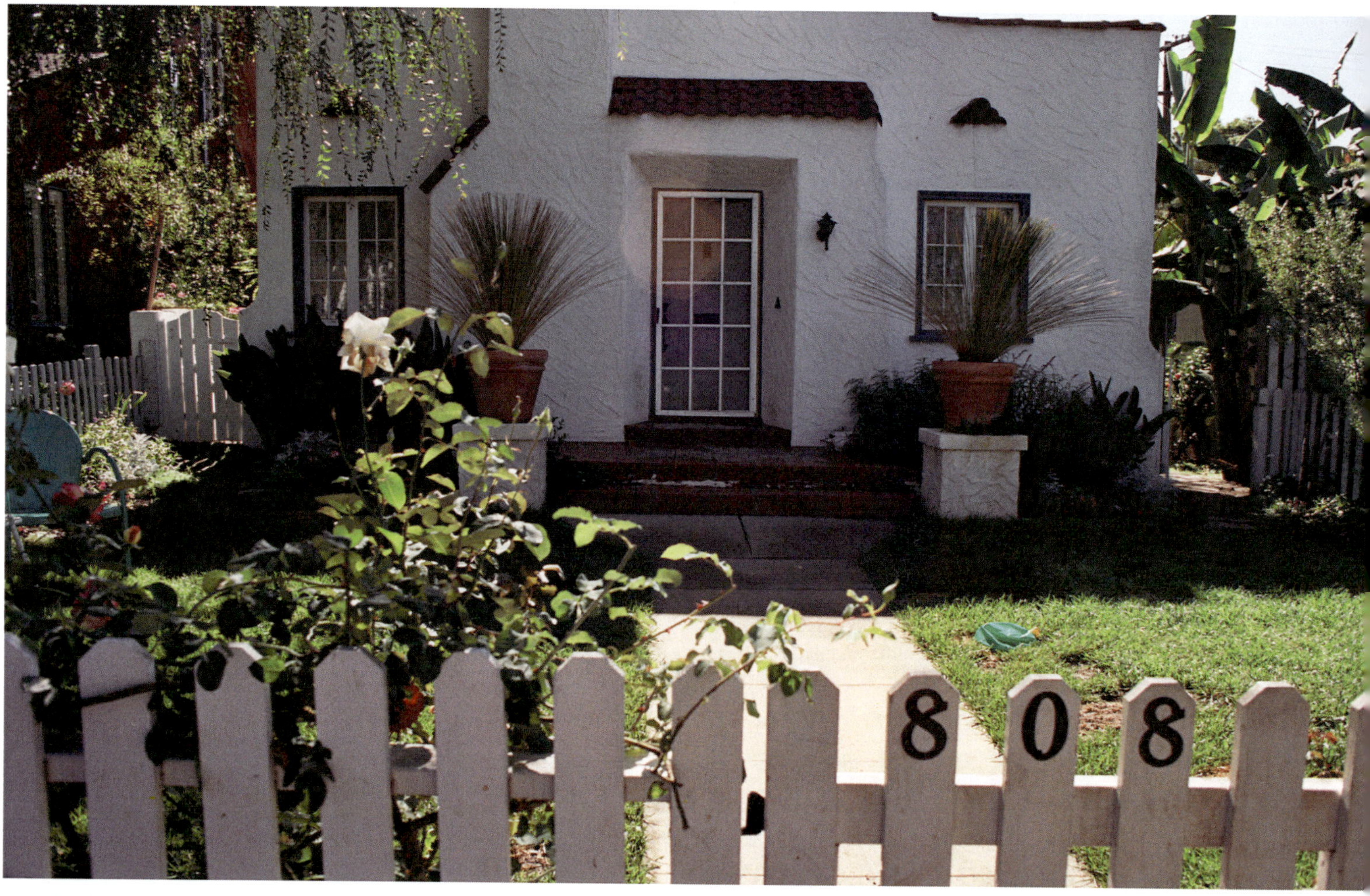

808

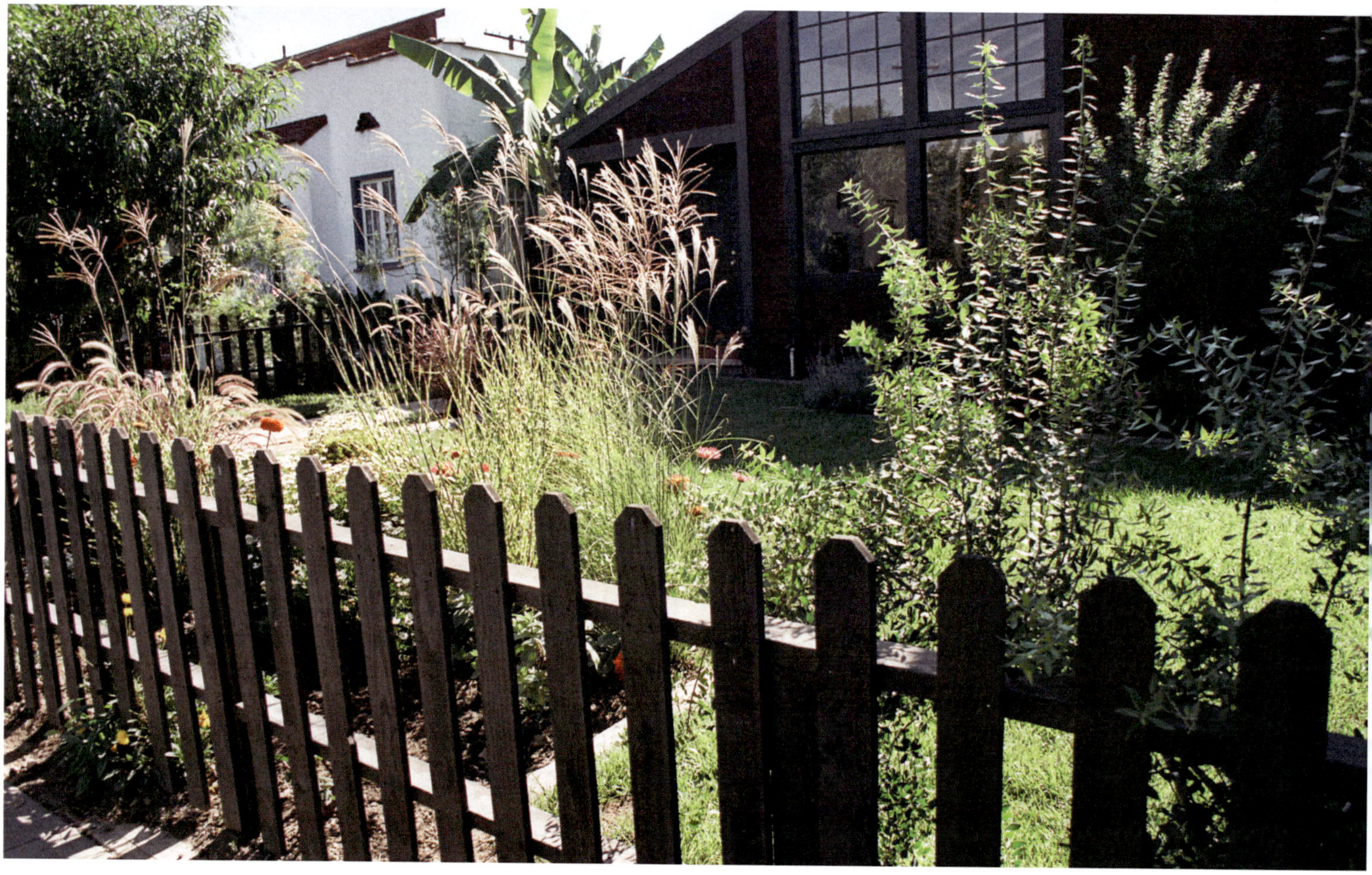

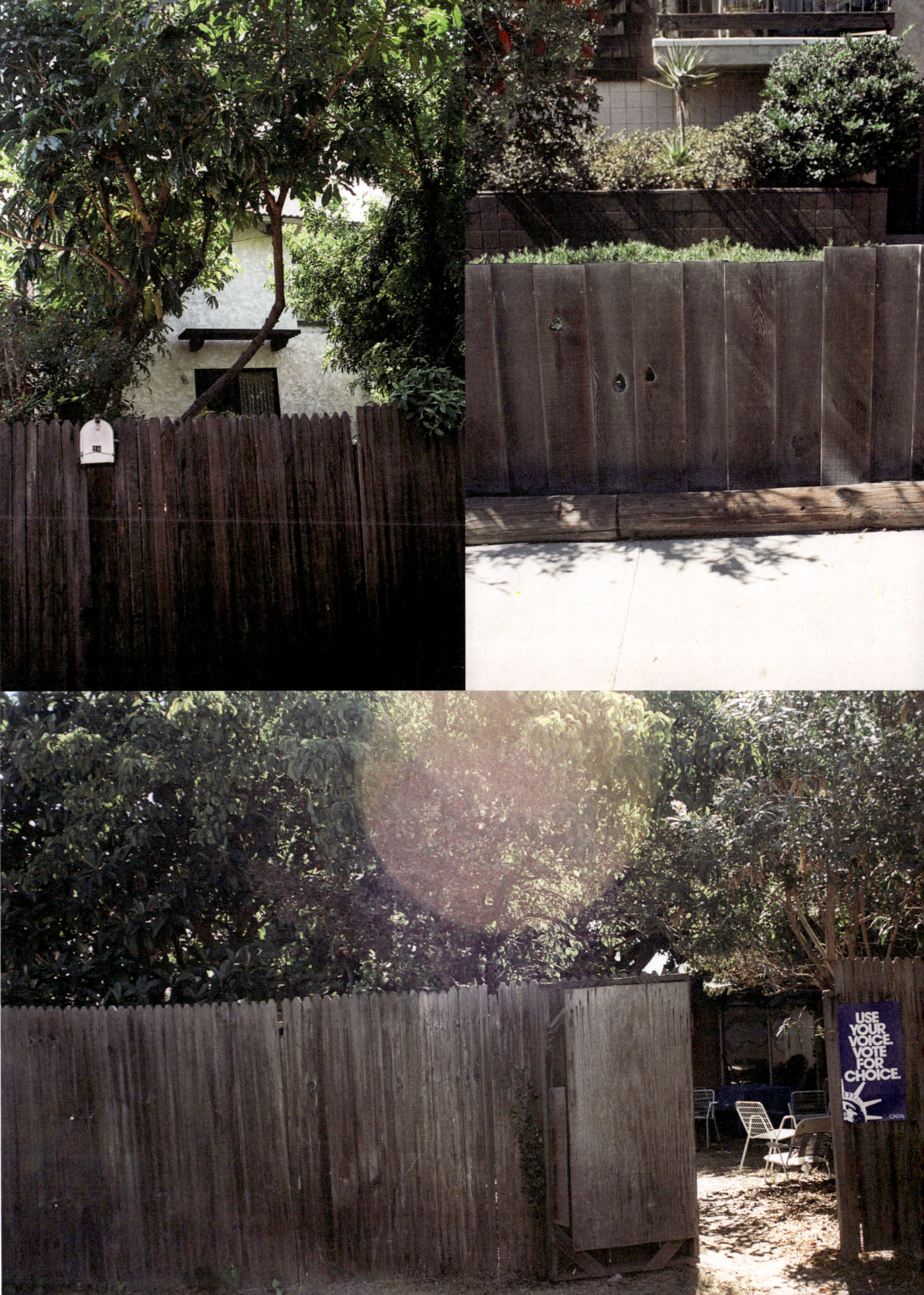
USE
YOUR
VOICE.
VOTE
FOR
CHOICE.

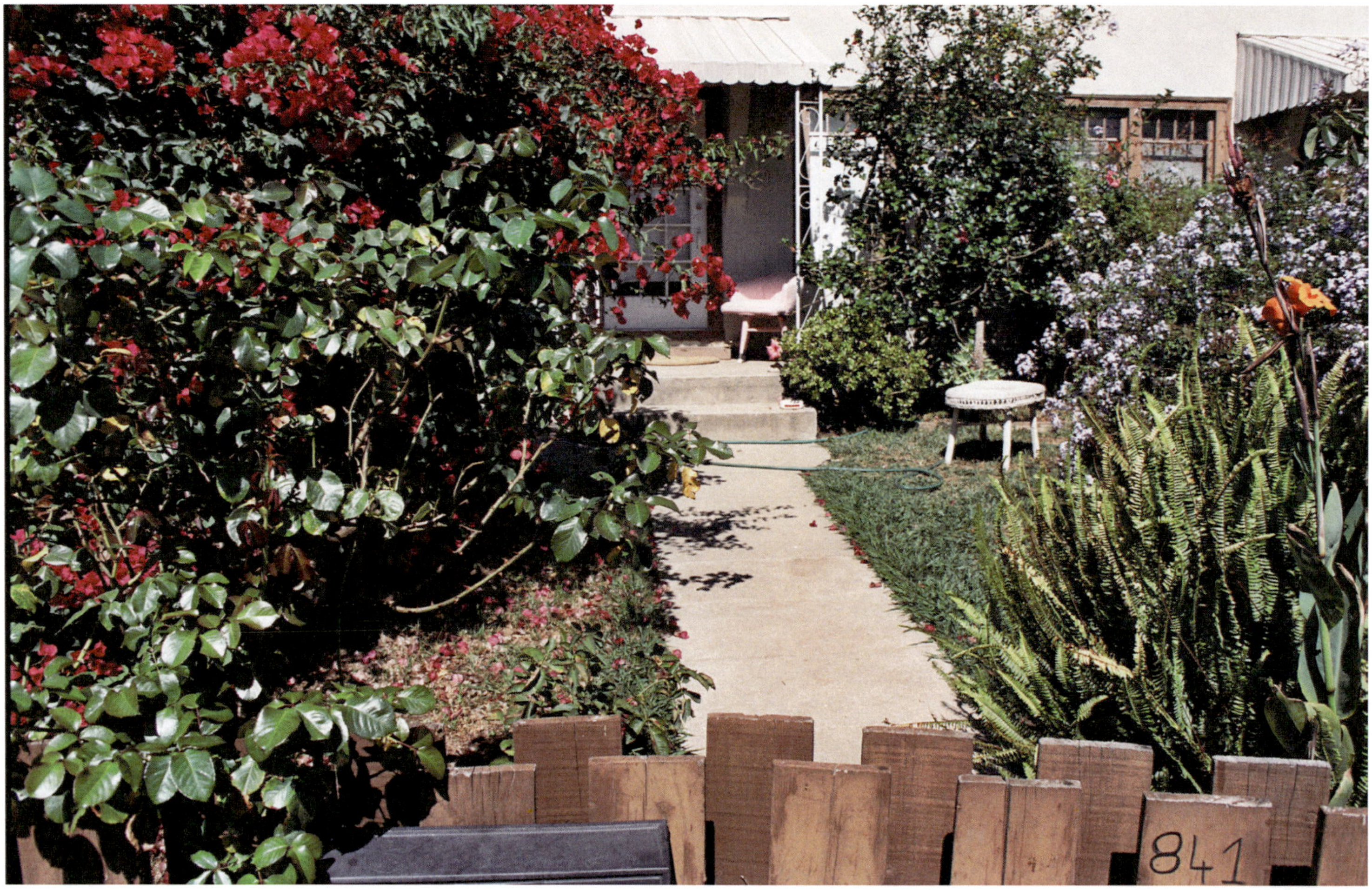

841

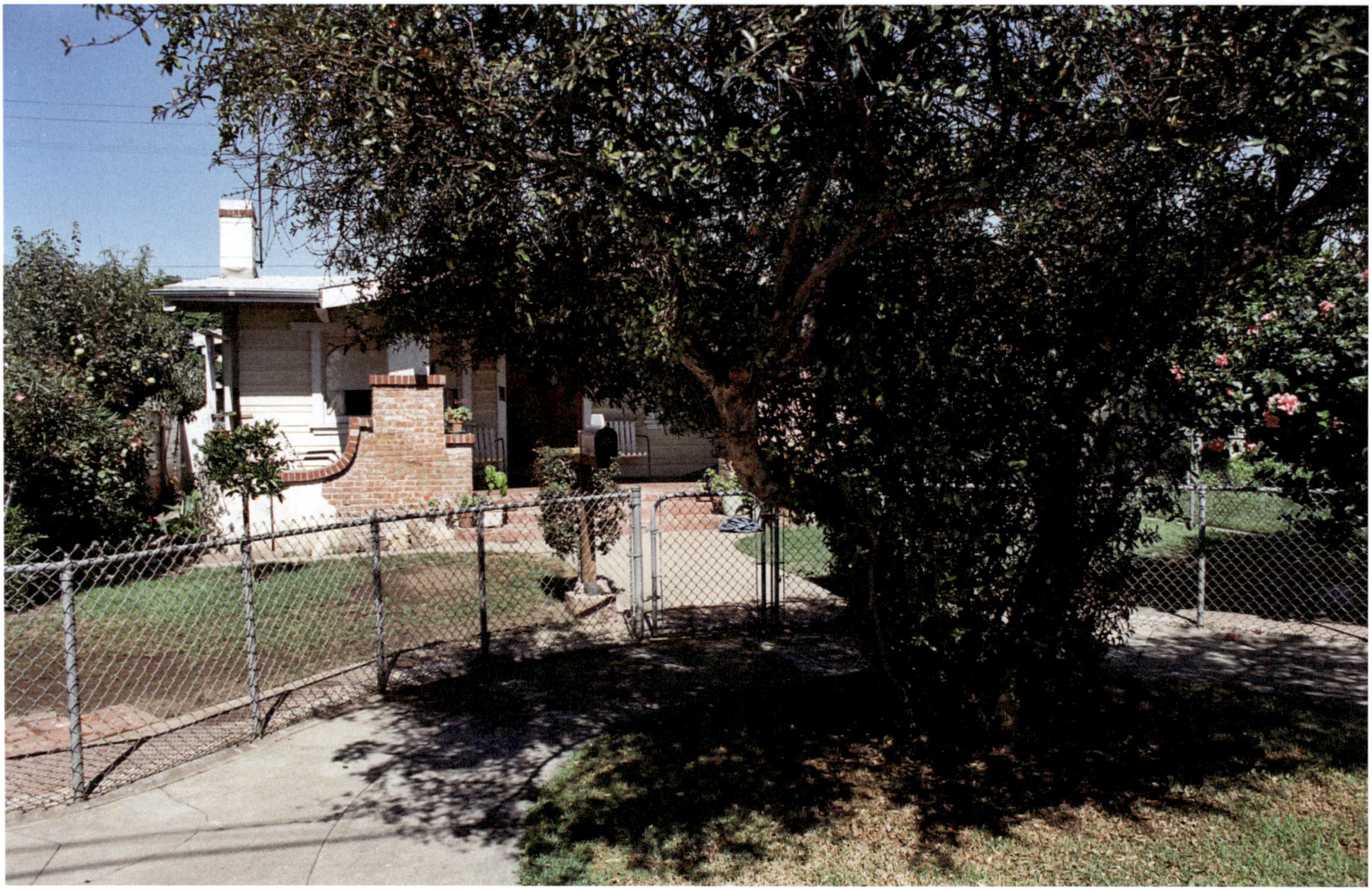

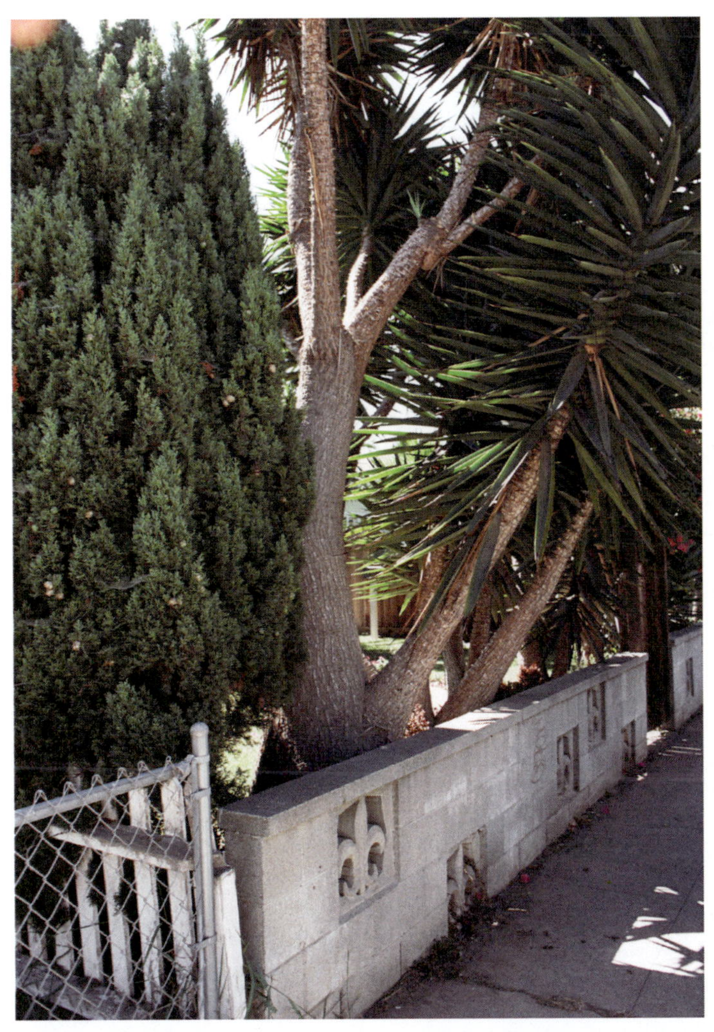
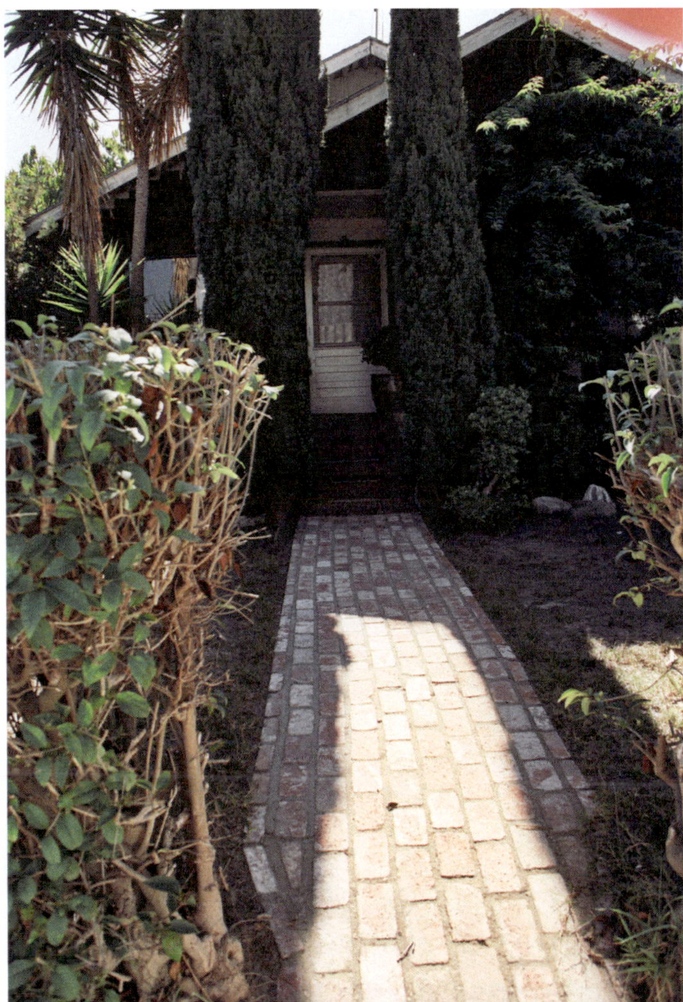

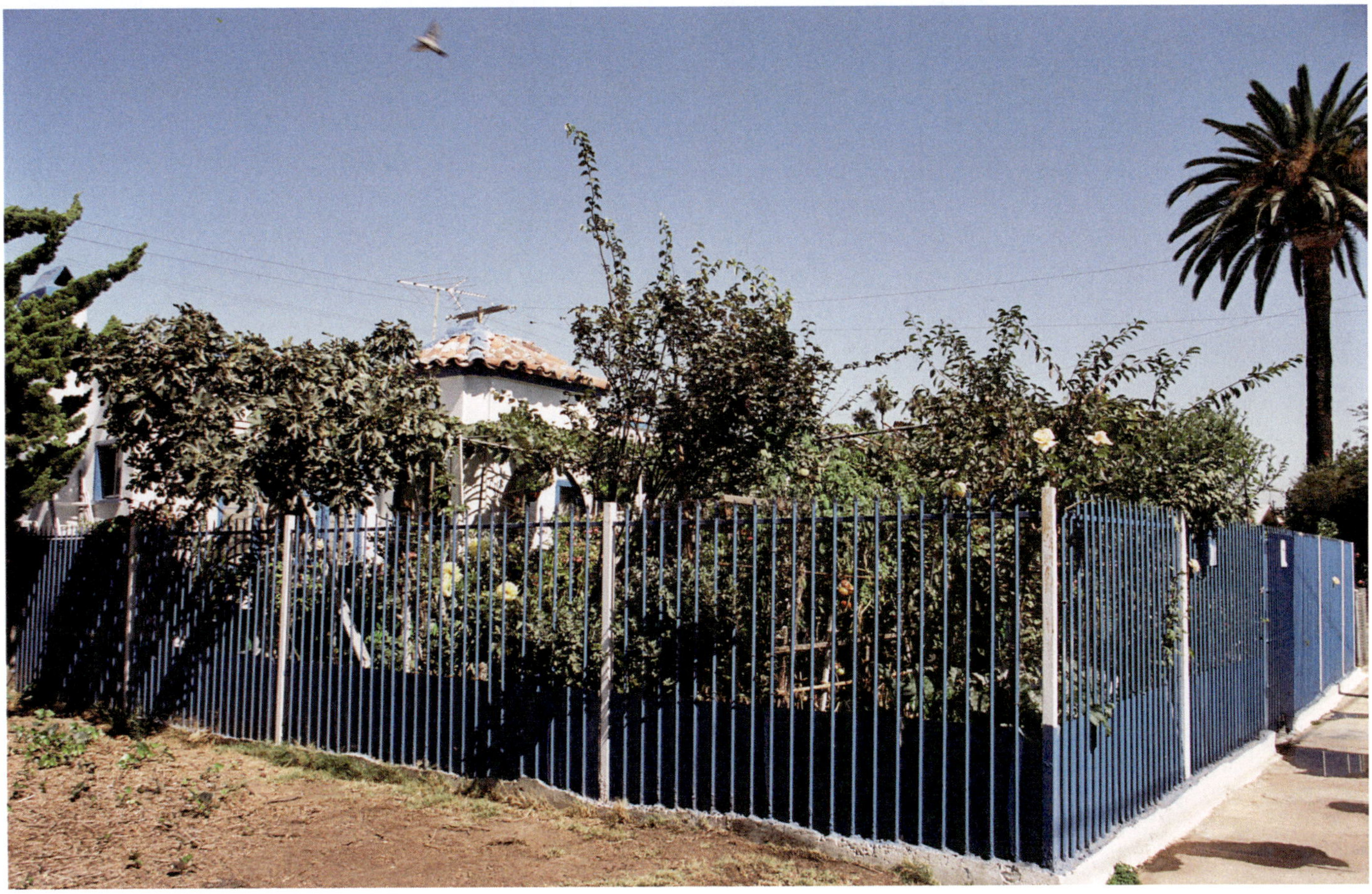

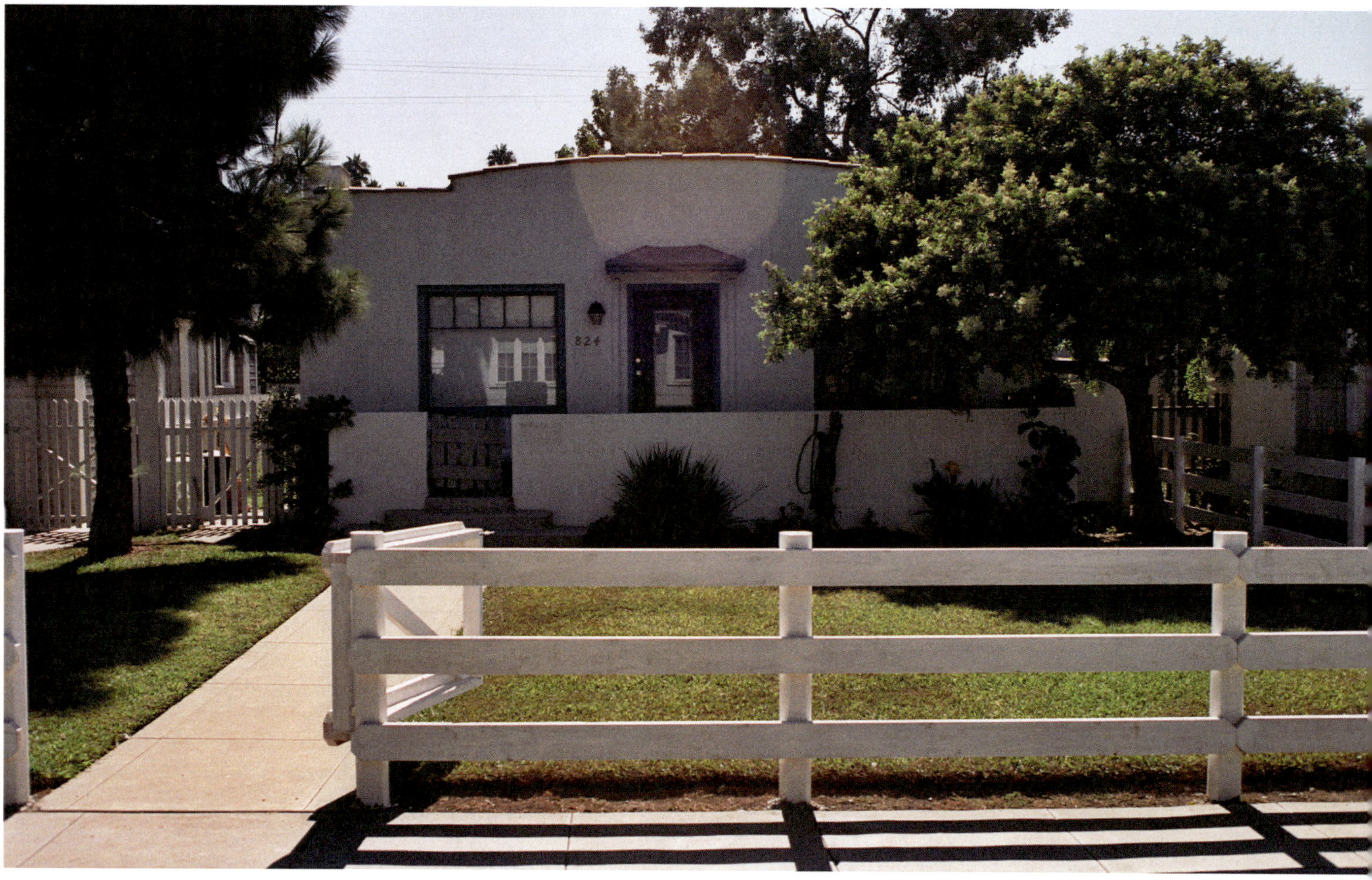

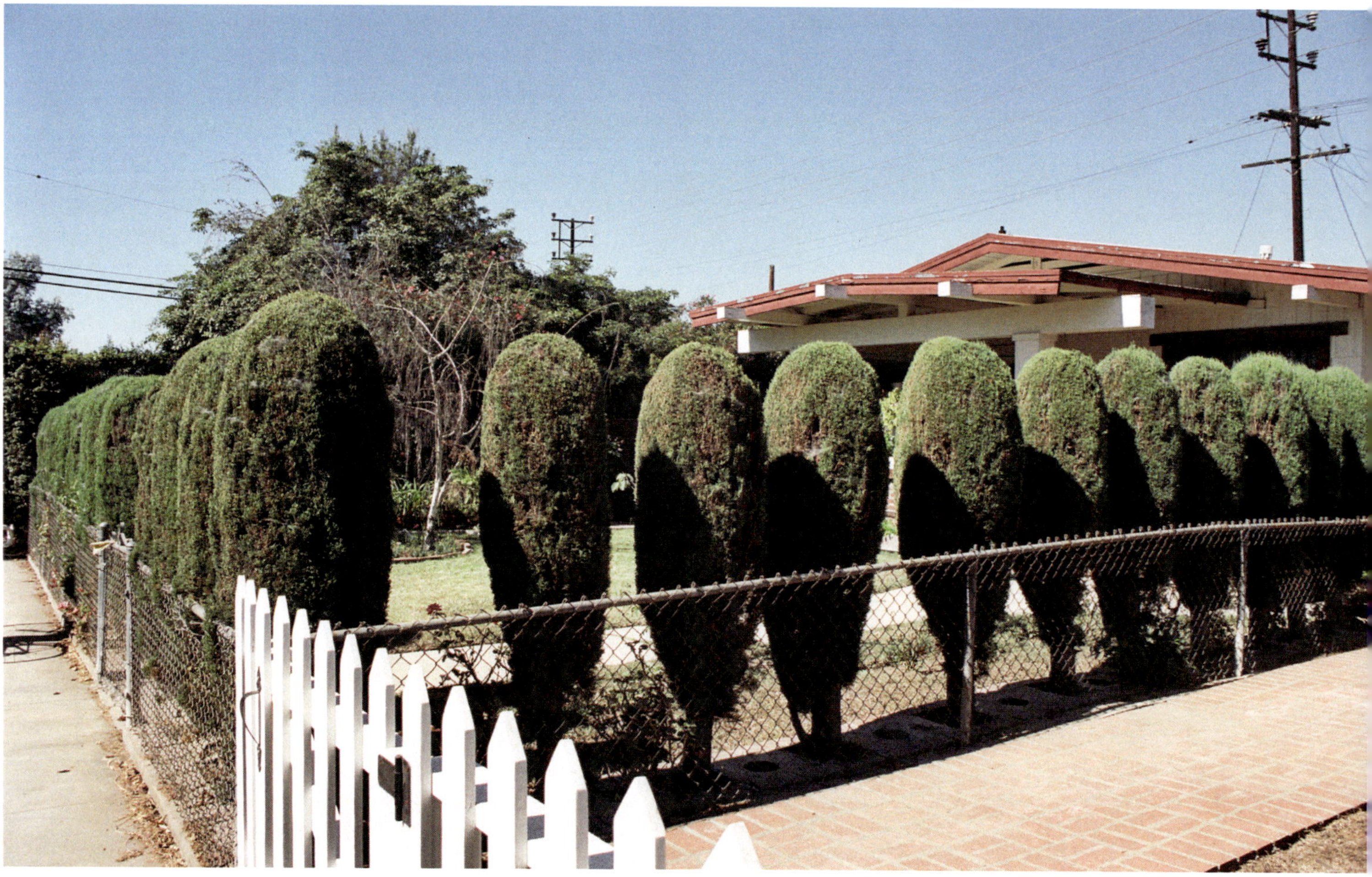

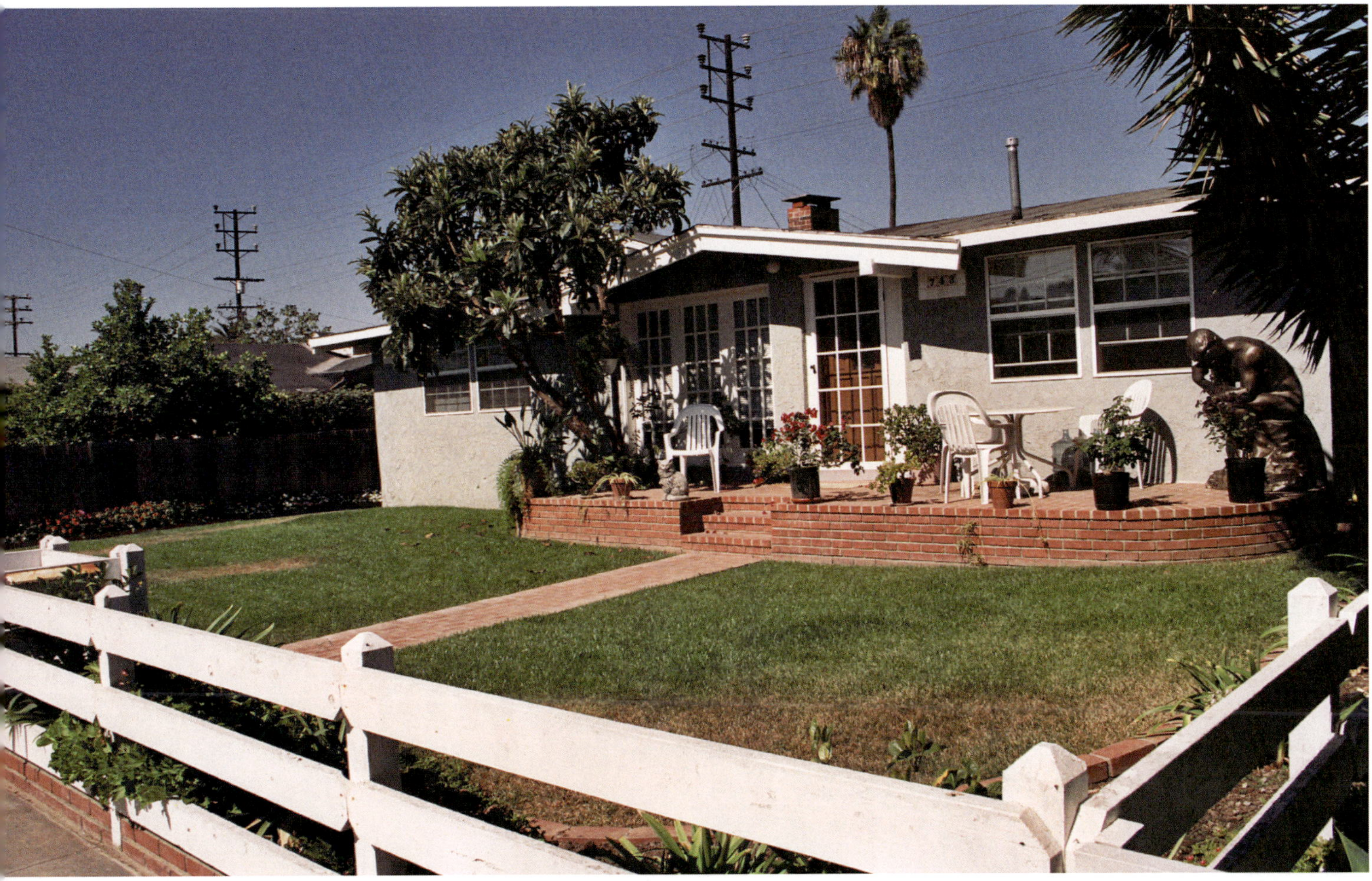

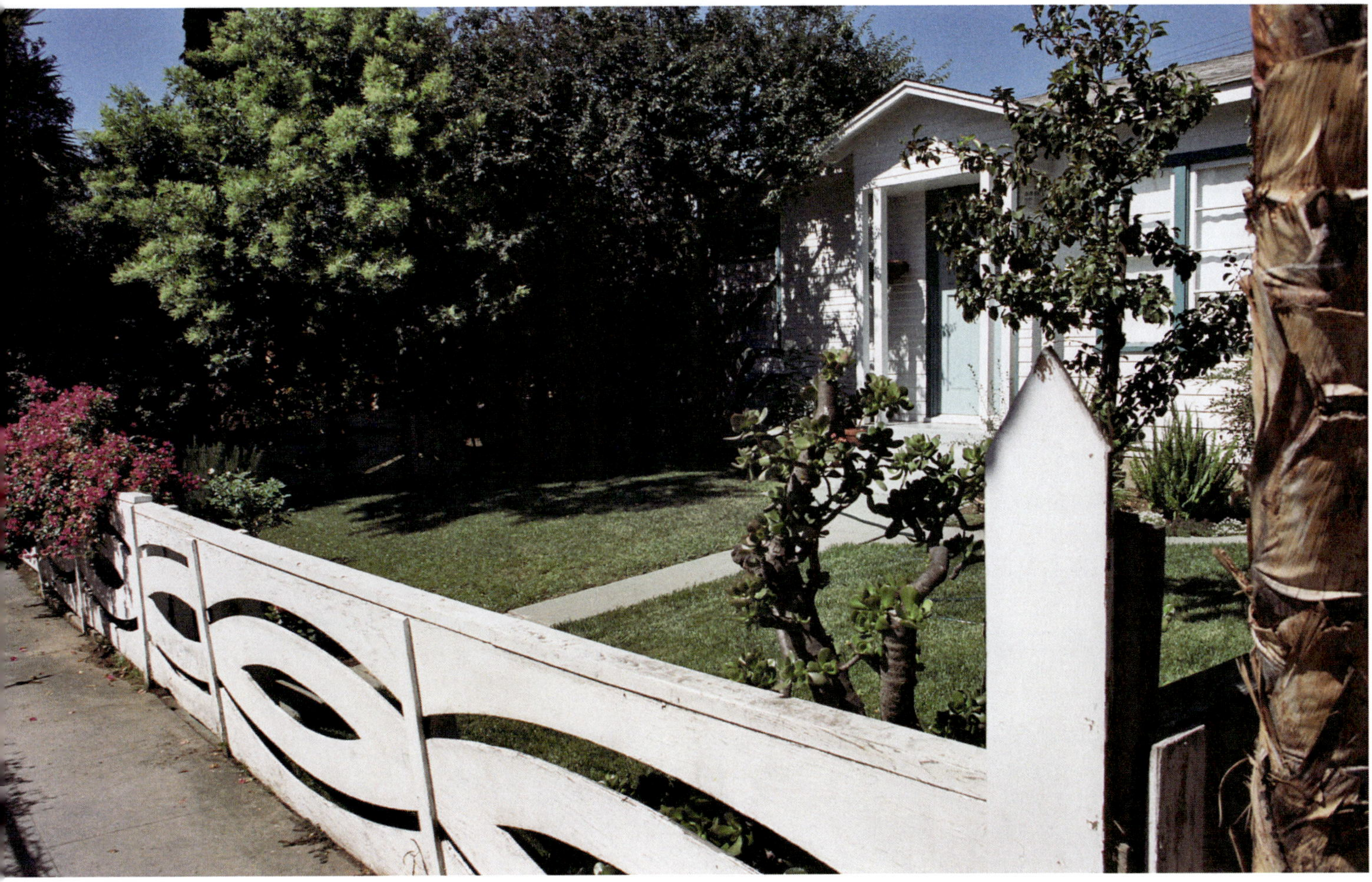

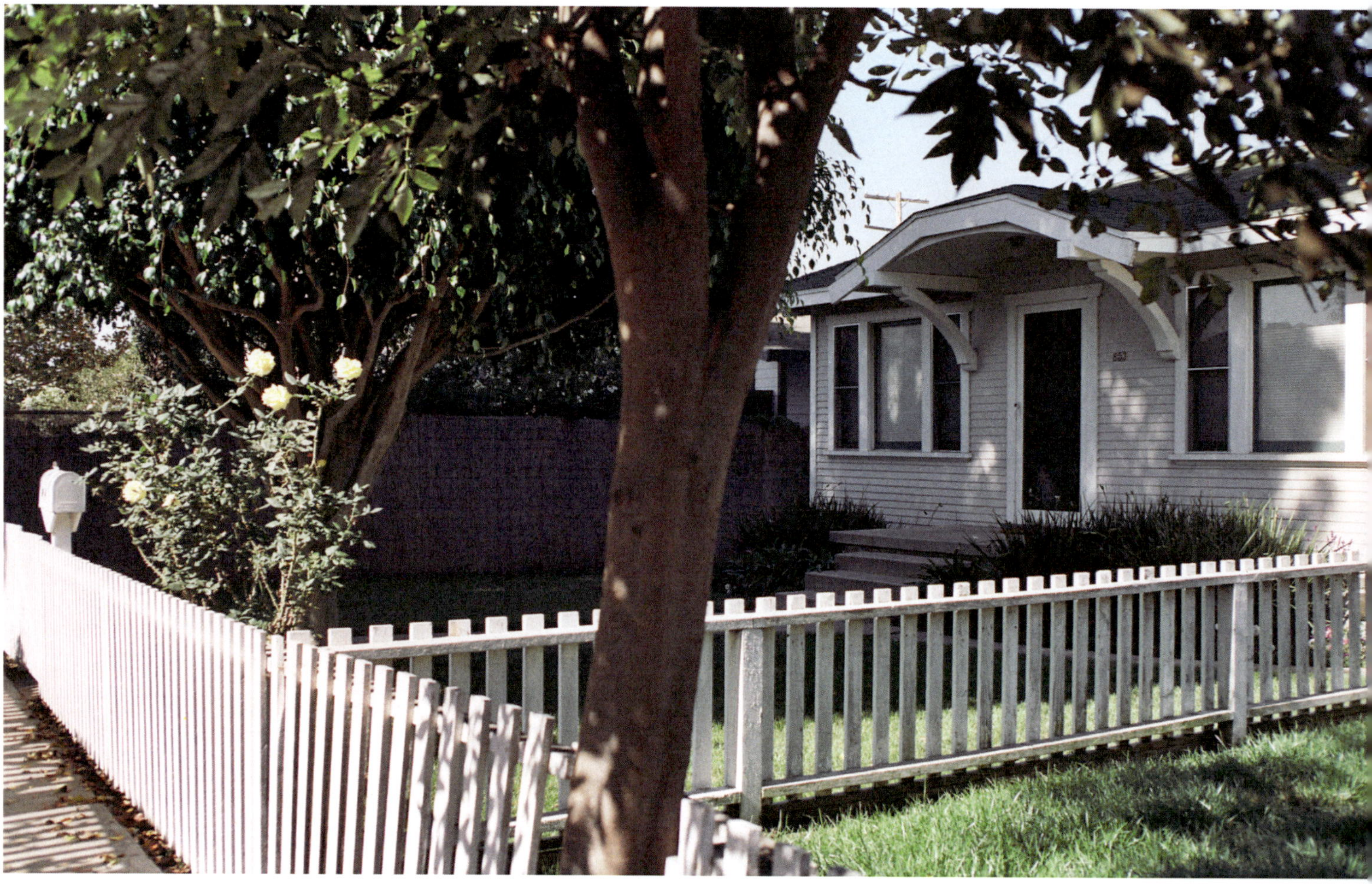

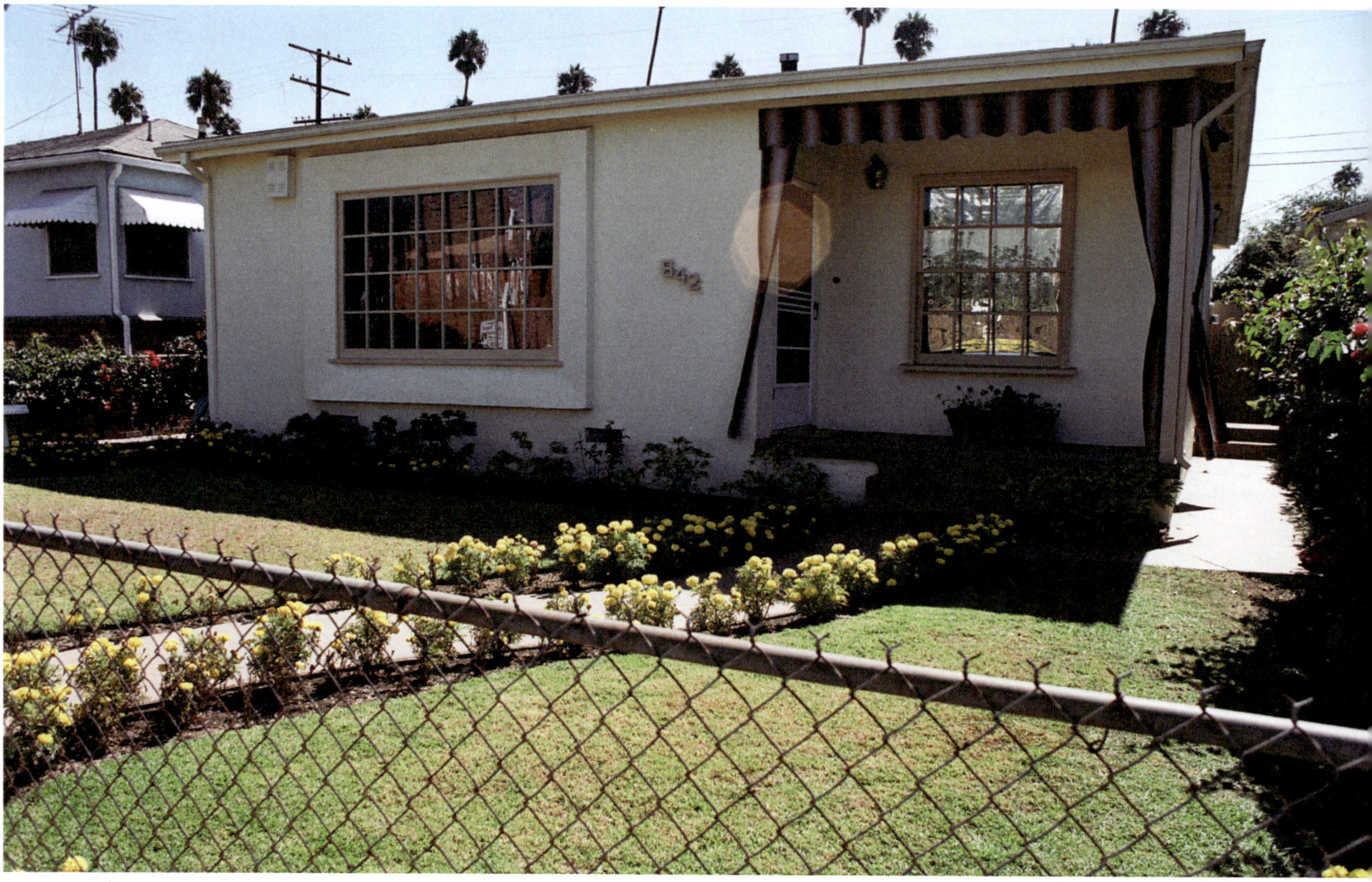

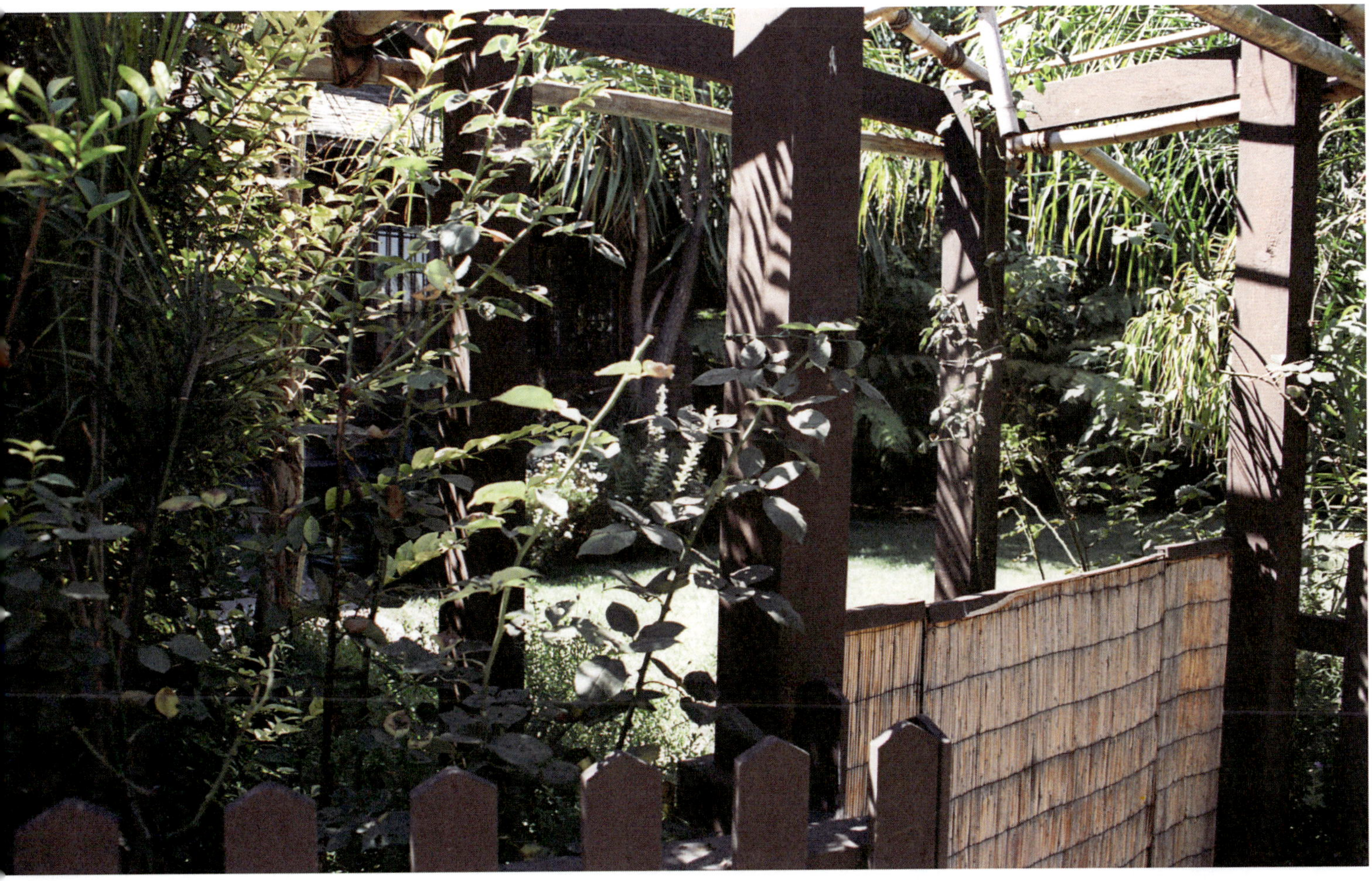

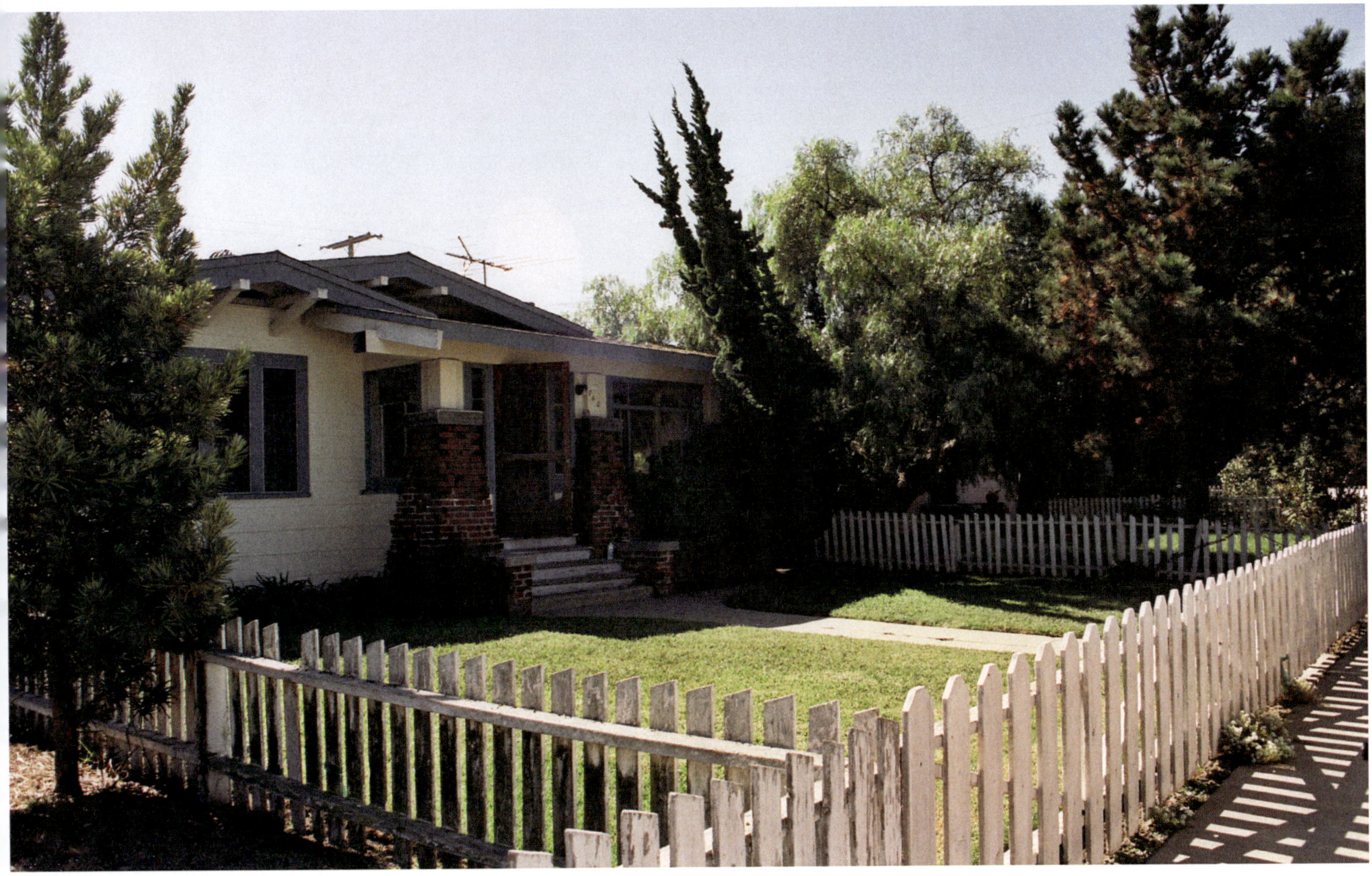

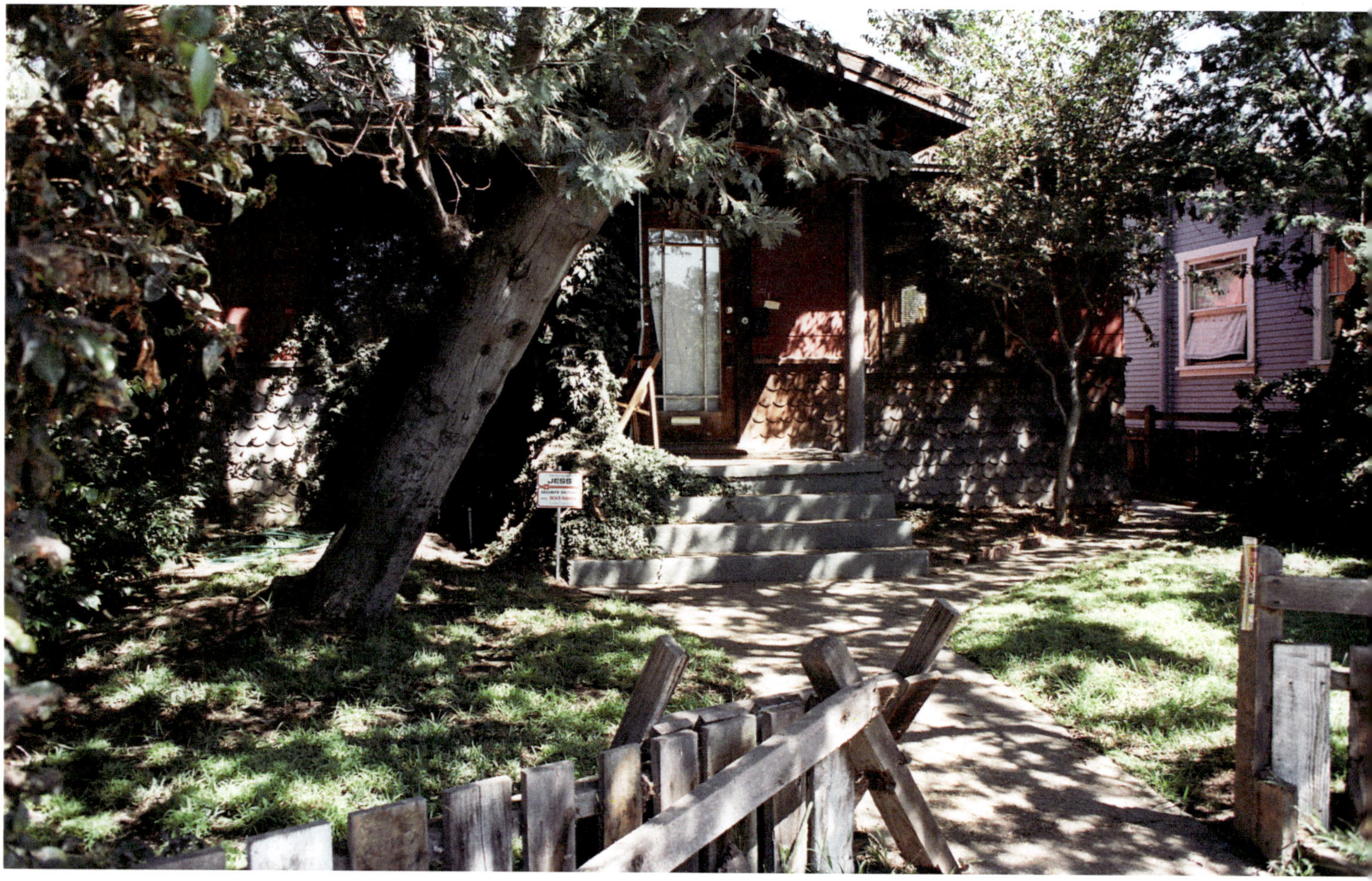

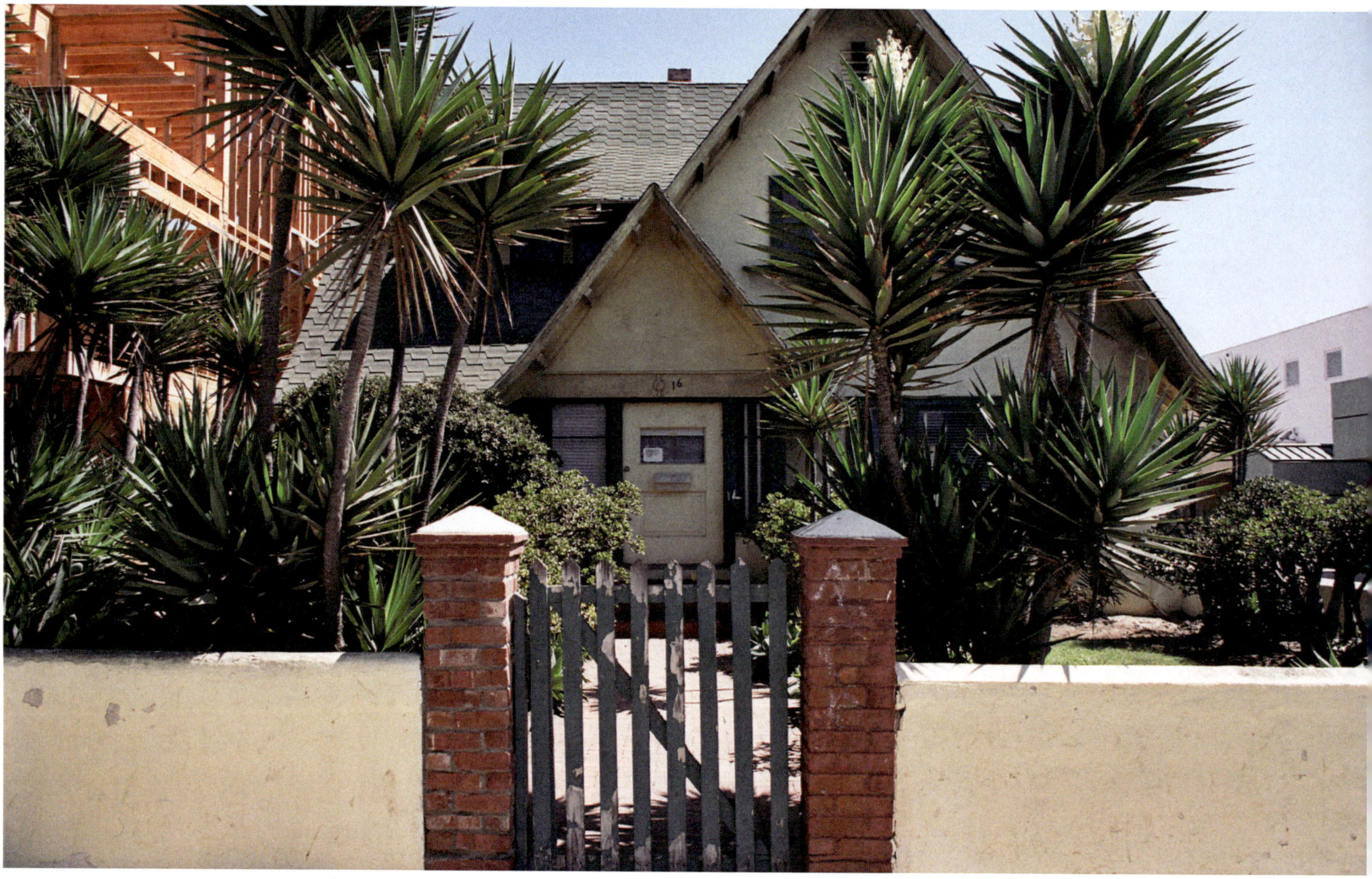

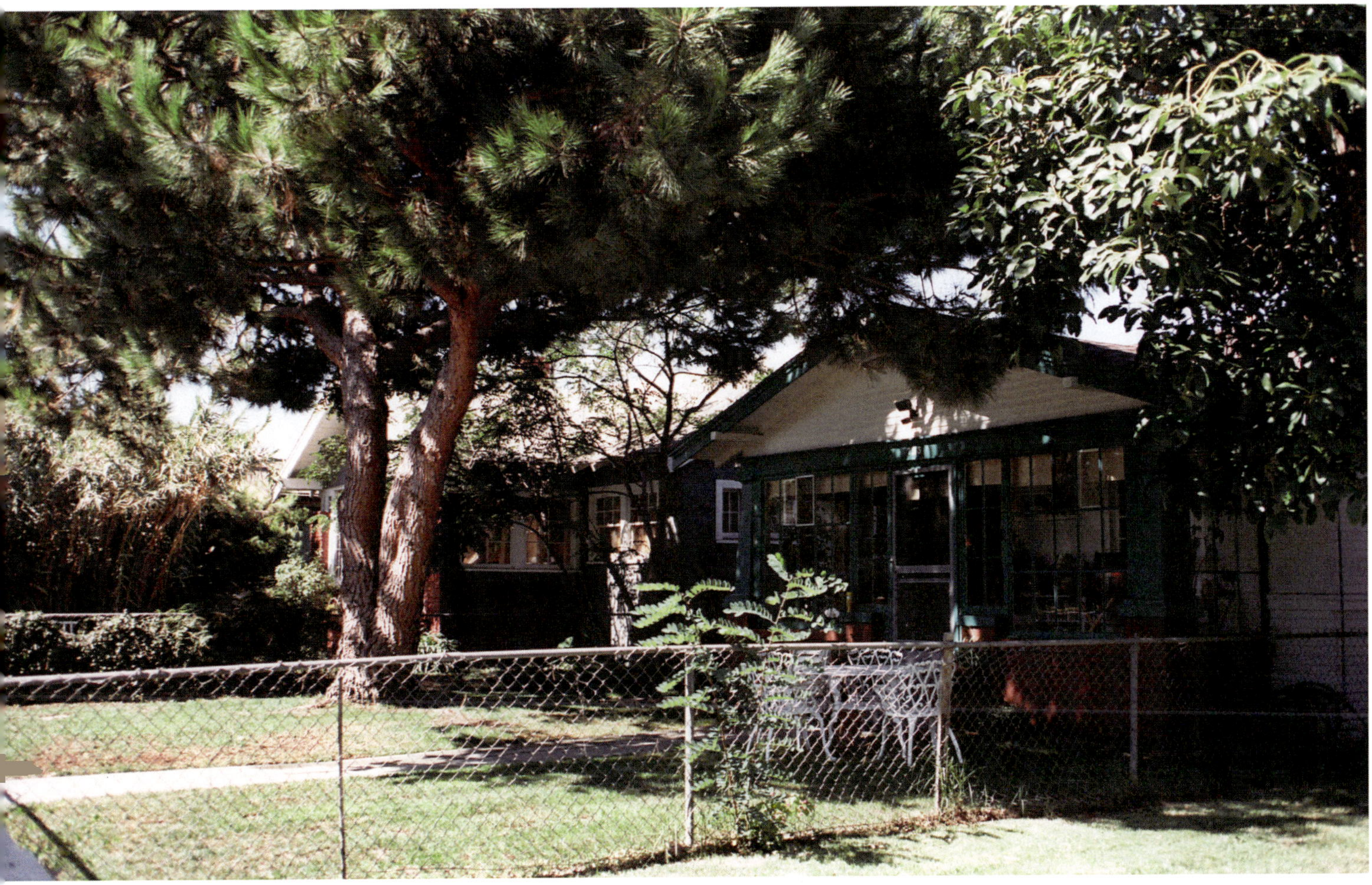

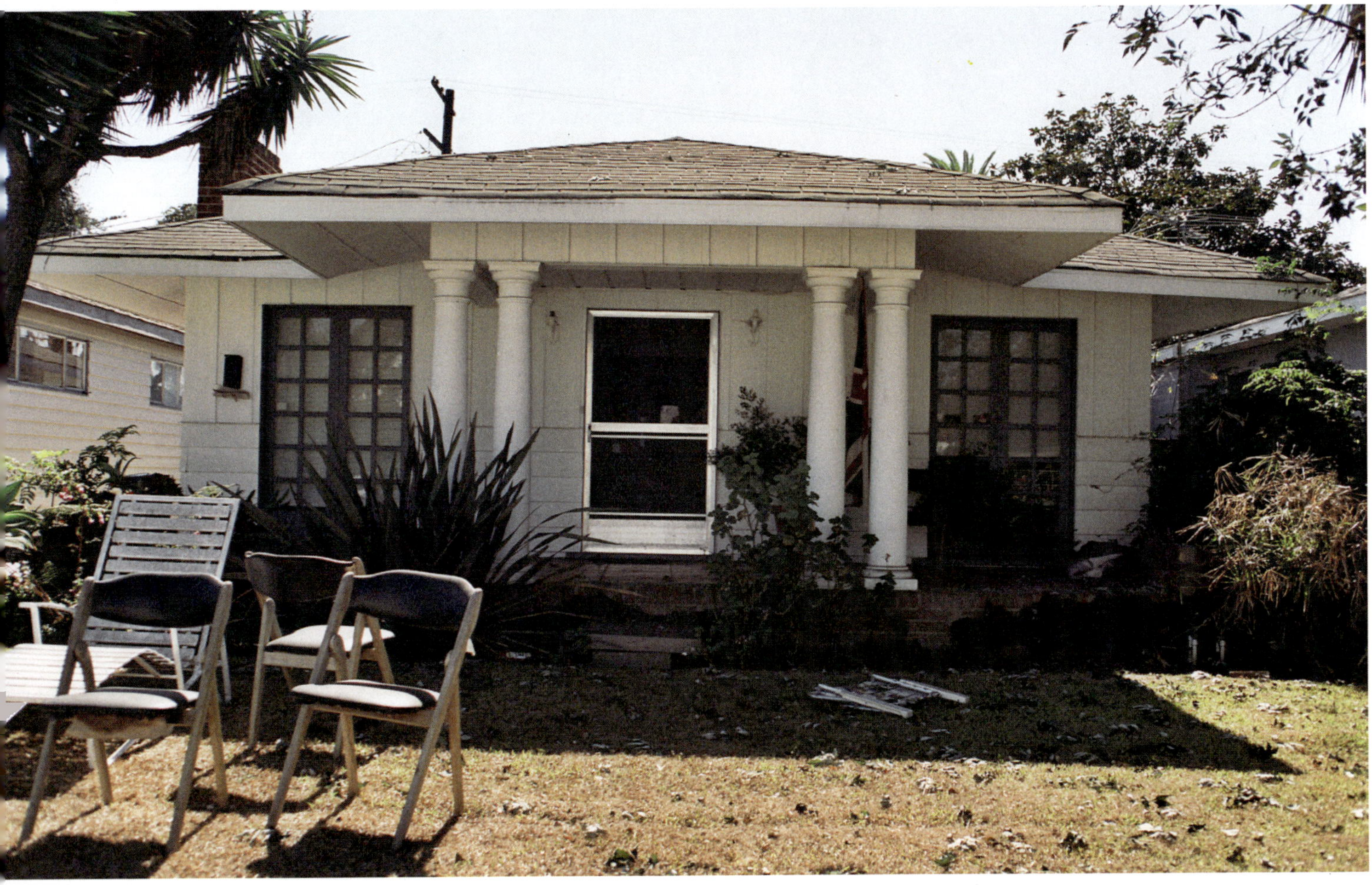

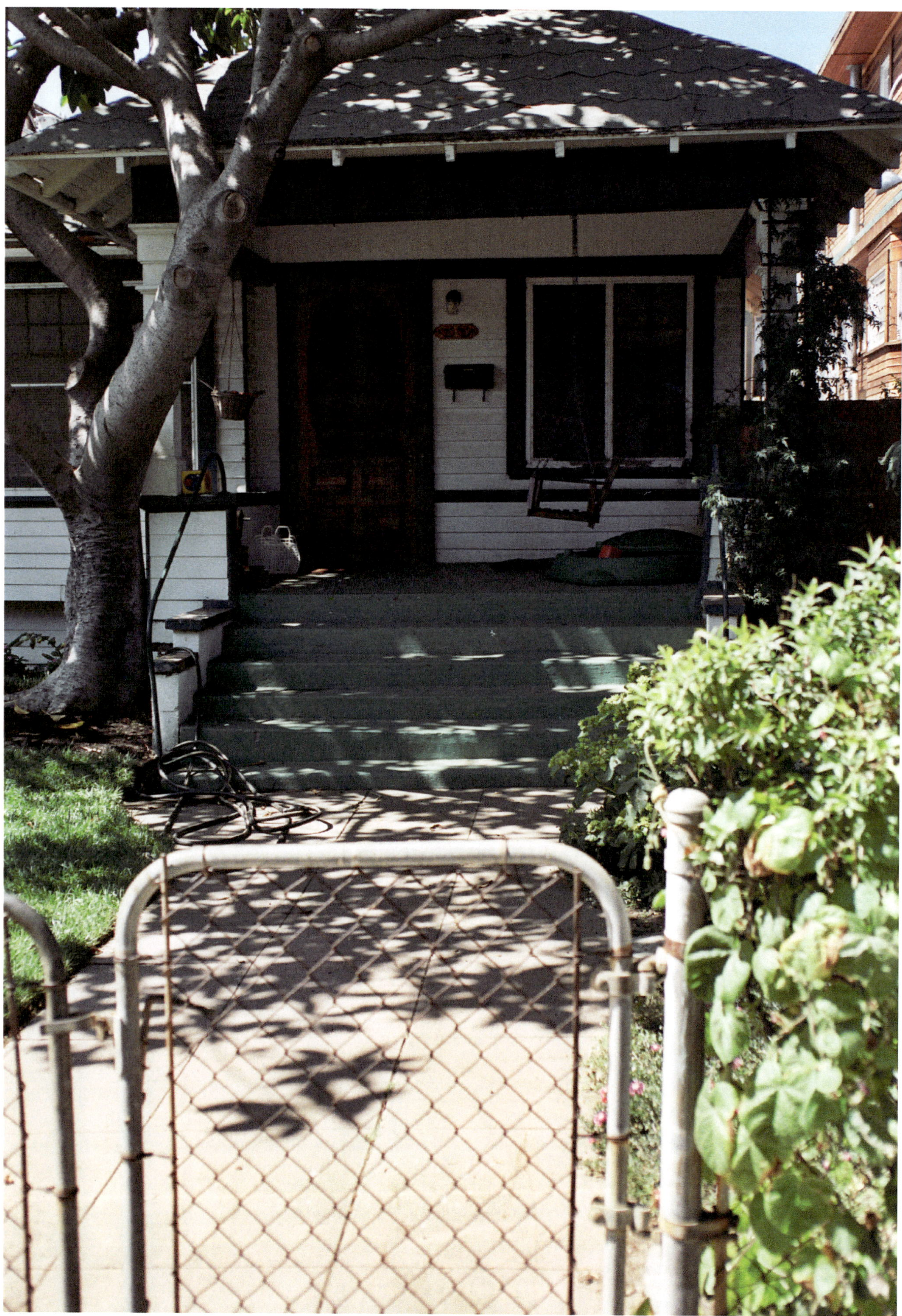

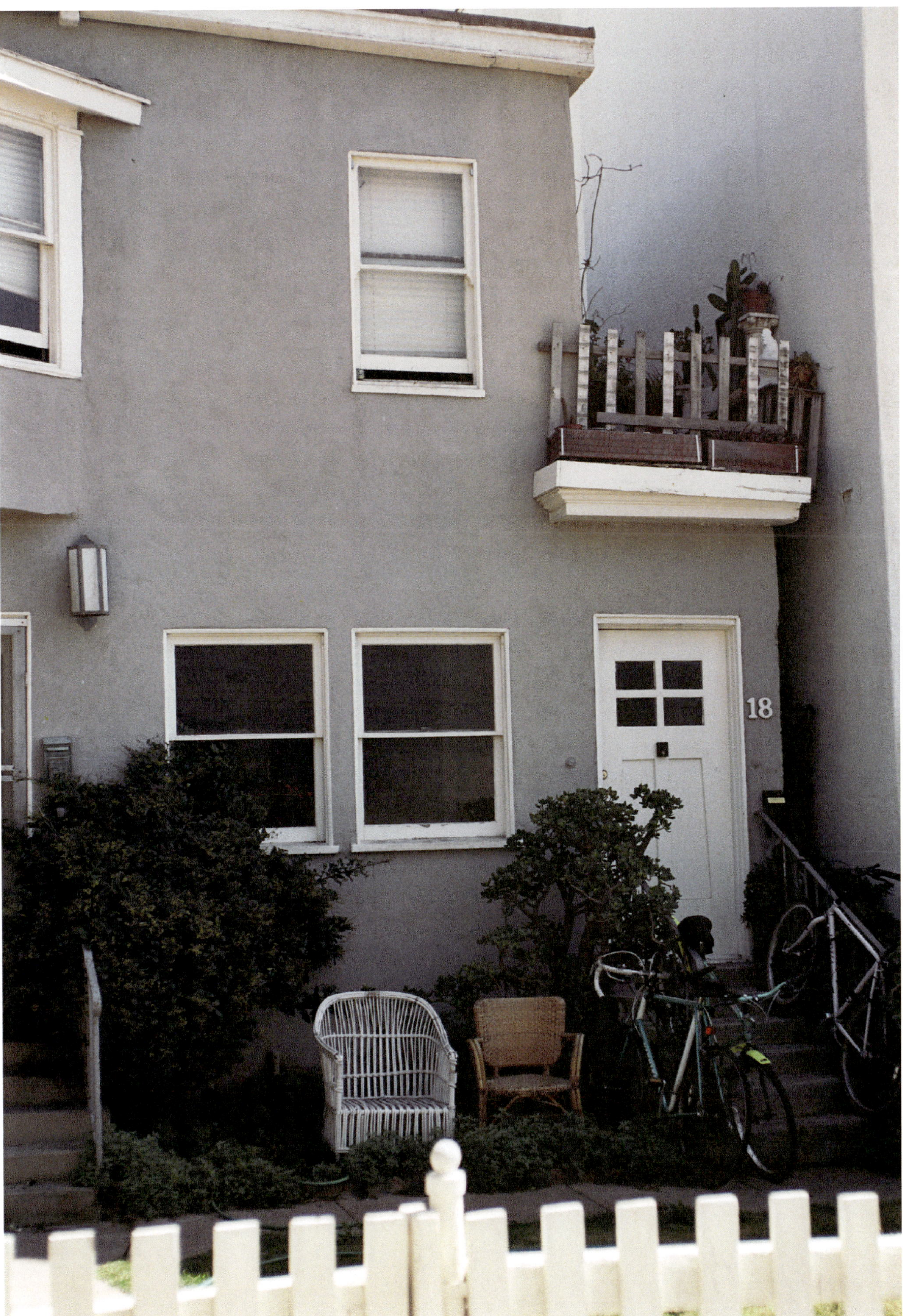

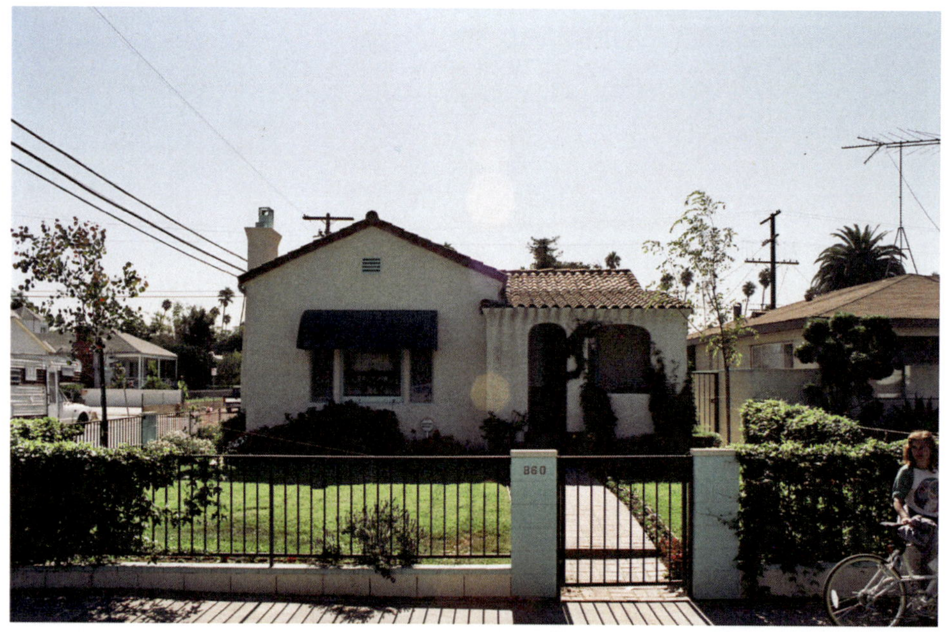

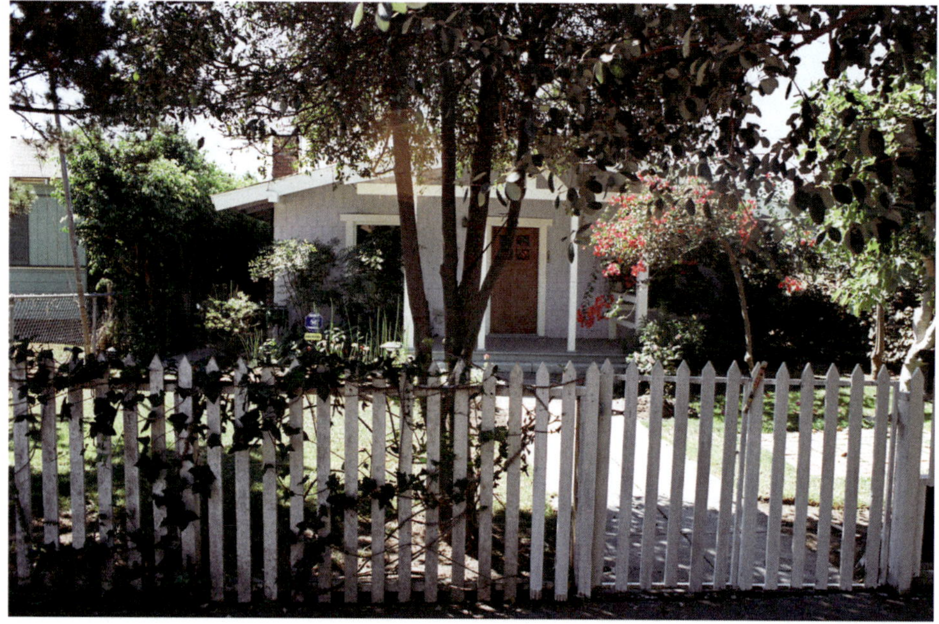

Removal of our
Walkstreets will make
our homes islands
surrounded by traffic.
Our front doors will be
steps from the street.
The street will still
be narrow and our
children will have no
safe place to play or
even walk to the beach.
—Jack Susser

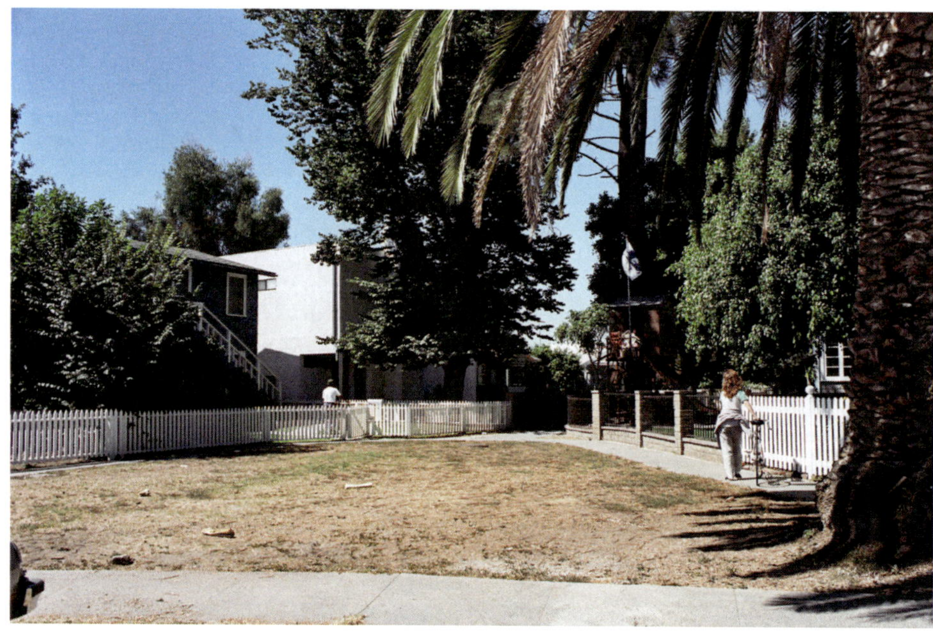

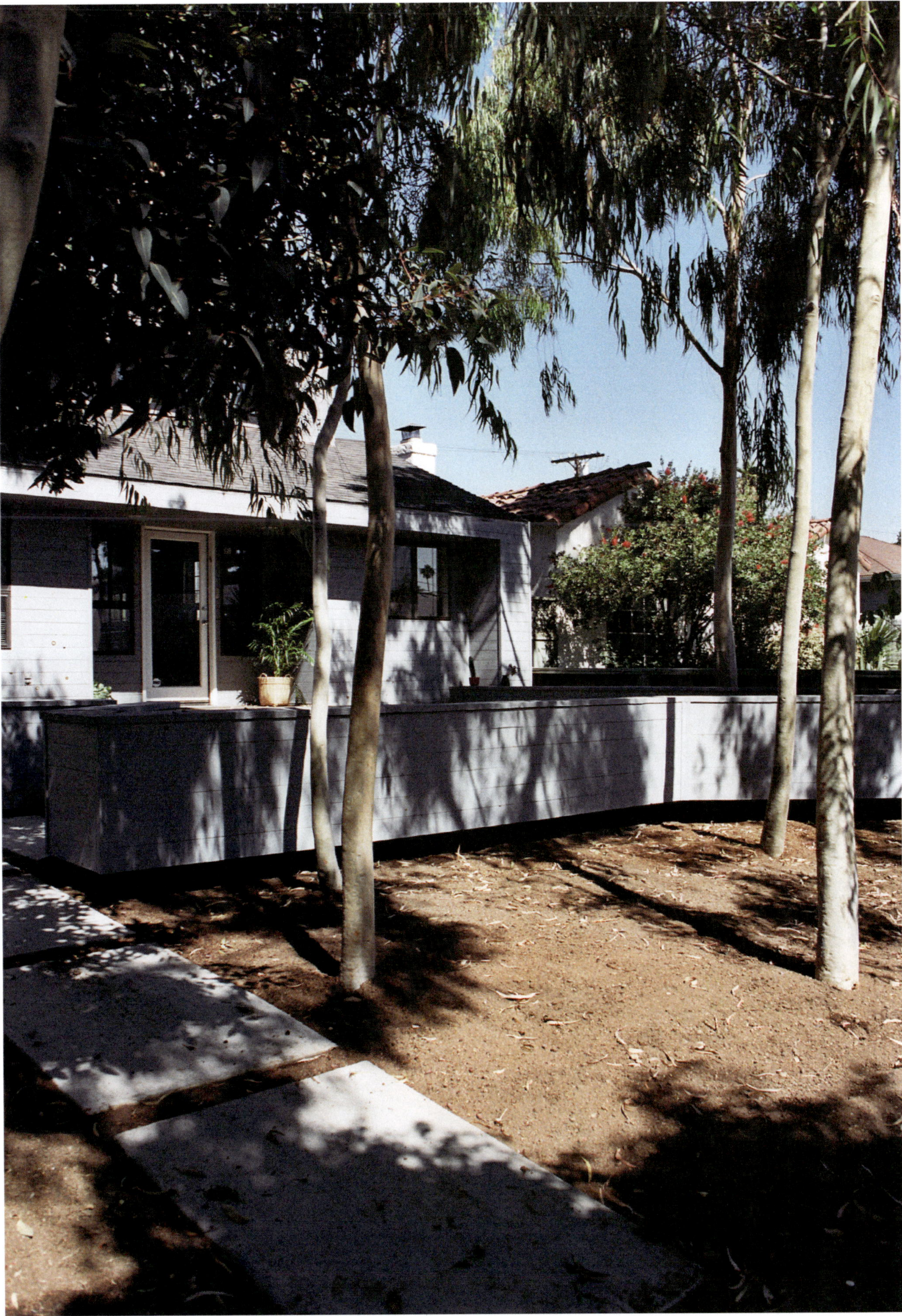

The walkstreets also provide an incomparable
place to feel a part of a real neighborhood.
The intimate and dense nature of the housing,
together with the common areas created by the
walkways, cause neighbors to feel much more of
a sense of shared responsibility and interest.
For instance, my block cooperated to create a
neighborhood vegetable garden, a neighborhood
watch group and several neighborhood holiday
parties and potlucks. Since everyone has to use
a fairly narrow walkway to get to their homes,
there is plenty of opportunity to chat and mix
with neighbors. This stands in stark contrast
against most Los Angeles neighborhoods where
residents balk at crossing the street to chat
with a neighbor, managing at best to yell cursory
salutations from driveway to driveway as they
get out of their cars.

Widening the walkways destroys this shared
intimacy and concomitantly the built-in incentives
for residents to create a neighborhood spirit.
If the walkstreets are widened, they will begin
to operate more as vehicular thoroughfares than
pedestrian ambling zones. The wider walkstreets
already attract too many motorcycles, bicycles,
skateboards and even cars. Such traffic deters from
an atmosphere where neighbors view the walkway as
a place to hang out leisurely and get to know one
another. —Jens Koepke

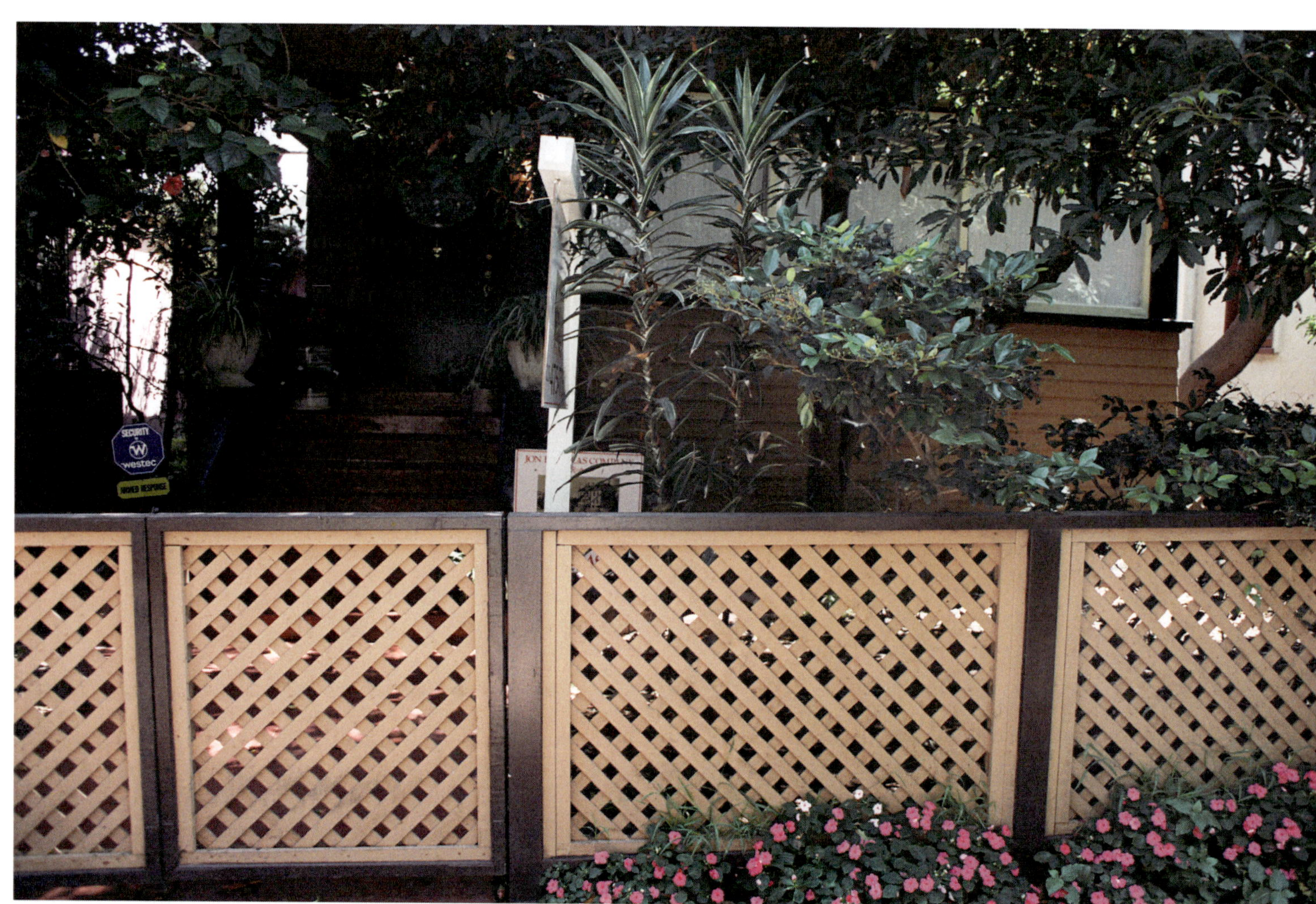

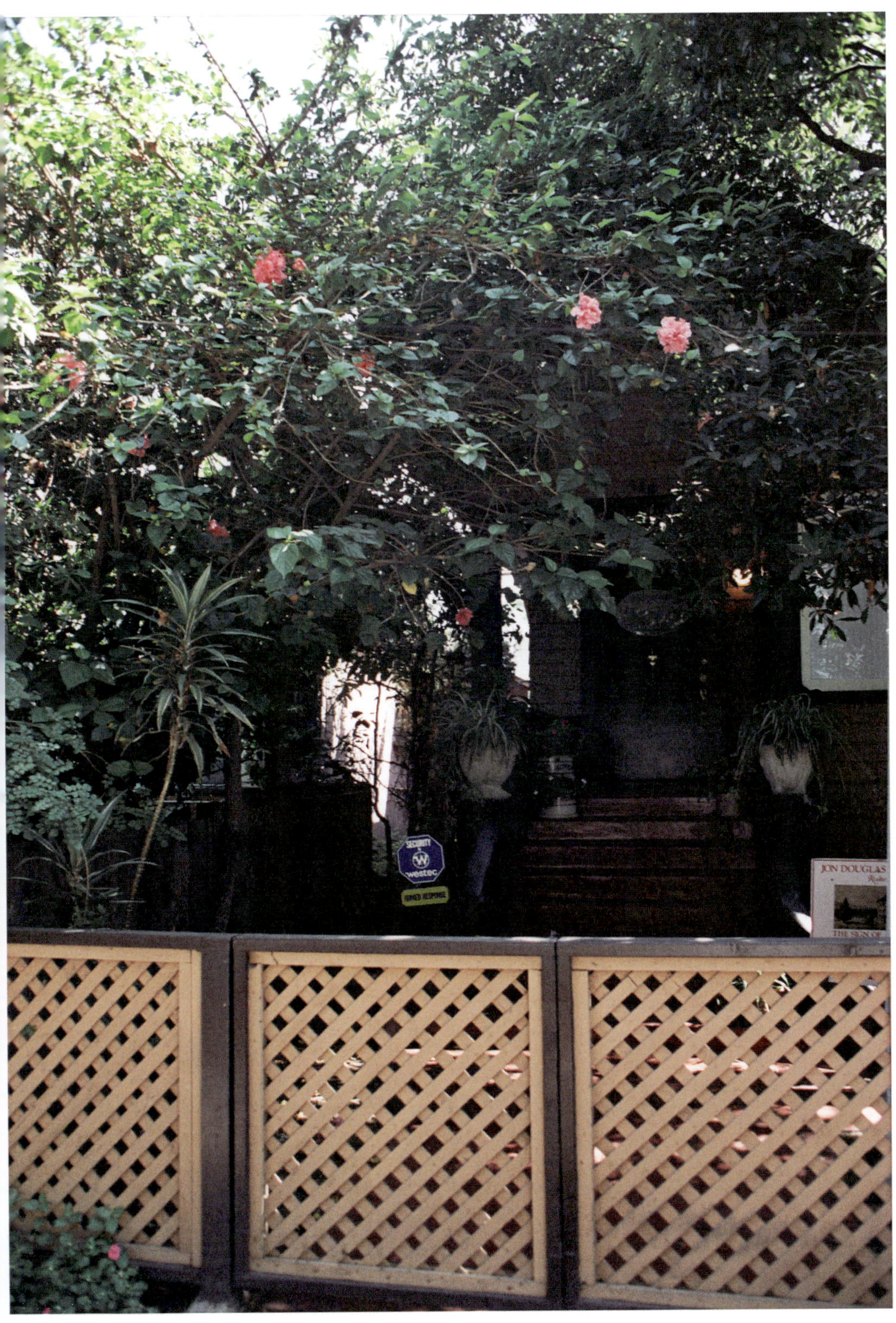

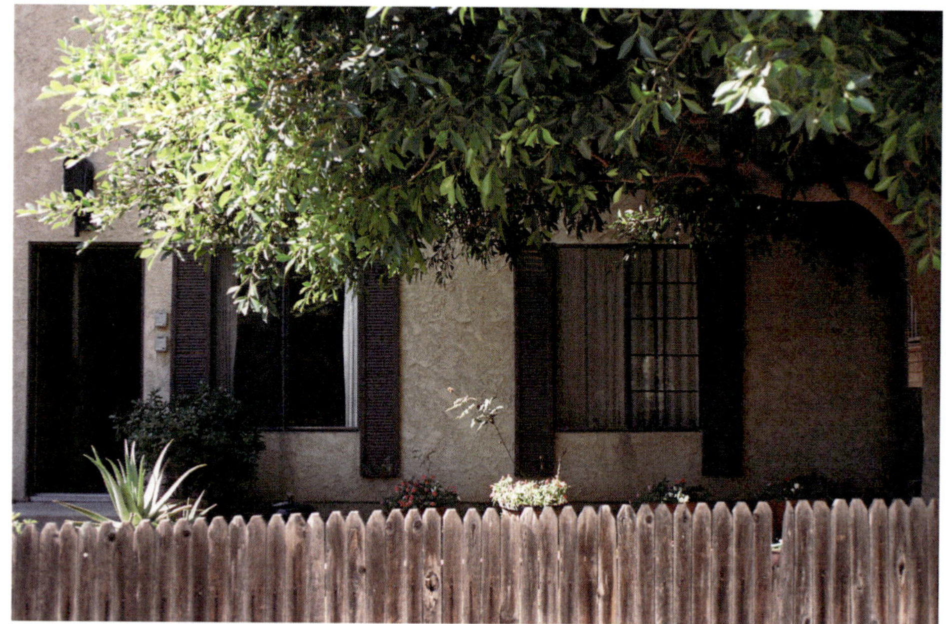

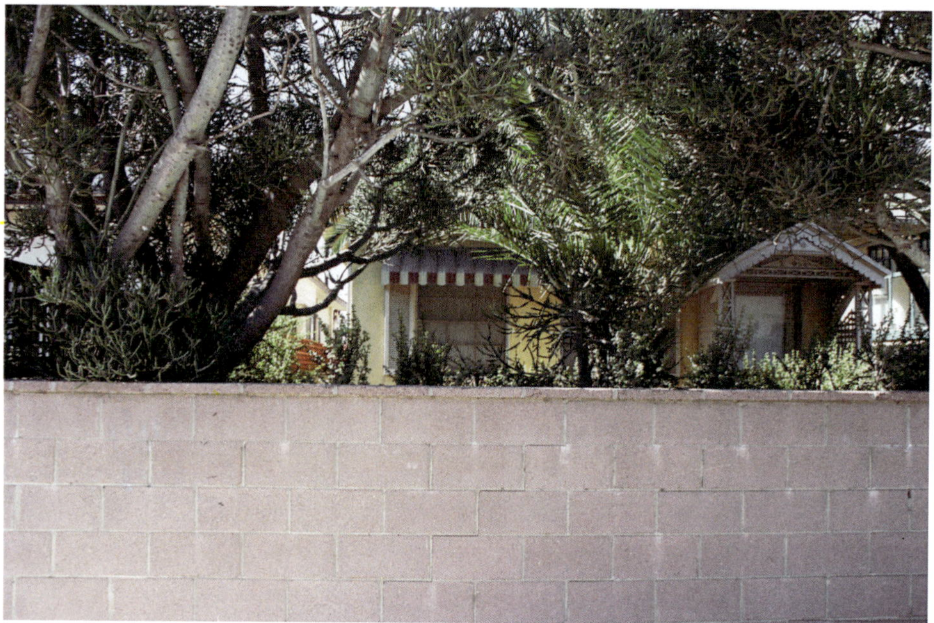

The creation of the Venice
walkways was a rare and
fortuitous event in the
history of Los Angeles
urban development. The
reasons for their design —
to provide residents with
a quiet environment free
from the noise and dan-
gerous intrusion of motor
vehicles — are as valid
today as when they were
first constructed. The city
leaders and planners of
Los Angeles have
consistently chosen the
unimpeded rights of
automobile drivers over
the privacy and safety
of persons not in
automobiles. The result
can be seen everywhere
— an inhuman environment
that is polluted, unsafe
for pedestrians, noisy
and ugly. —Peter Forge

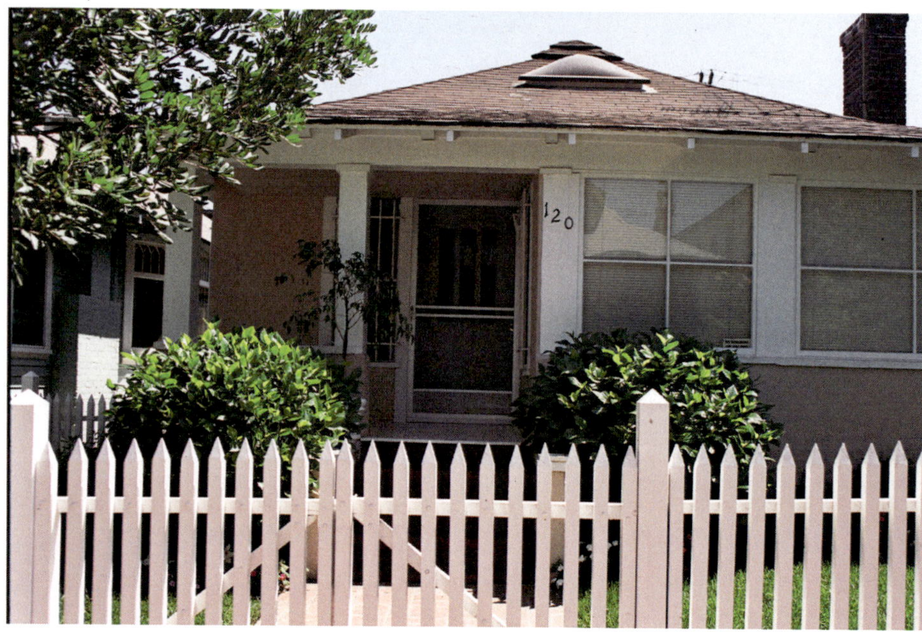

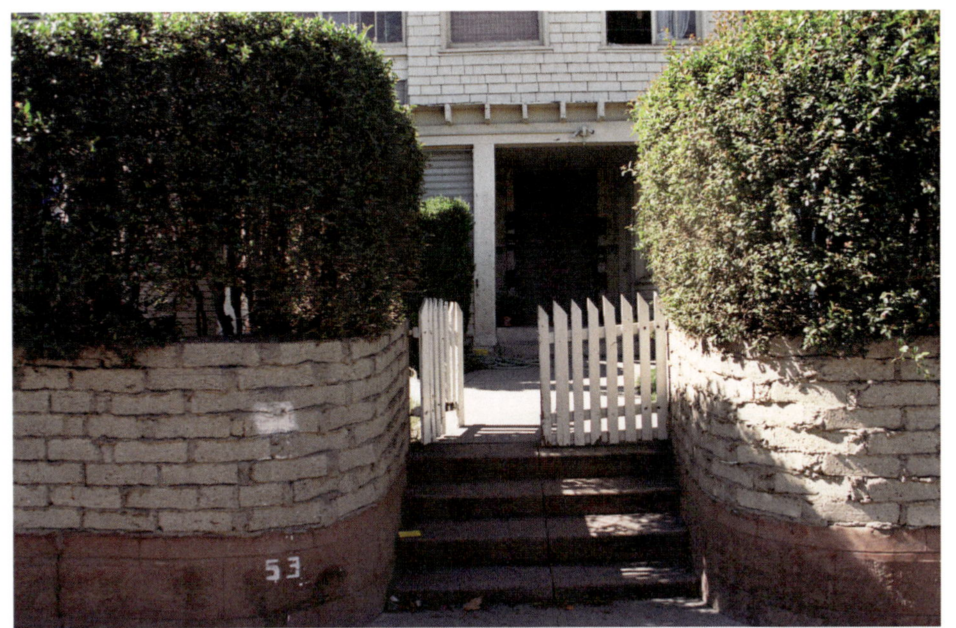

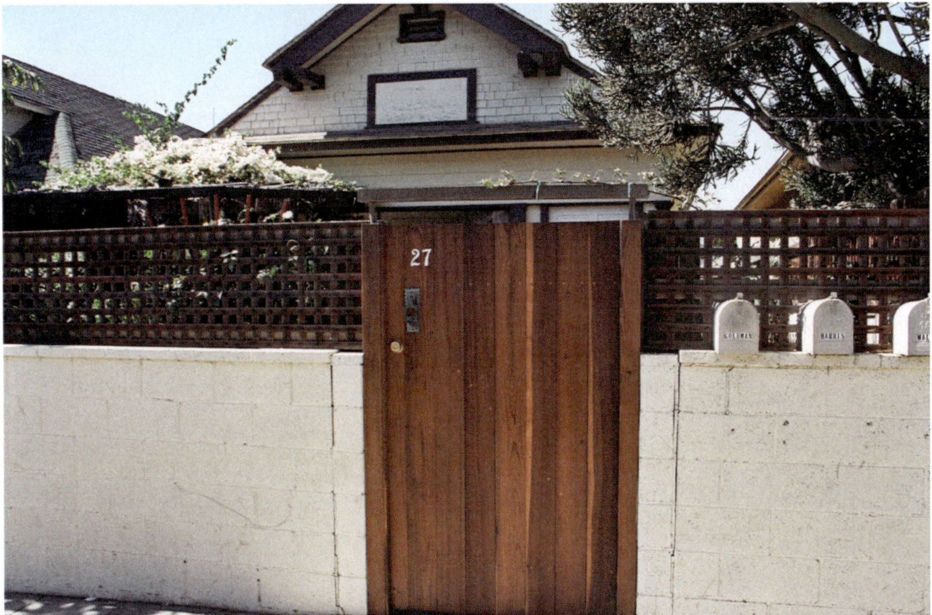

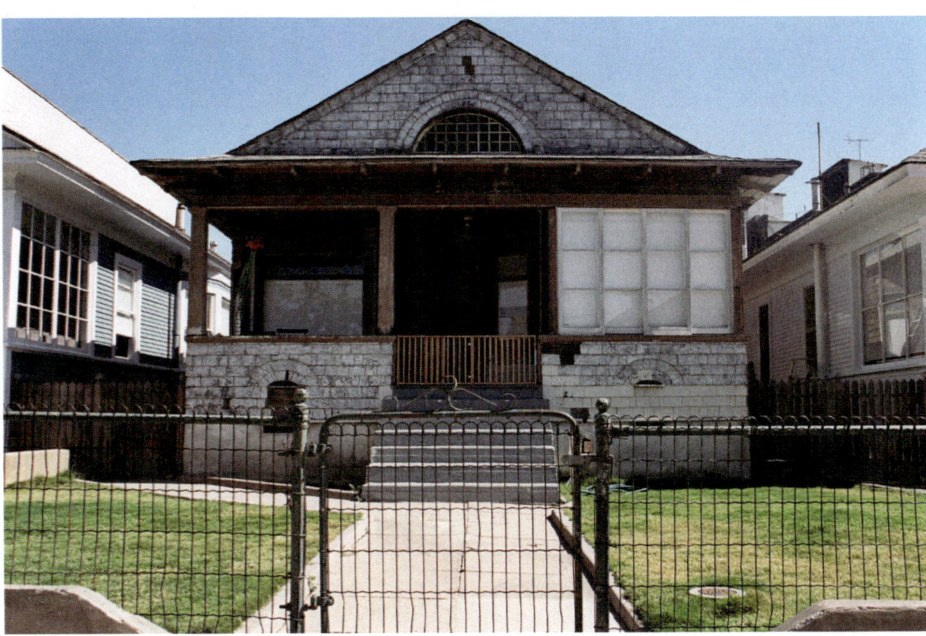

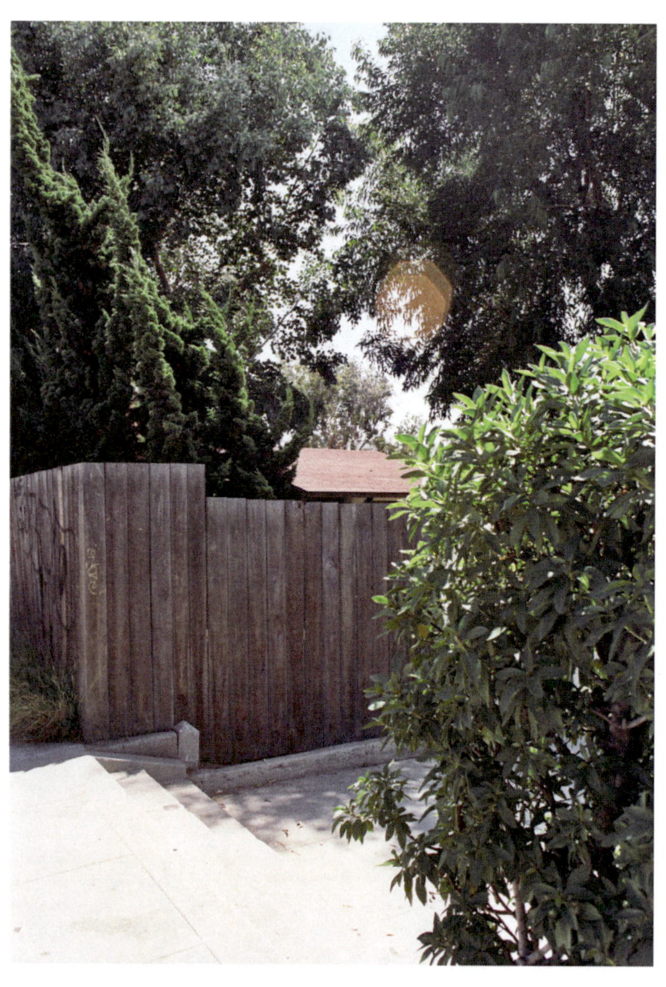

Another important element is the
intimate scale. The common areas
created by the walkstreets have
an almost garden-like quality. The
beautiful yards provide an aesthetic
delight. There is a feeling of safety
and solitude away from the hustle and
bustle of vehicular traffic. There is
a sense of shared responsibility and
interest to maintain the neighborhood.
—Betsy Goldman

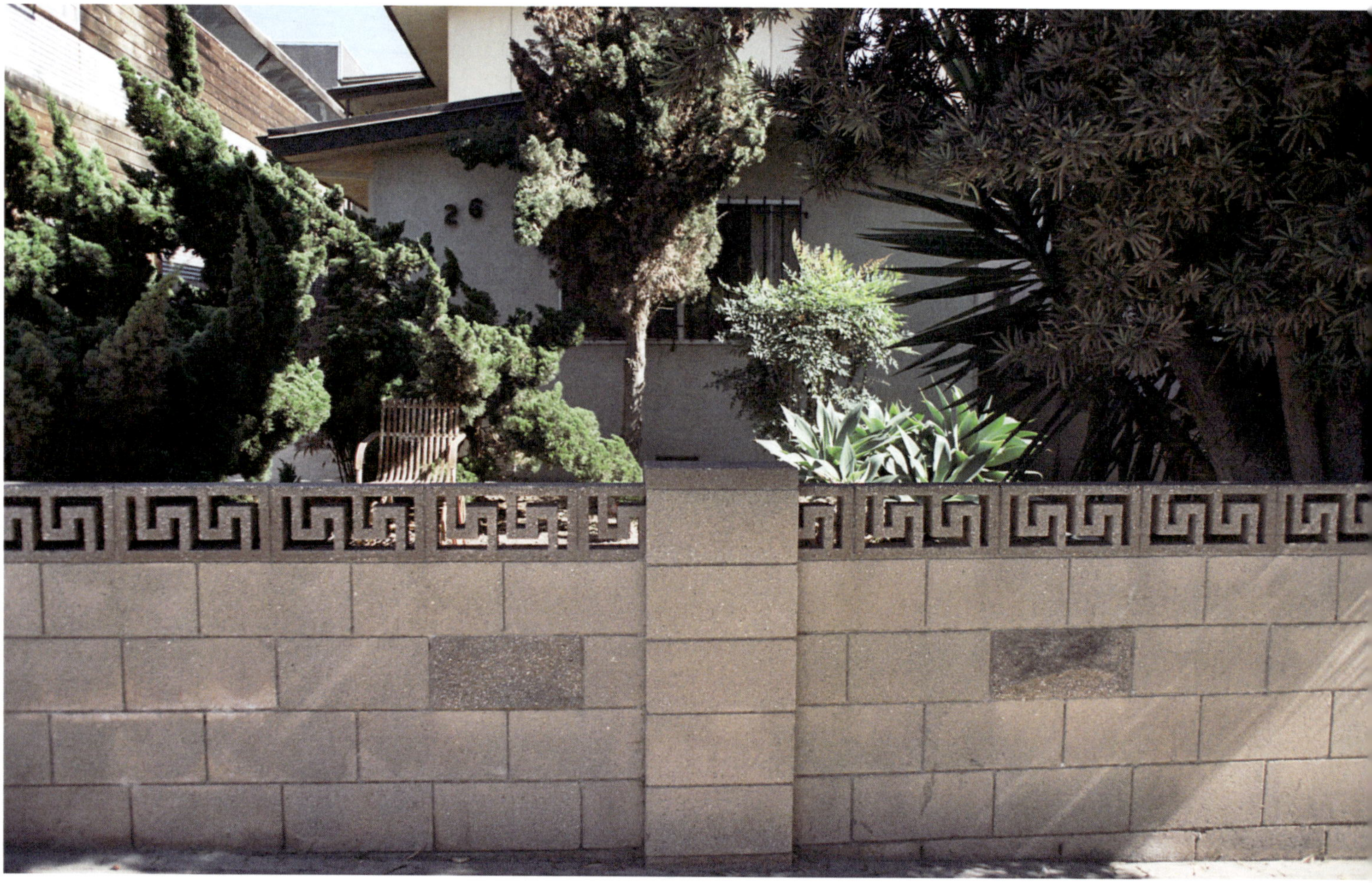

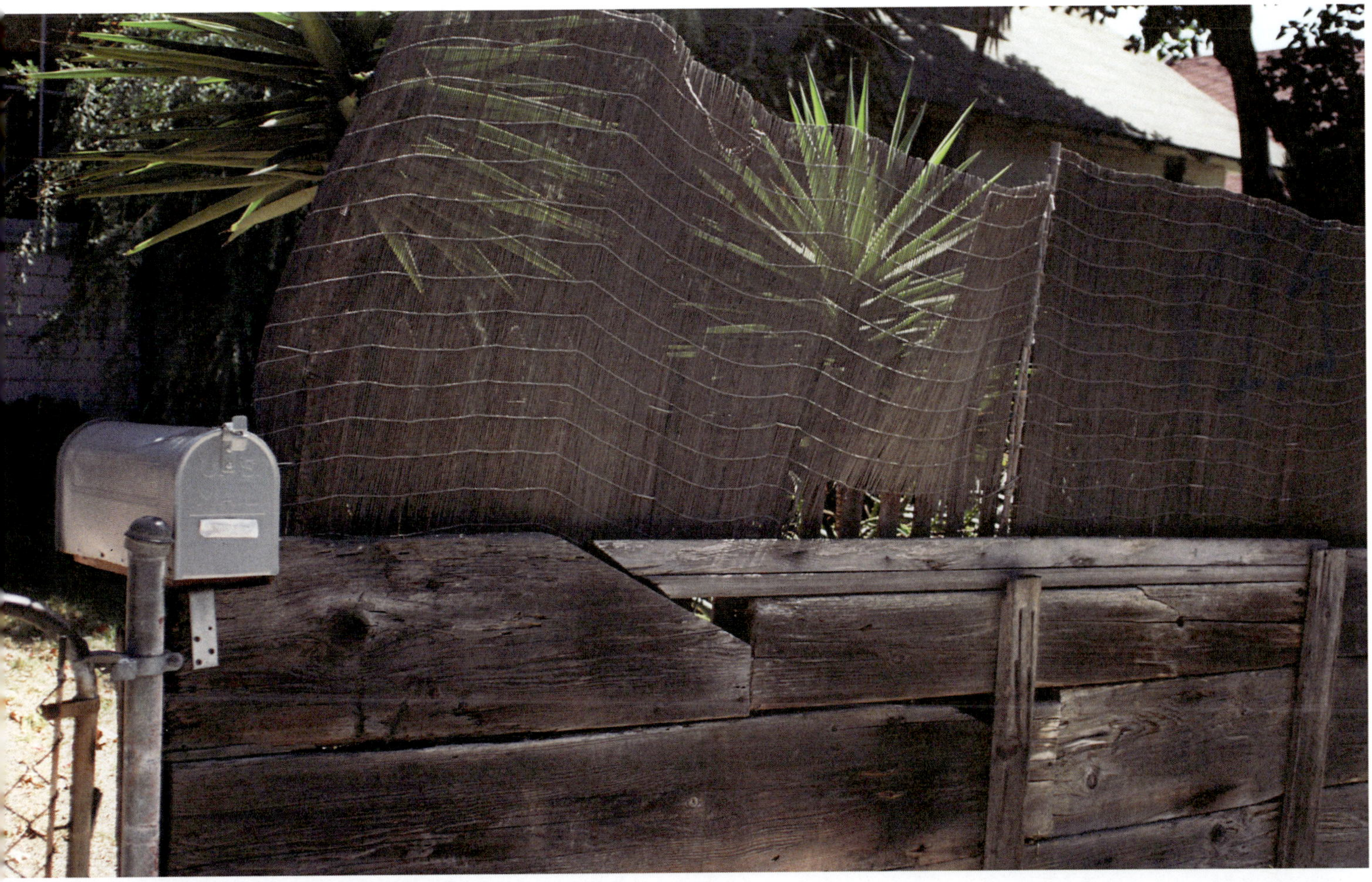

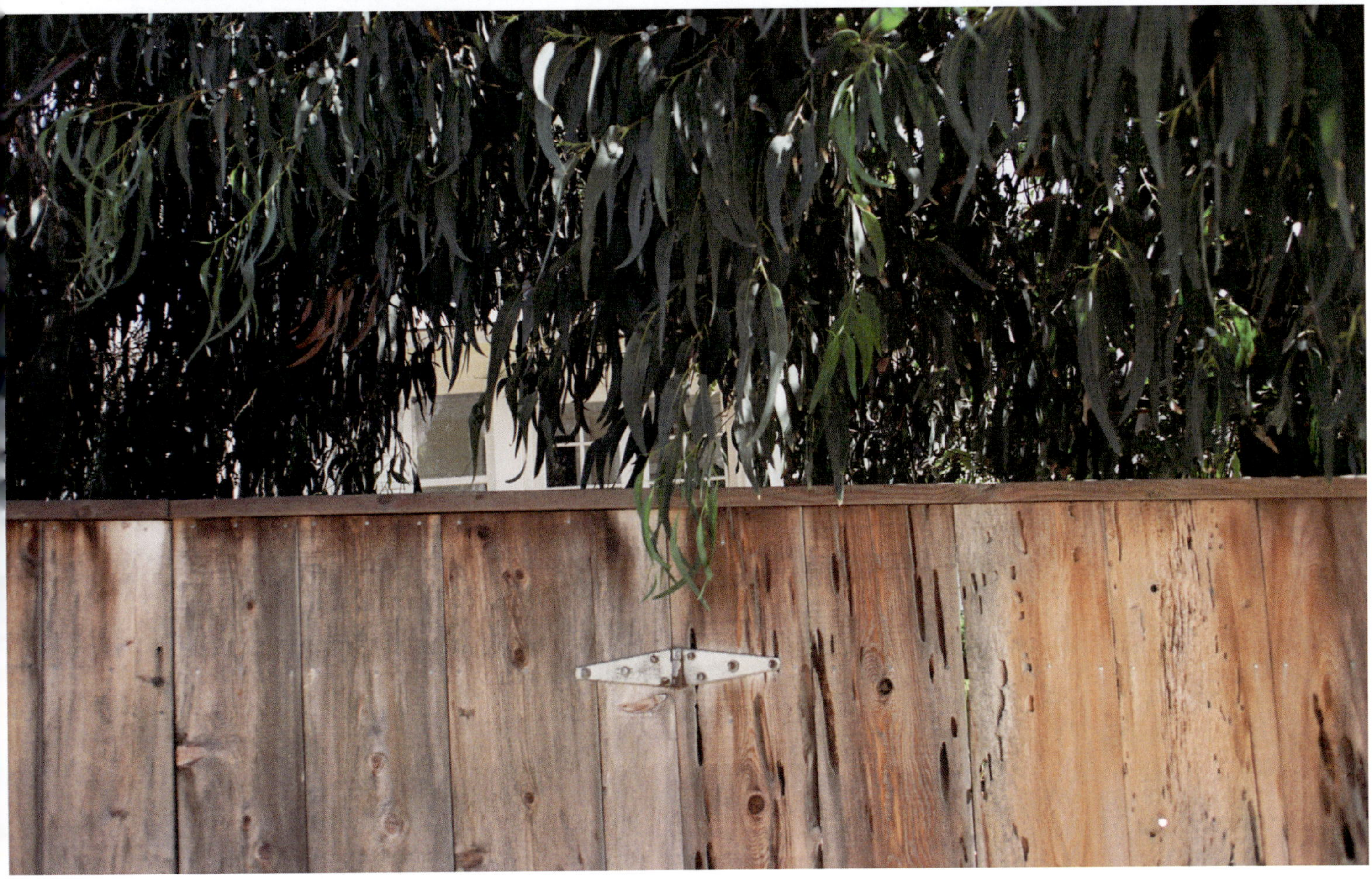

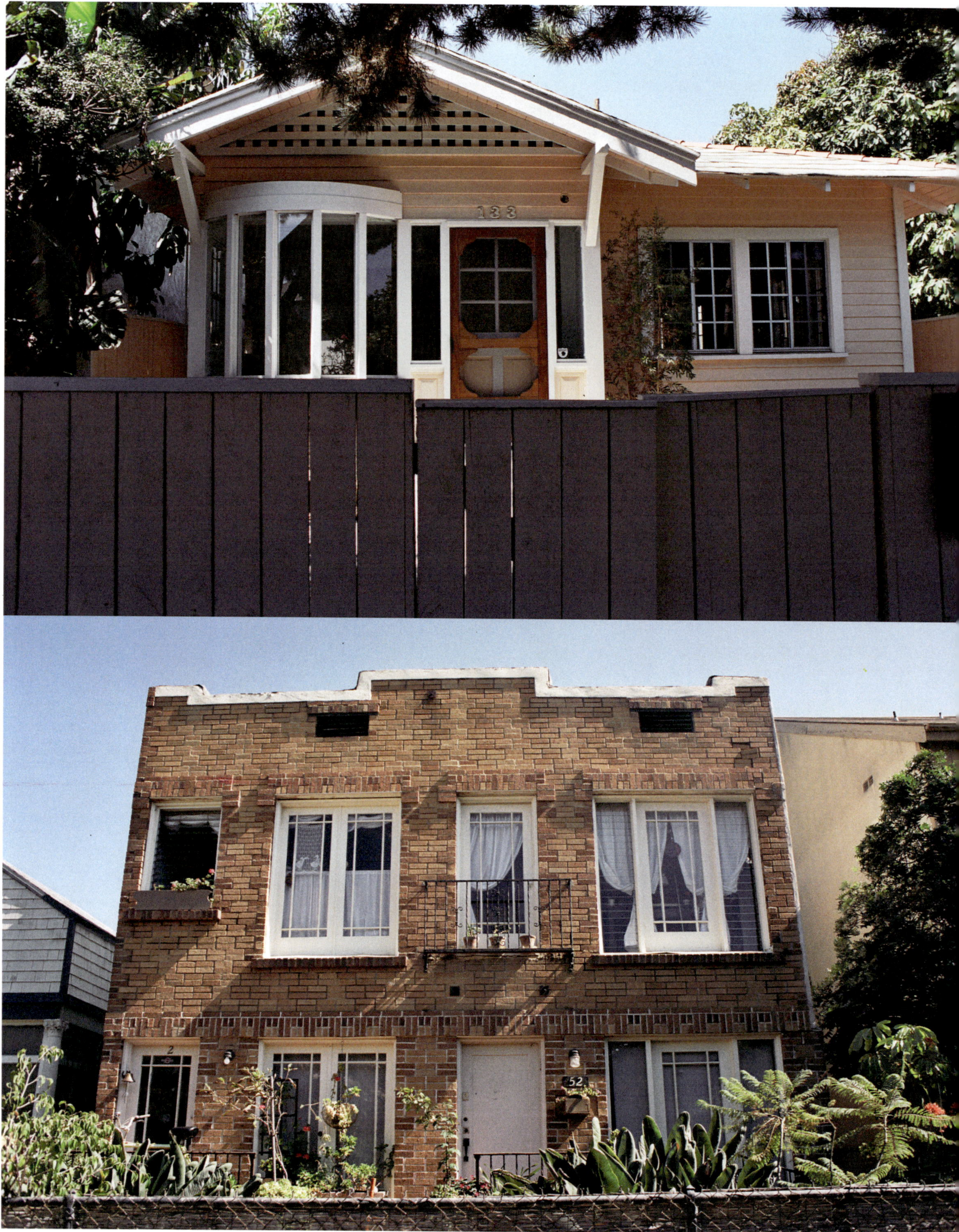

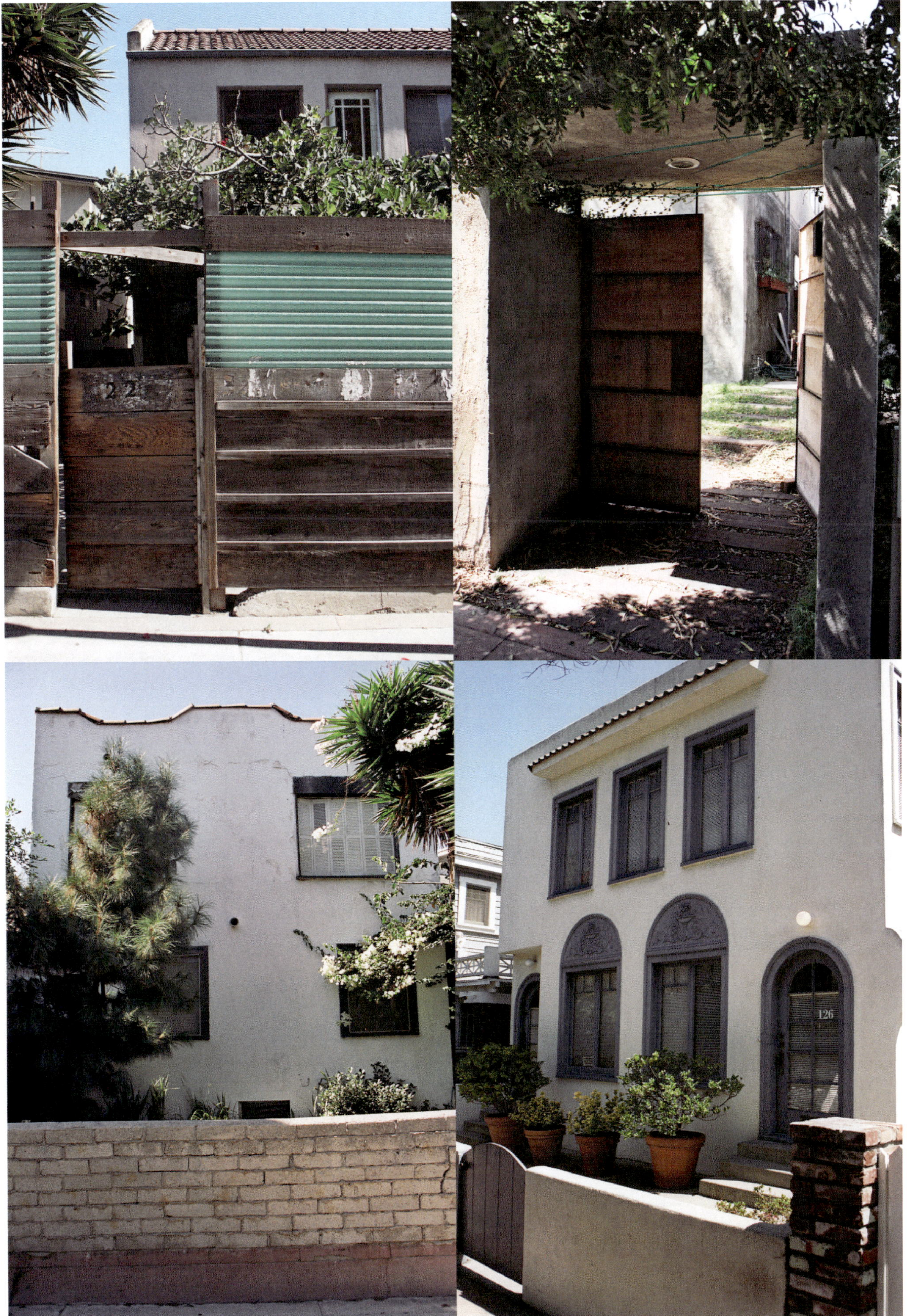

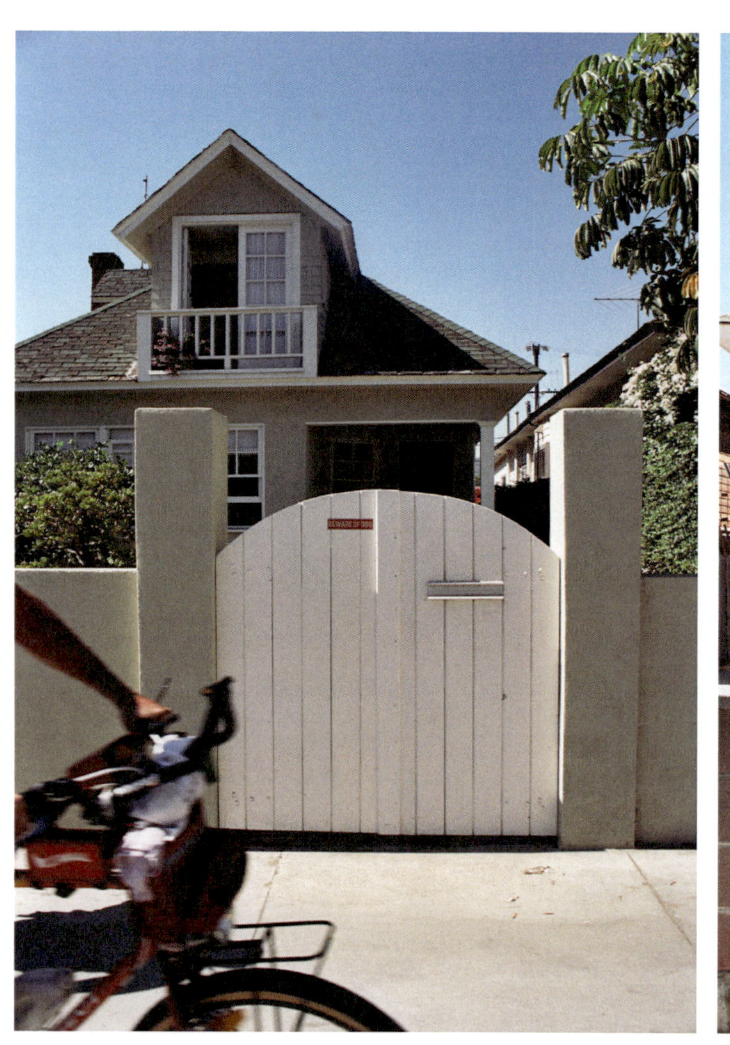

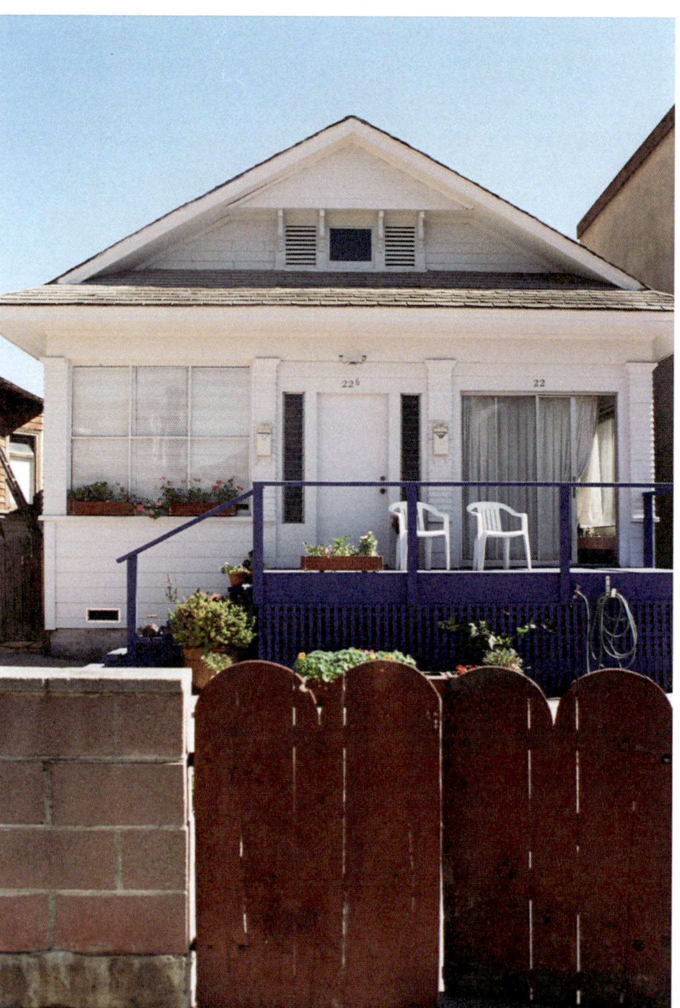

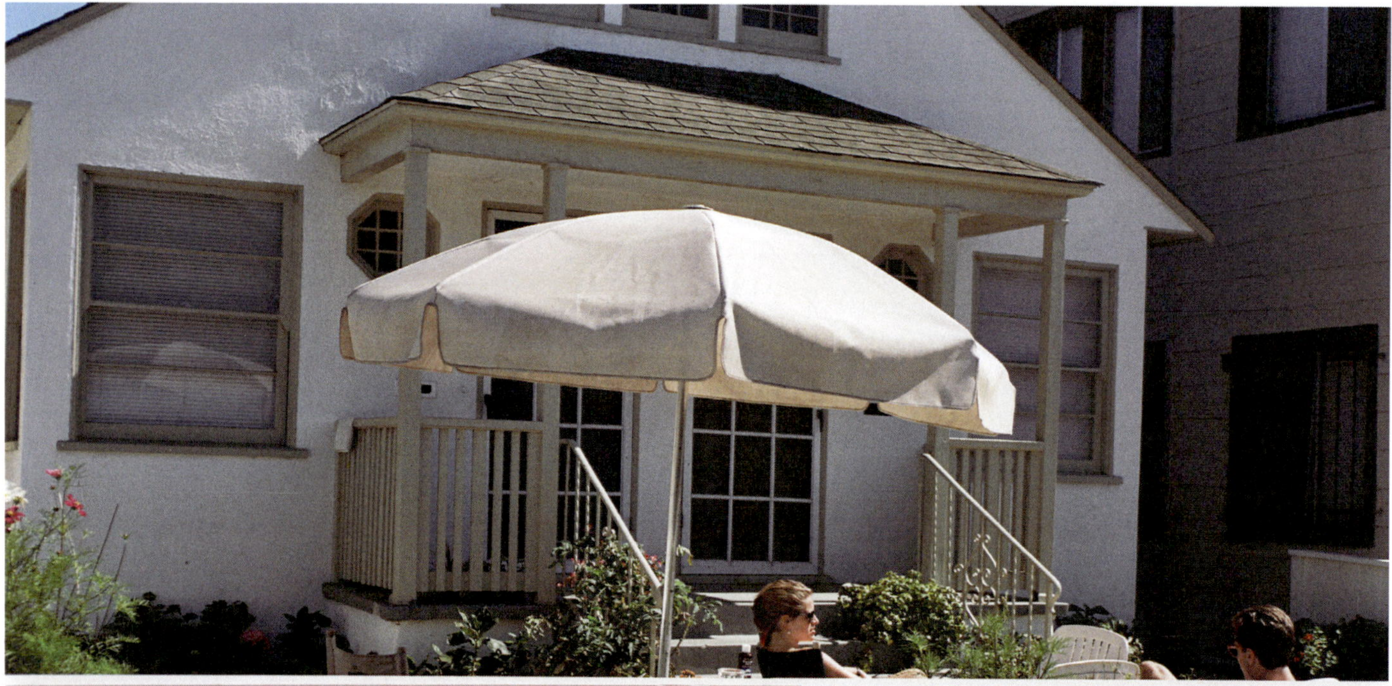

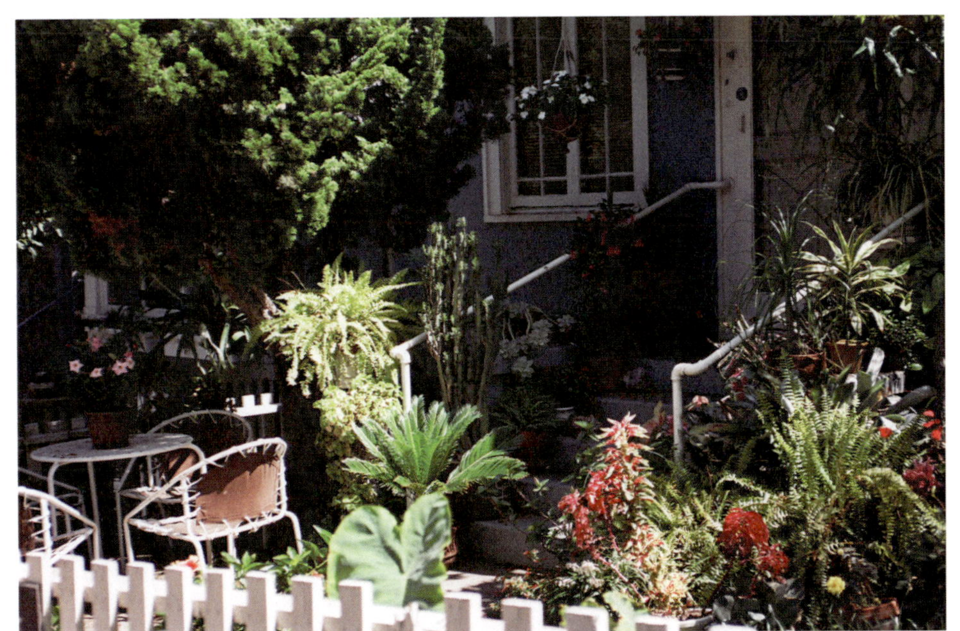

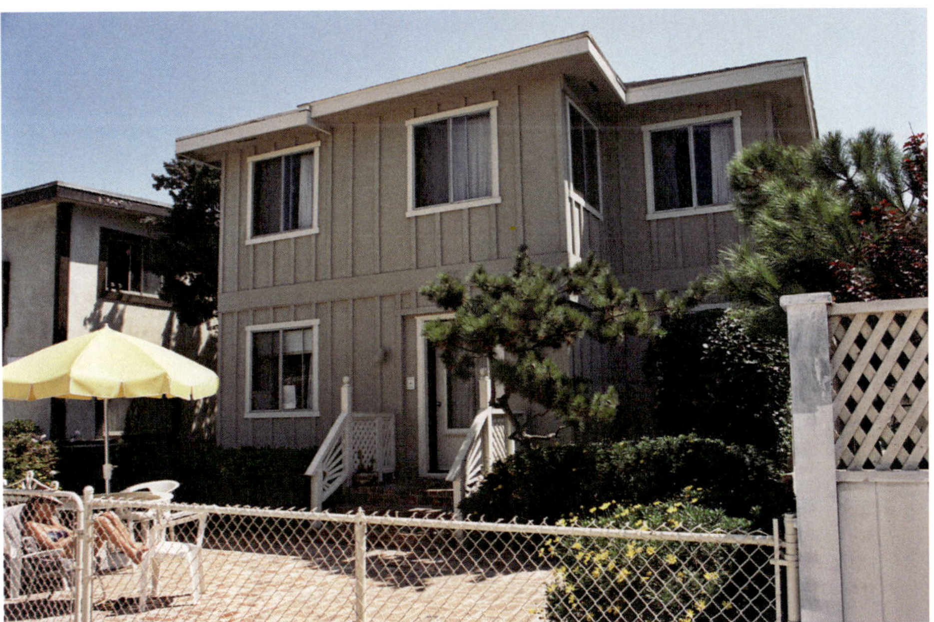

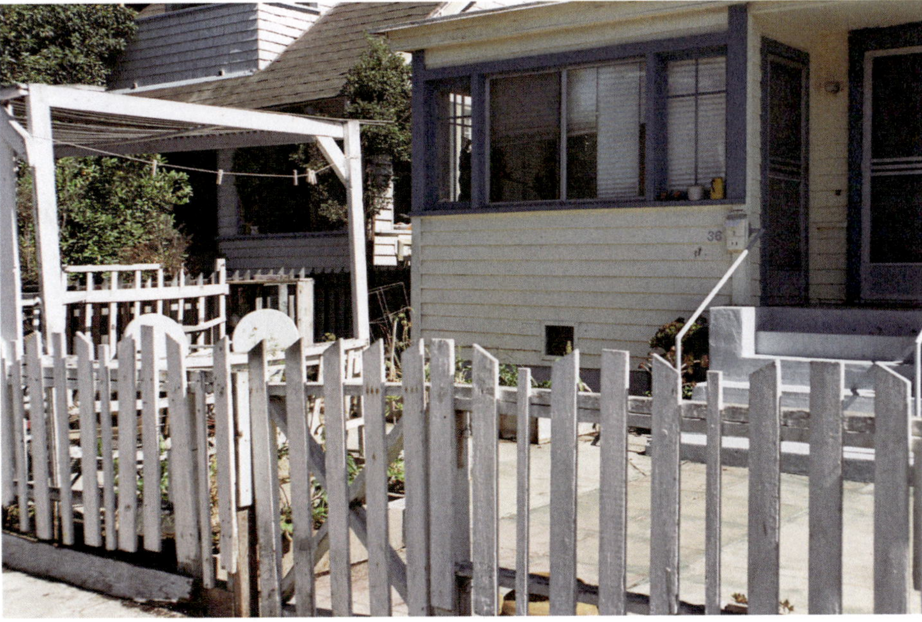

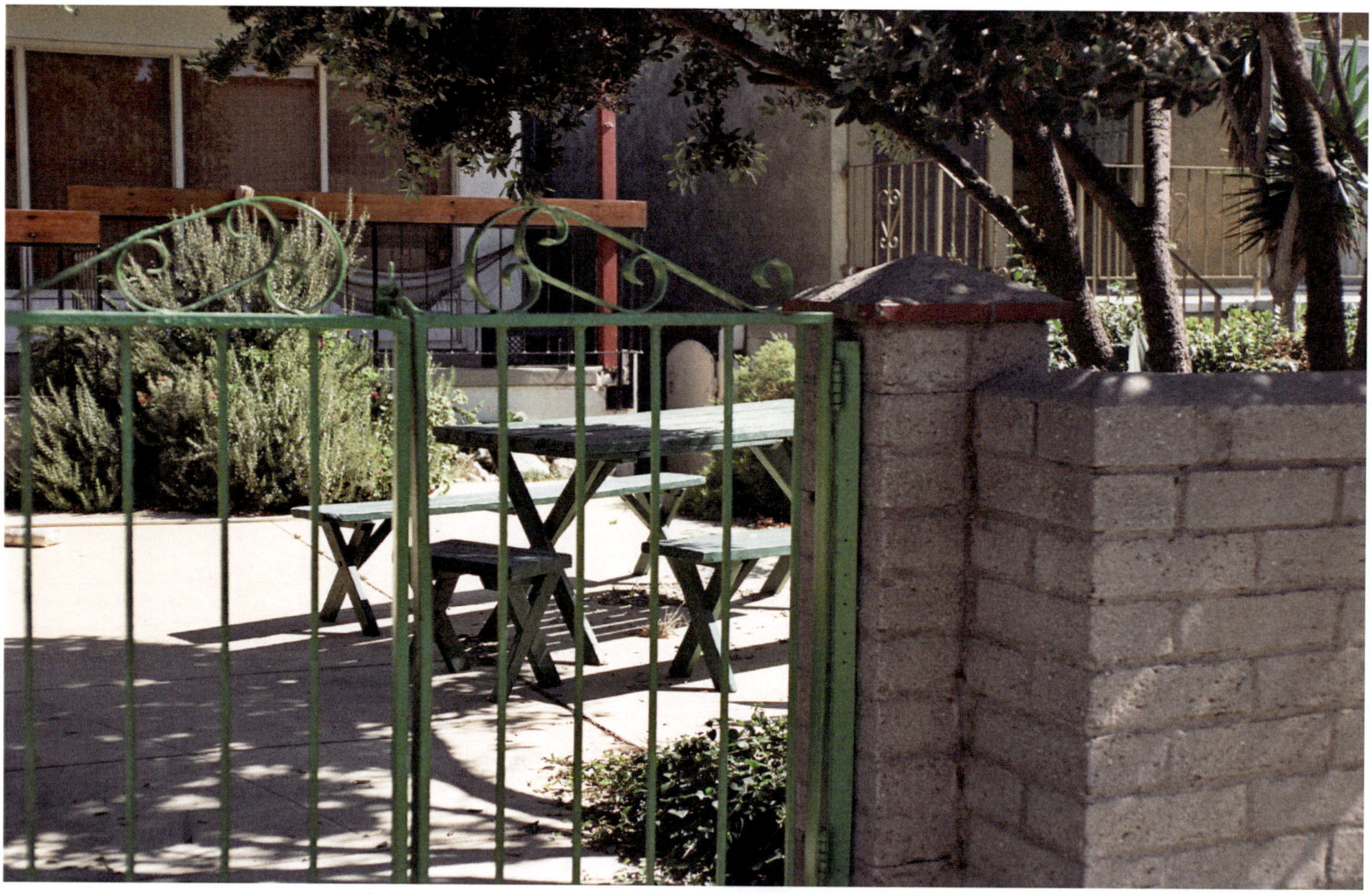

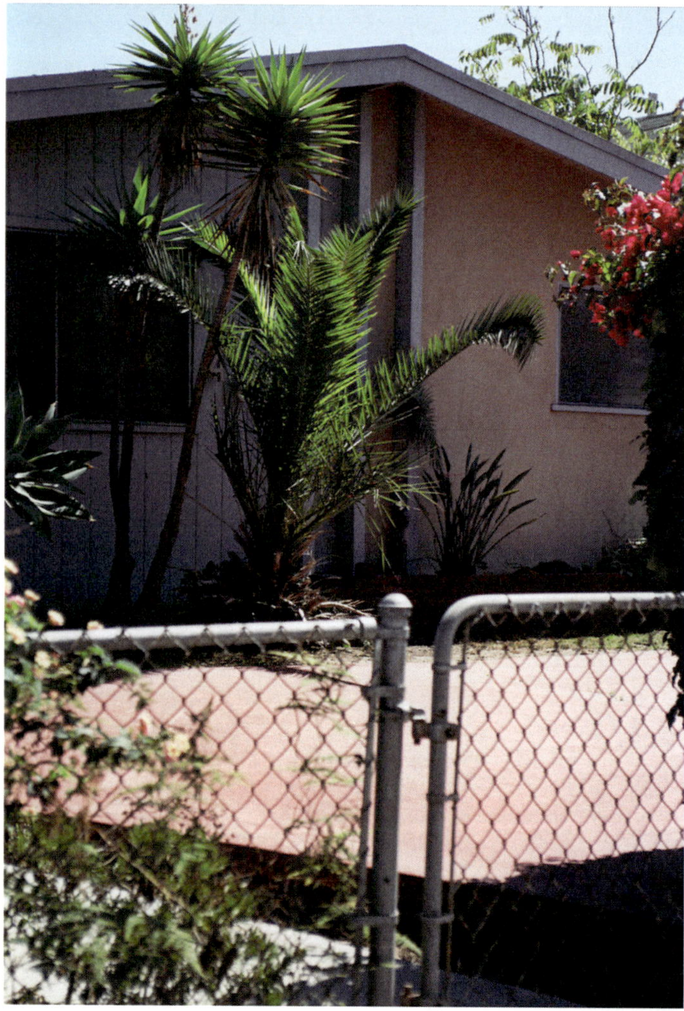
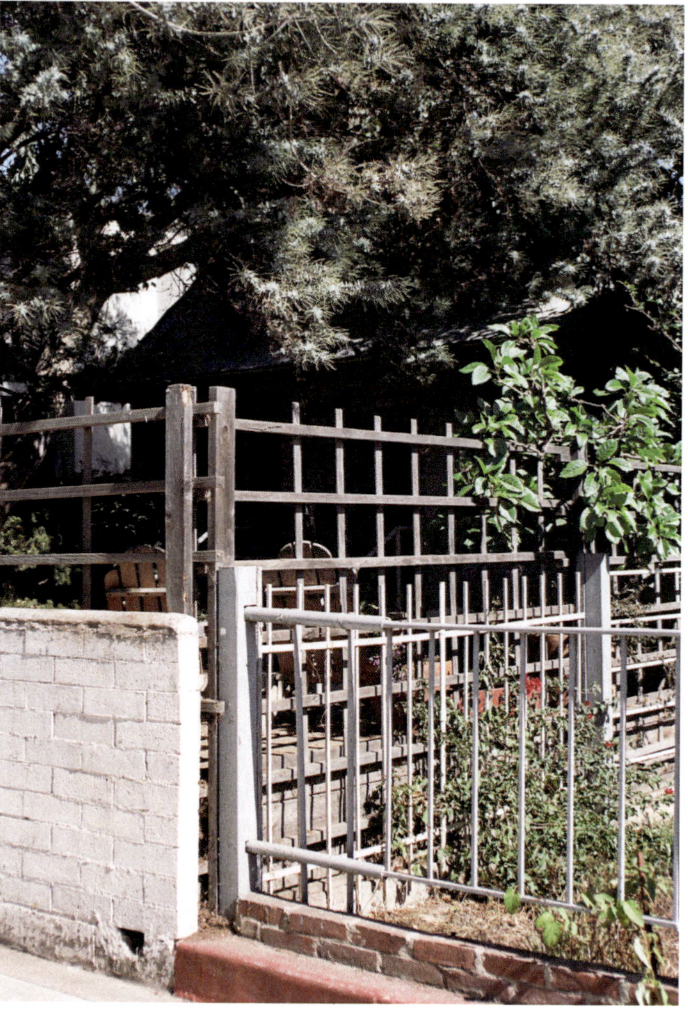

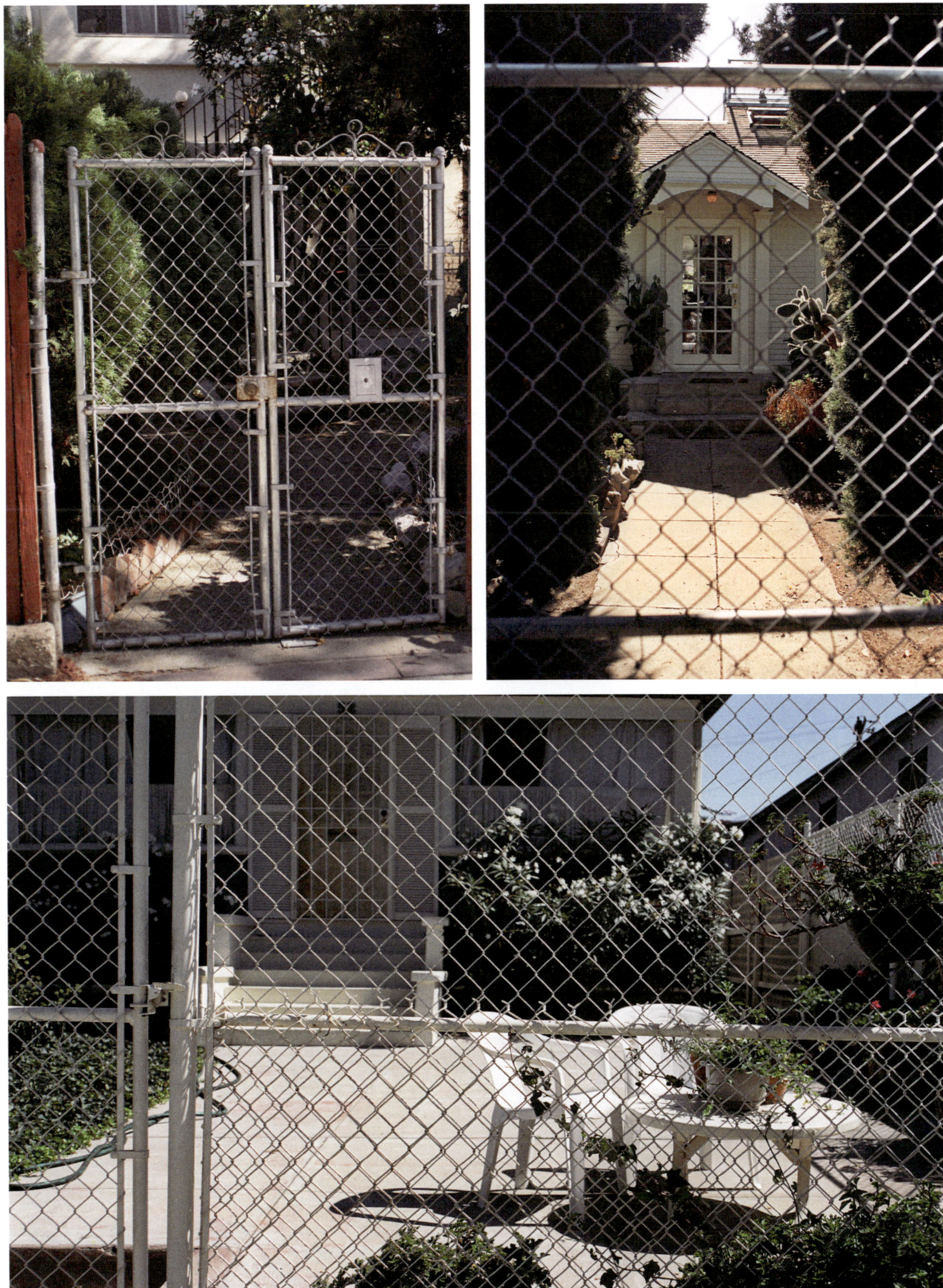

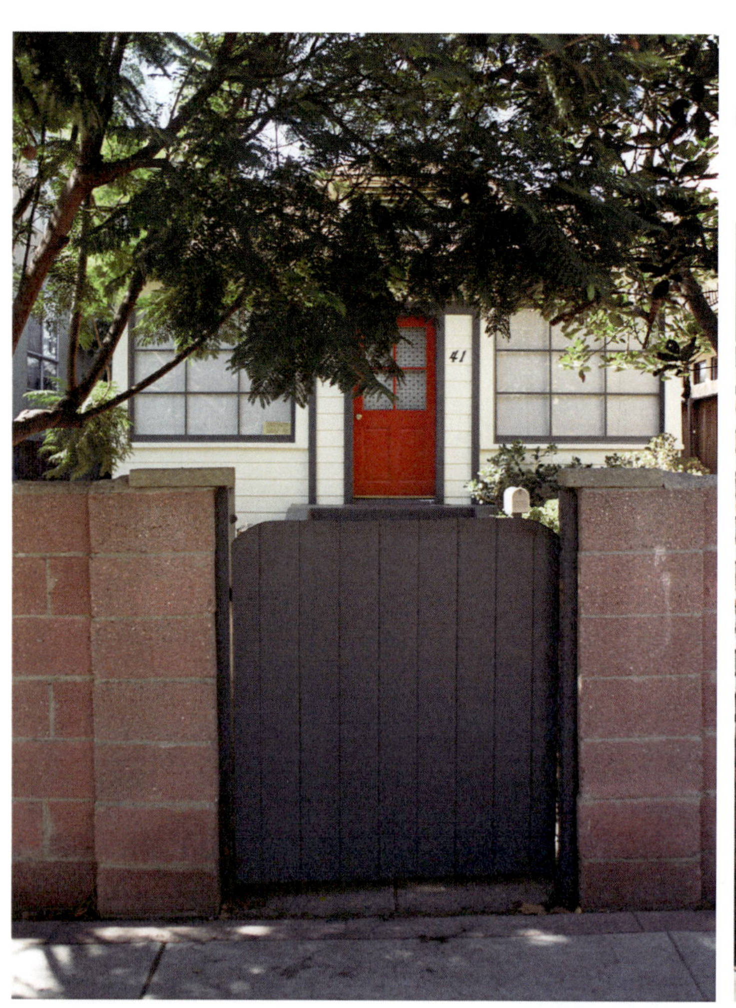
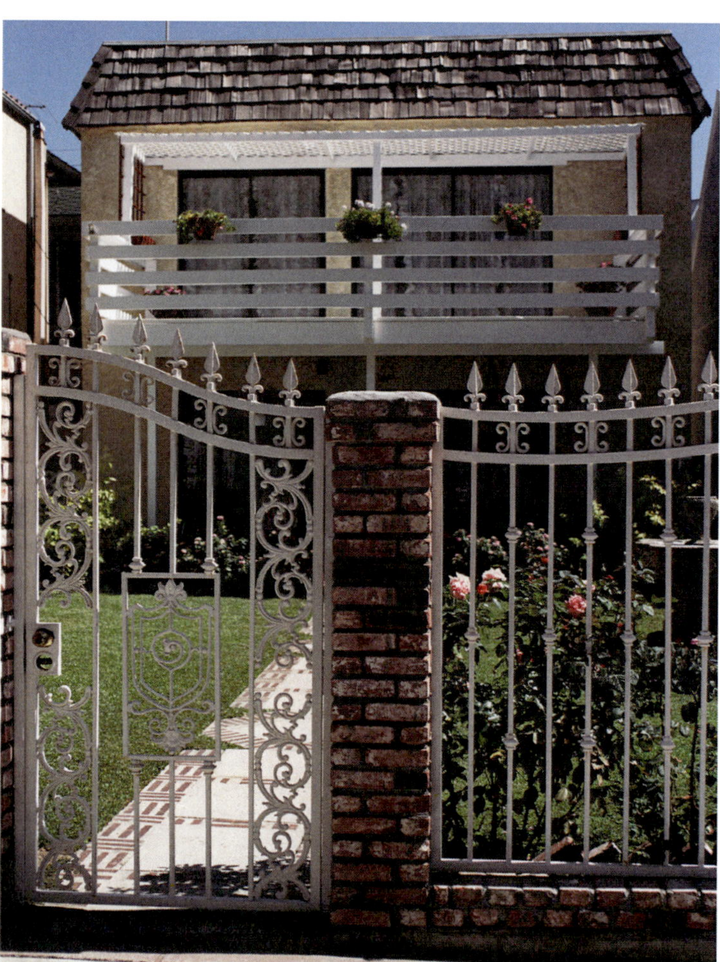

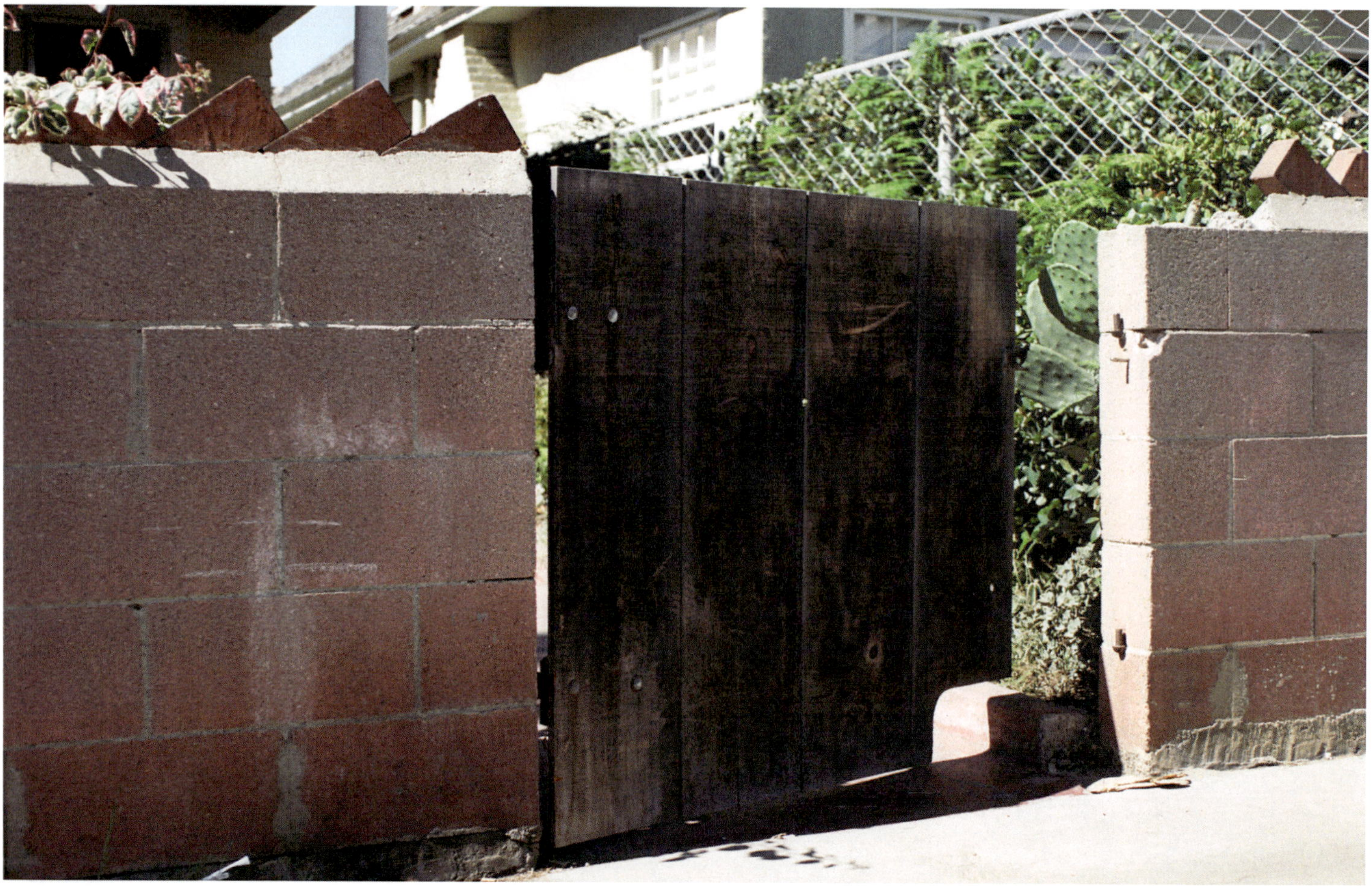

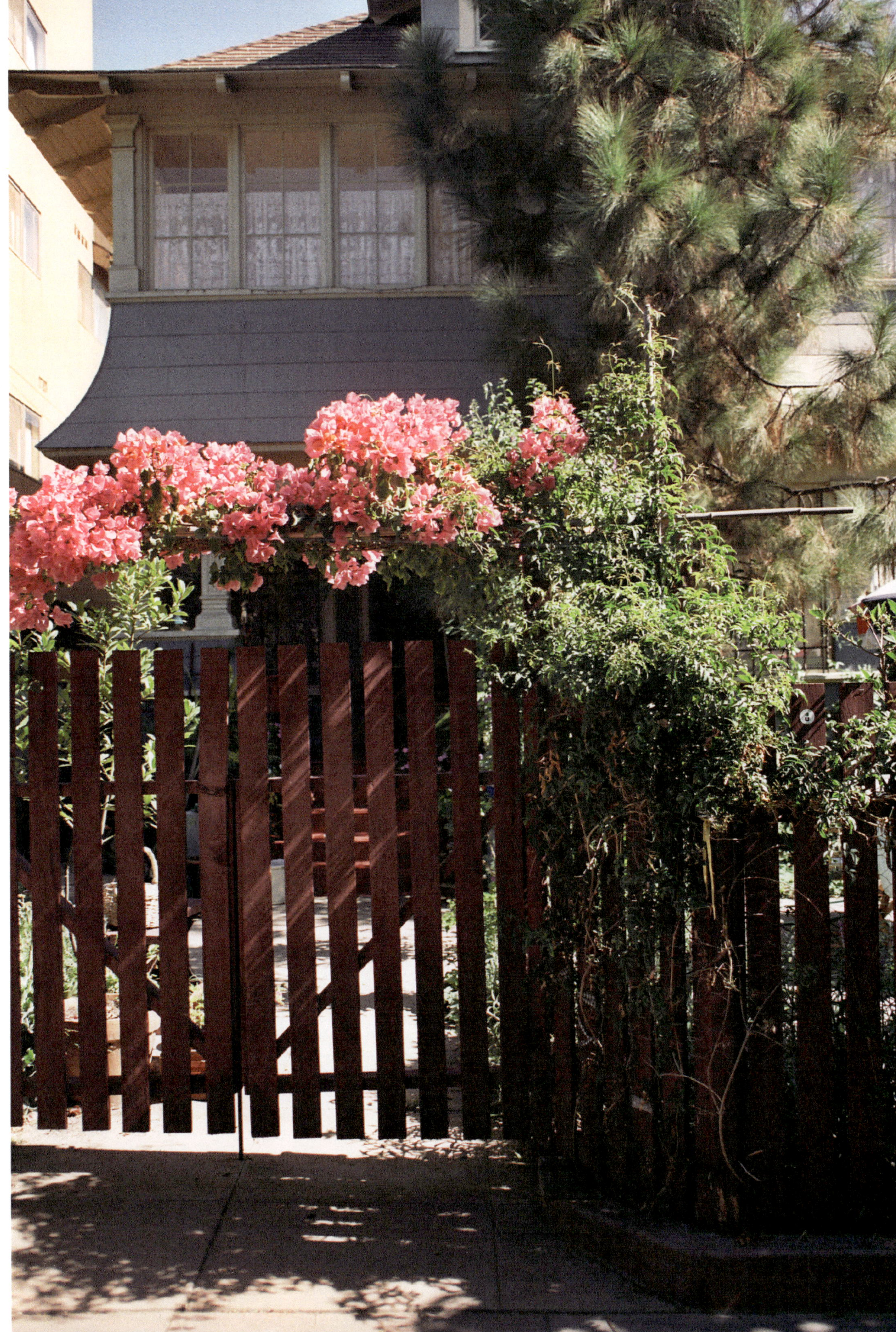

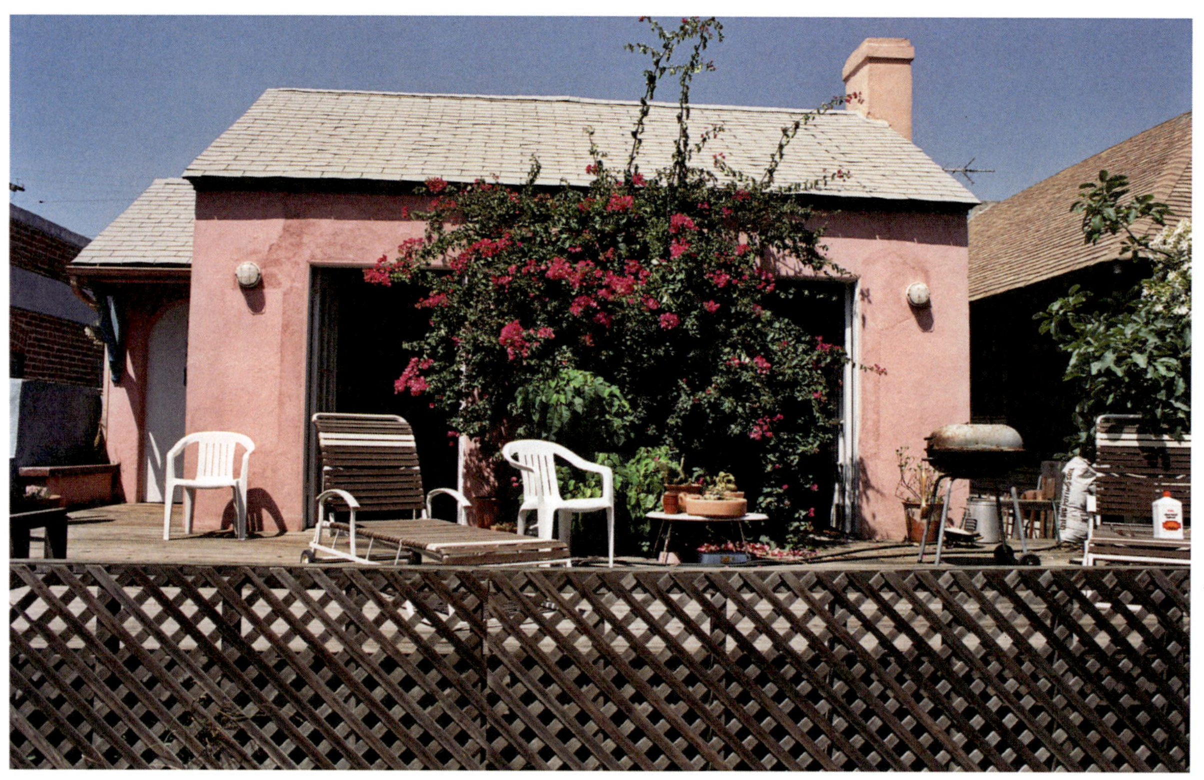

As the parents of two young children, we would be
very dismayed at the widening of our walk street.
We have no yards to speak of other than the few
feet fronting our property. The beach has become
a not altogether safe place for children these
days and we do feel that the only place for our
kids and the many neighboring children is on our
unique and not too well traveled walk street.
The value of our street as a pleasant place to
live would be greatly compromised." —Susan Moray
and Serzy Bilizuk

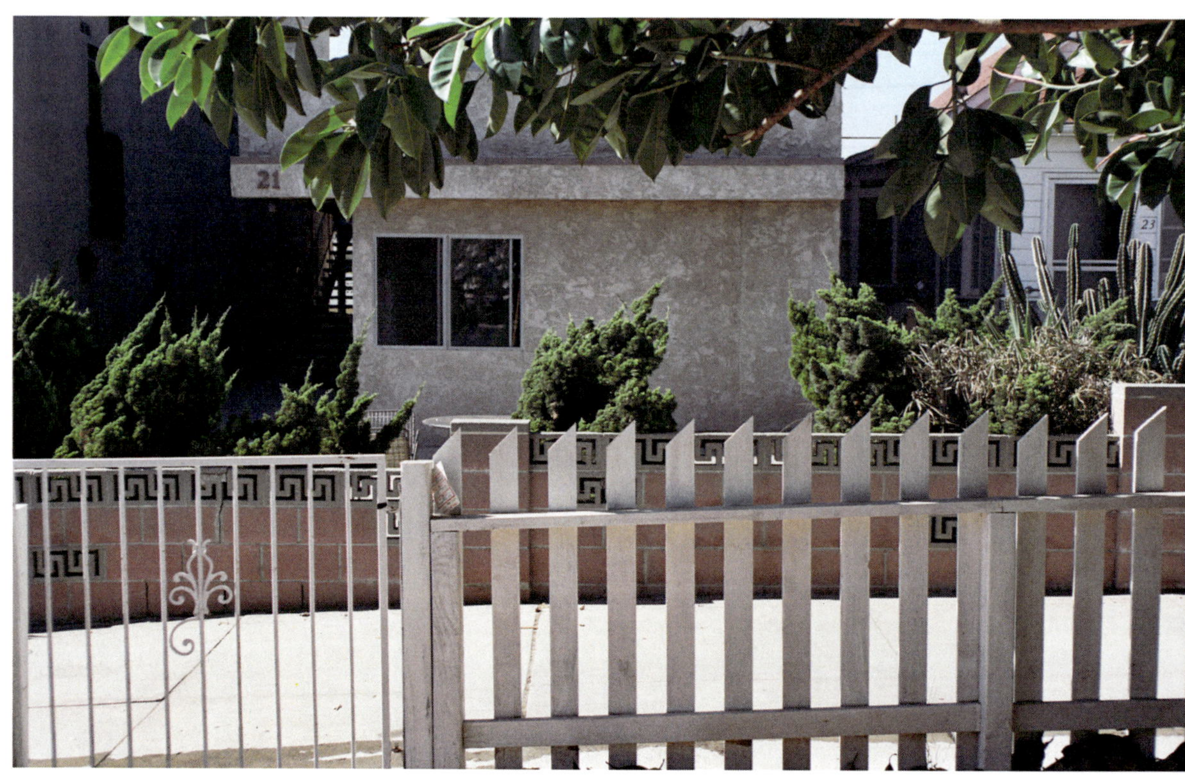

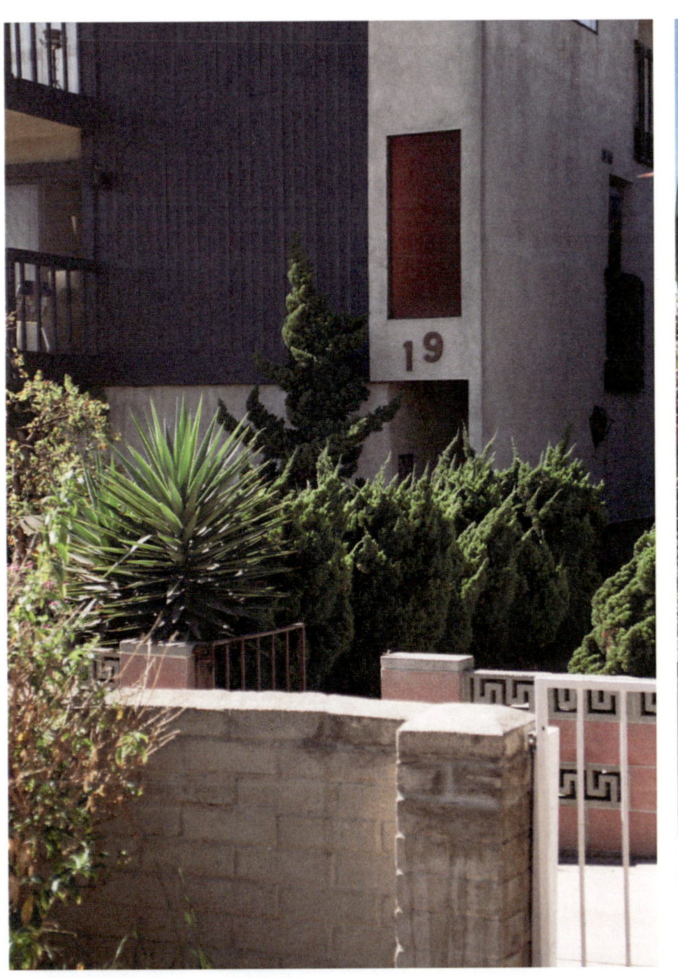
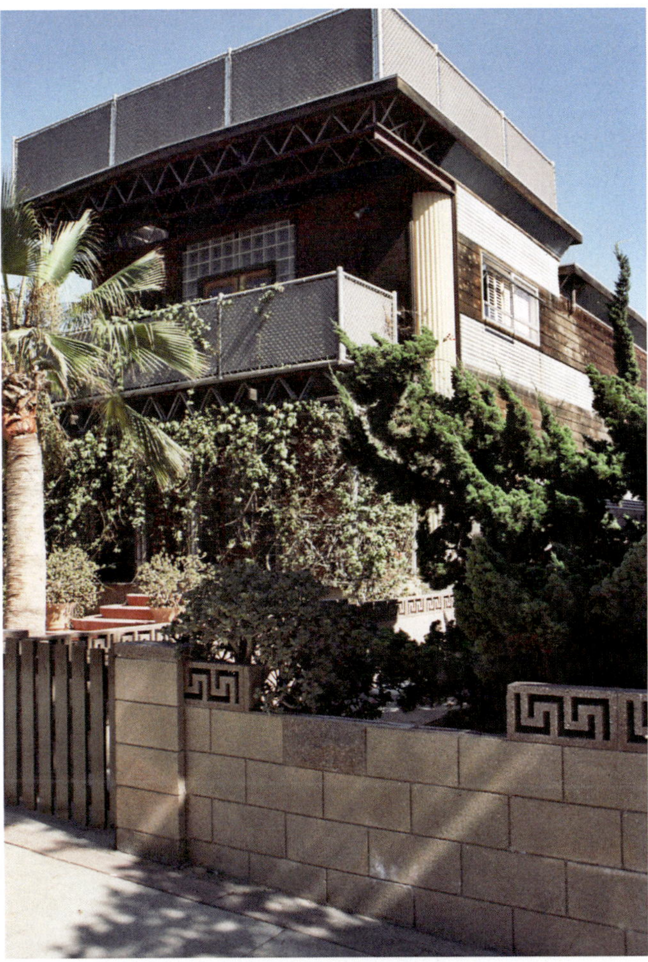
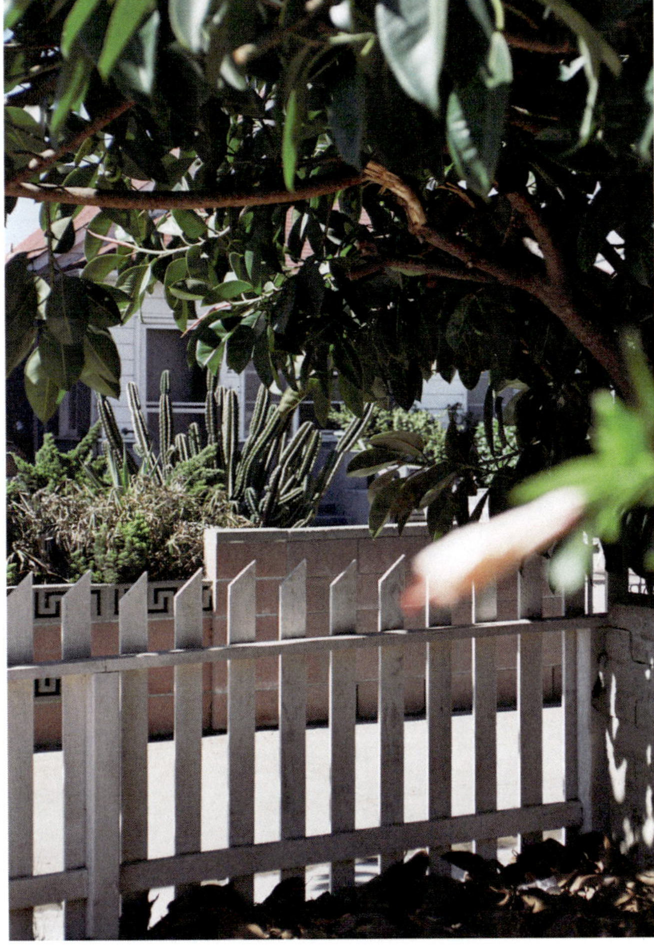
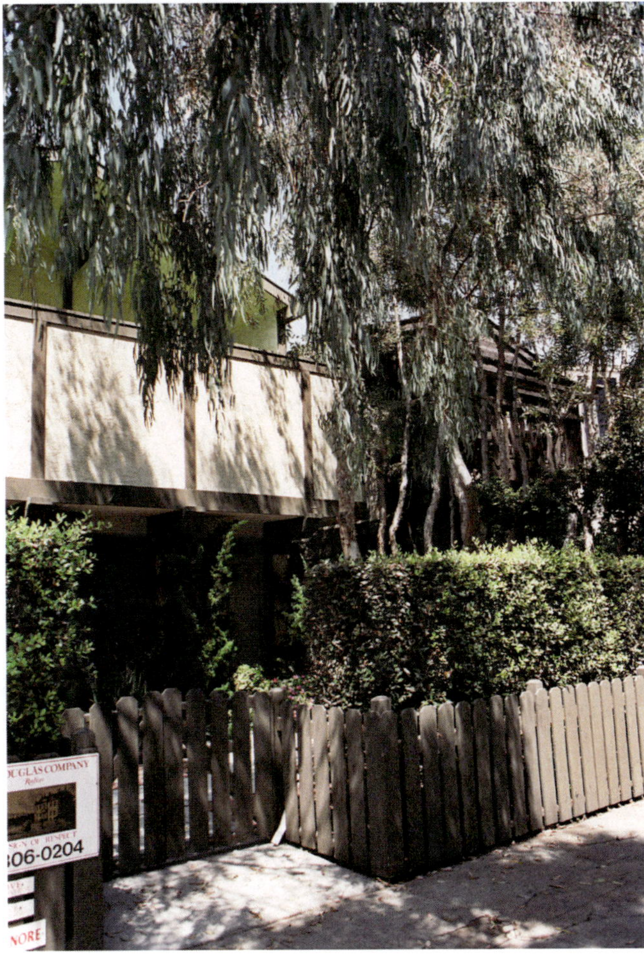

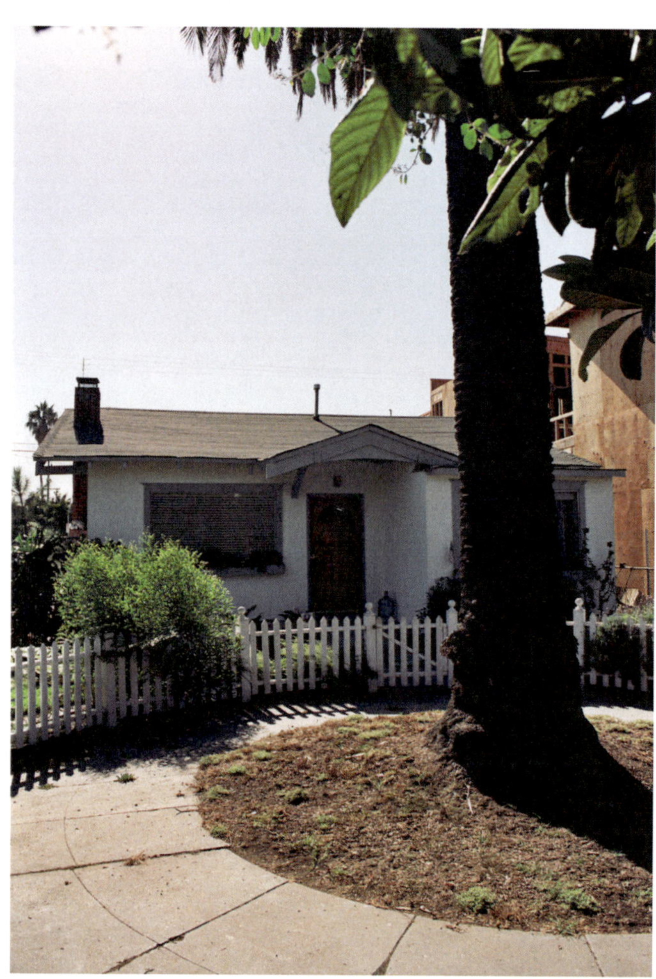
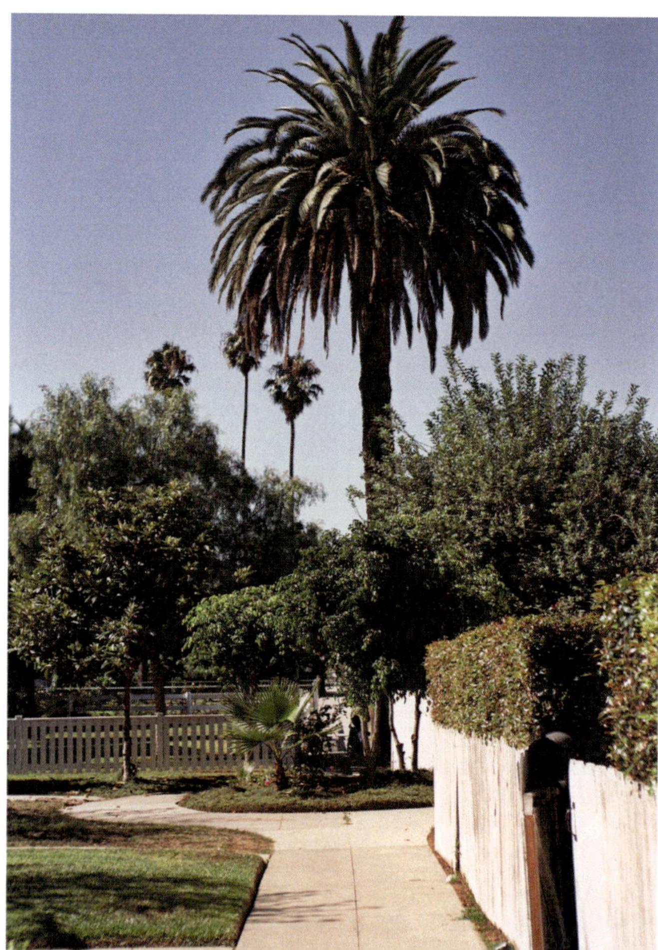
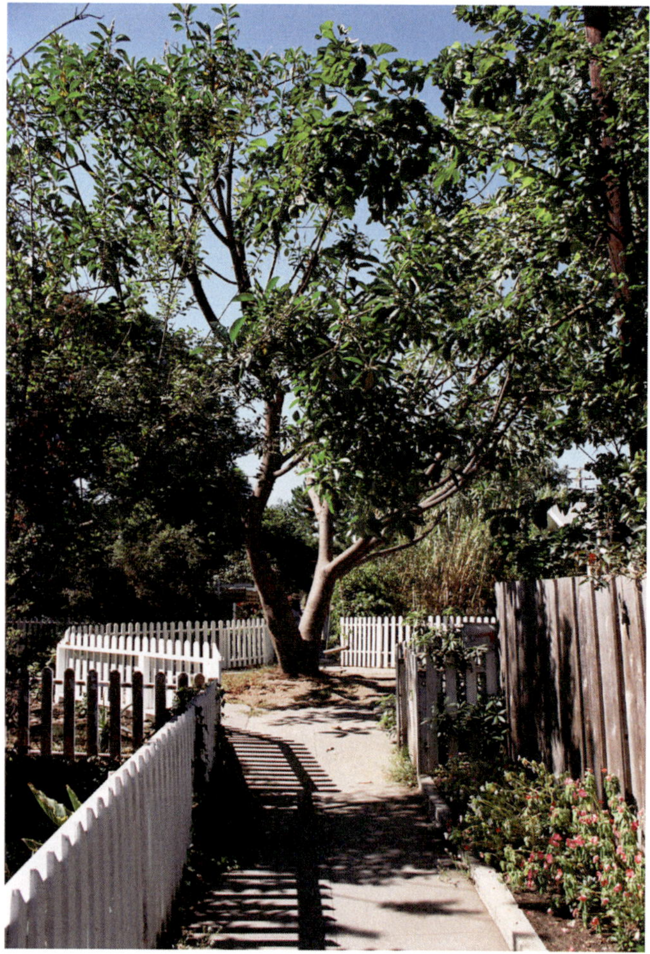
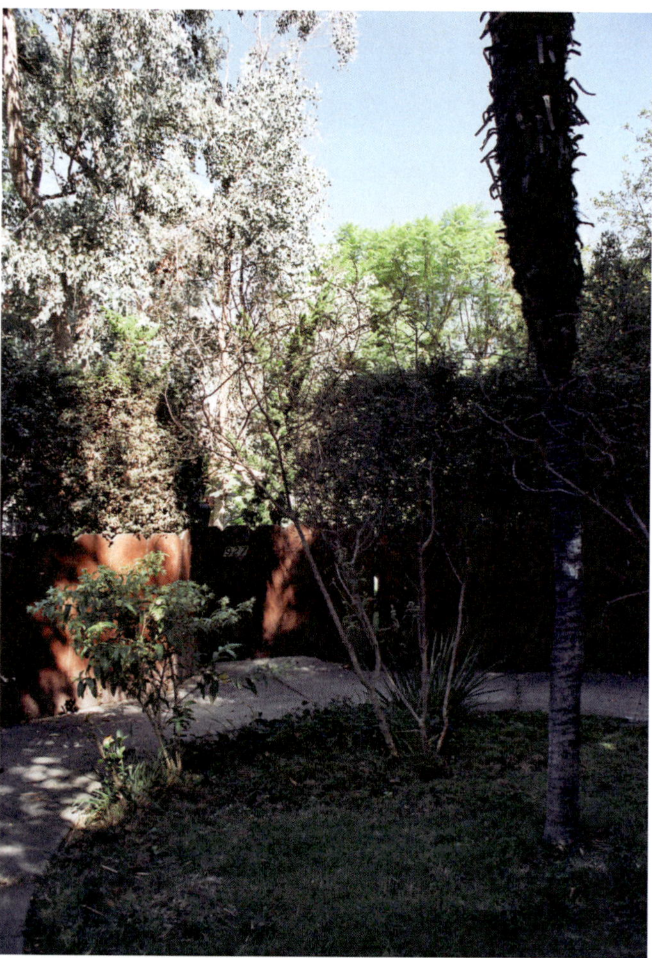

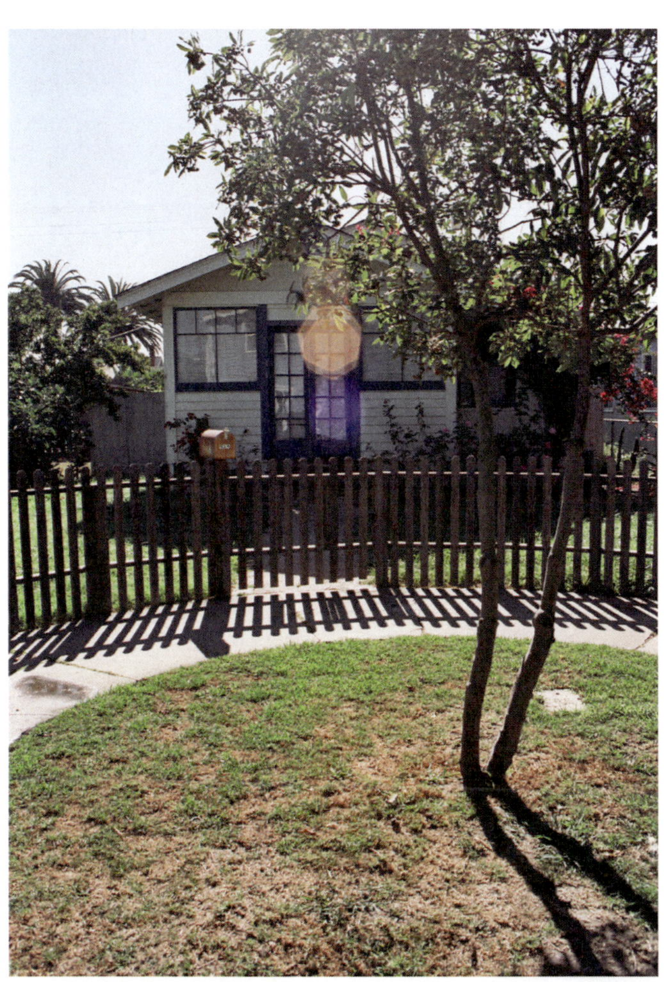

The Walkstreets which are between West Washington and Lincoln Boulevards (including Crescent Place, Nowita, Marco and Amoroso) have six foot sidewalks. Increasing them to 20' would take seven feet of already small front yards on each side of the Walkstreets. Since many of the homes are significantly less than 30' from the middle of the Walkstreets (as a result of legal variance or pre-building code construction), a new 20' street would leave some "front yards" with as little as 13' to the street edge. More importantly, it would wipe out most of the mature landscaping including 100-year-old fig, palm, pine, eucalyptus and other tall trees. In the case of several of these walk streets, Crescent Place in particular, this street widening would destroy small neighborhood parks. —Eileen Pollack Erickson, President, Crescent Place Preservation Committee

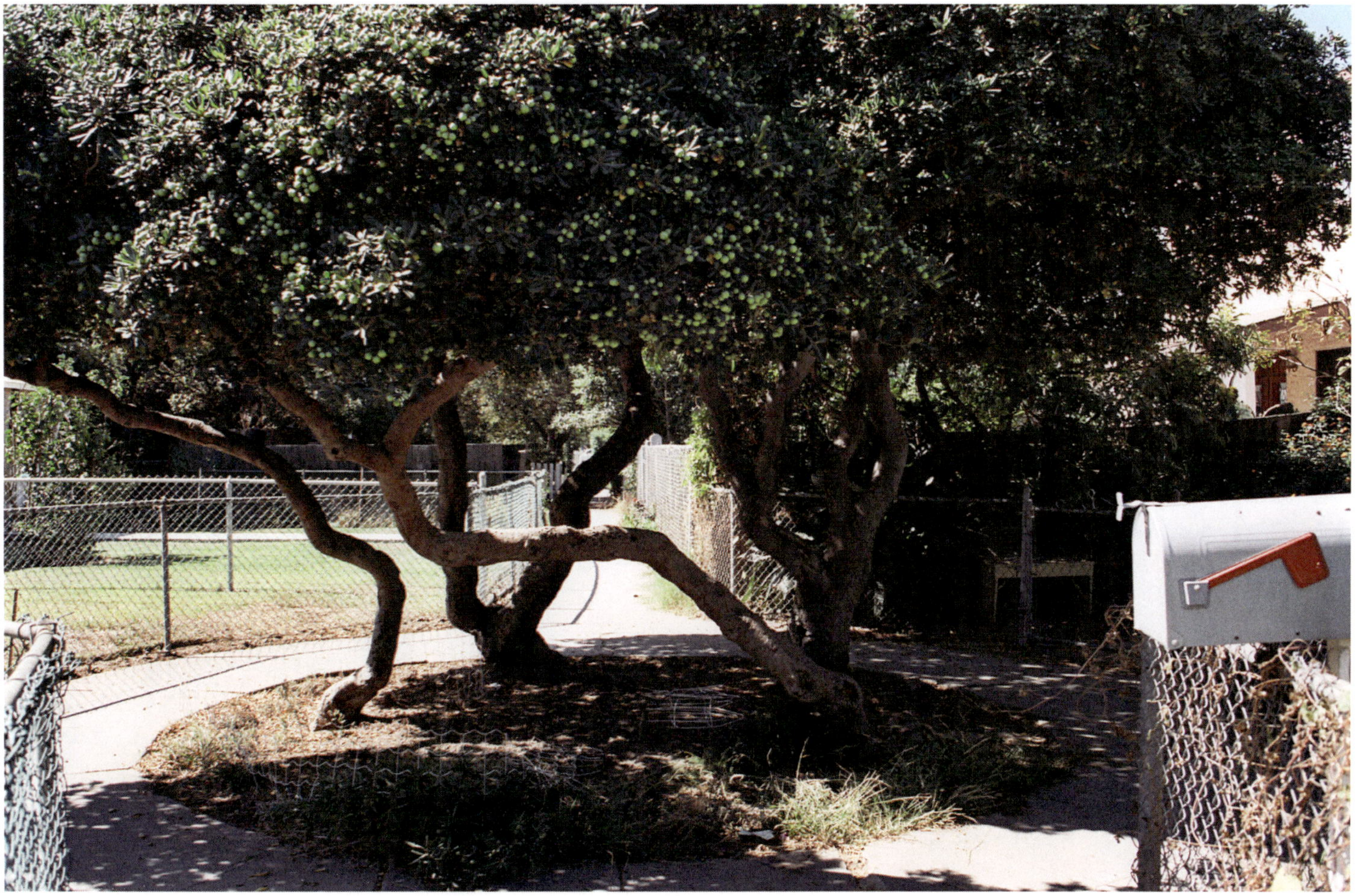

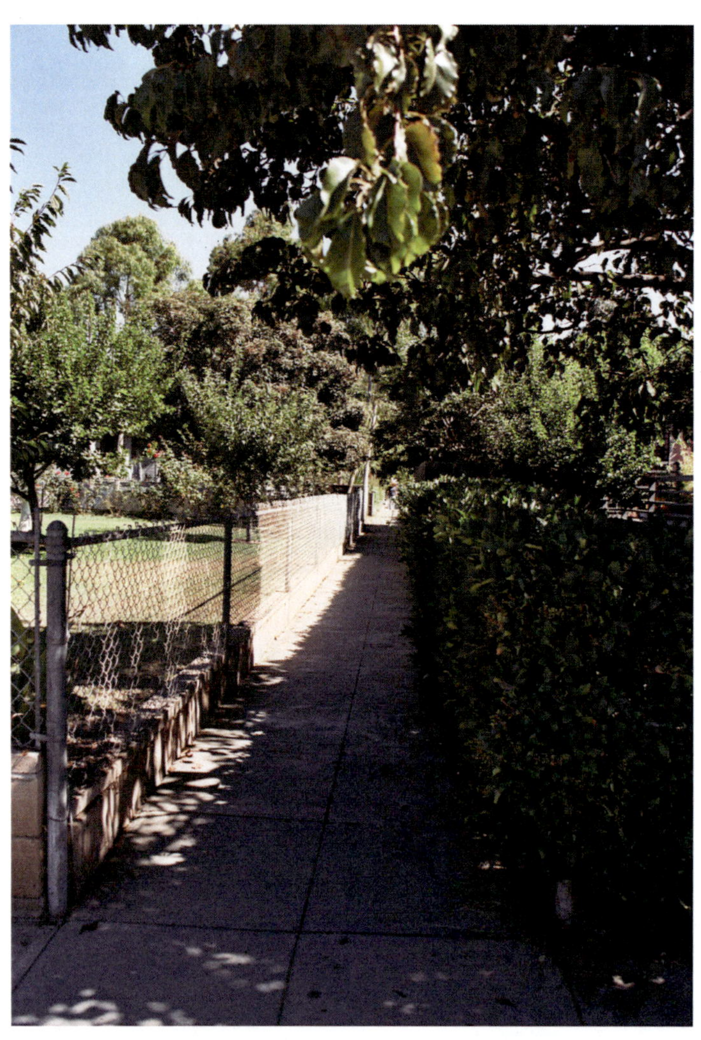
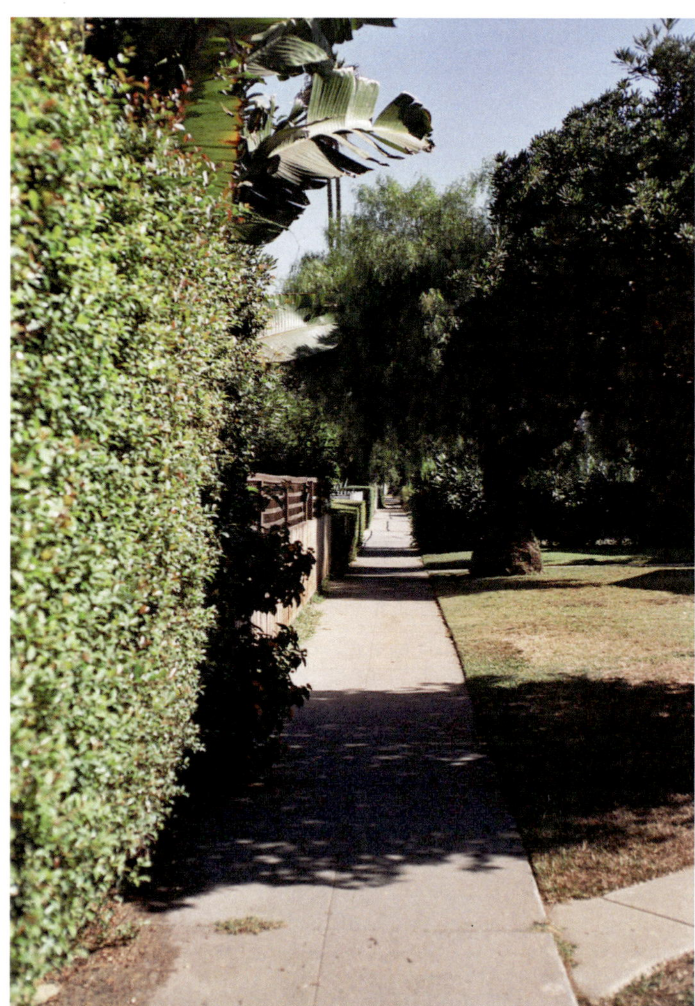

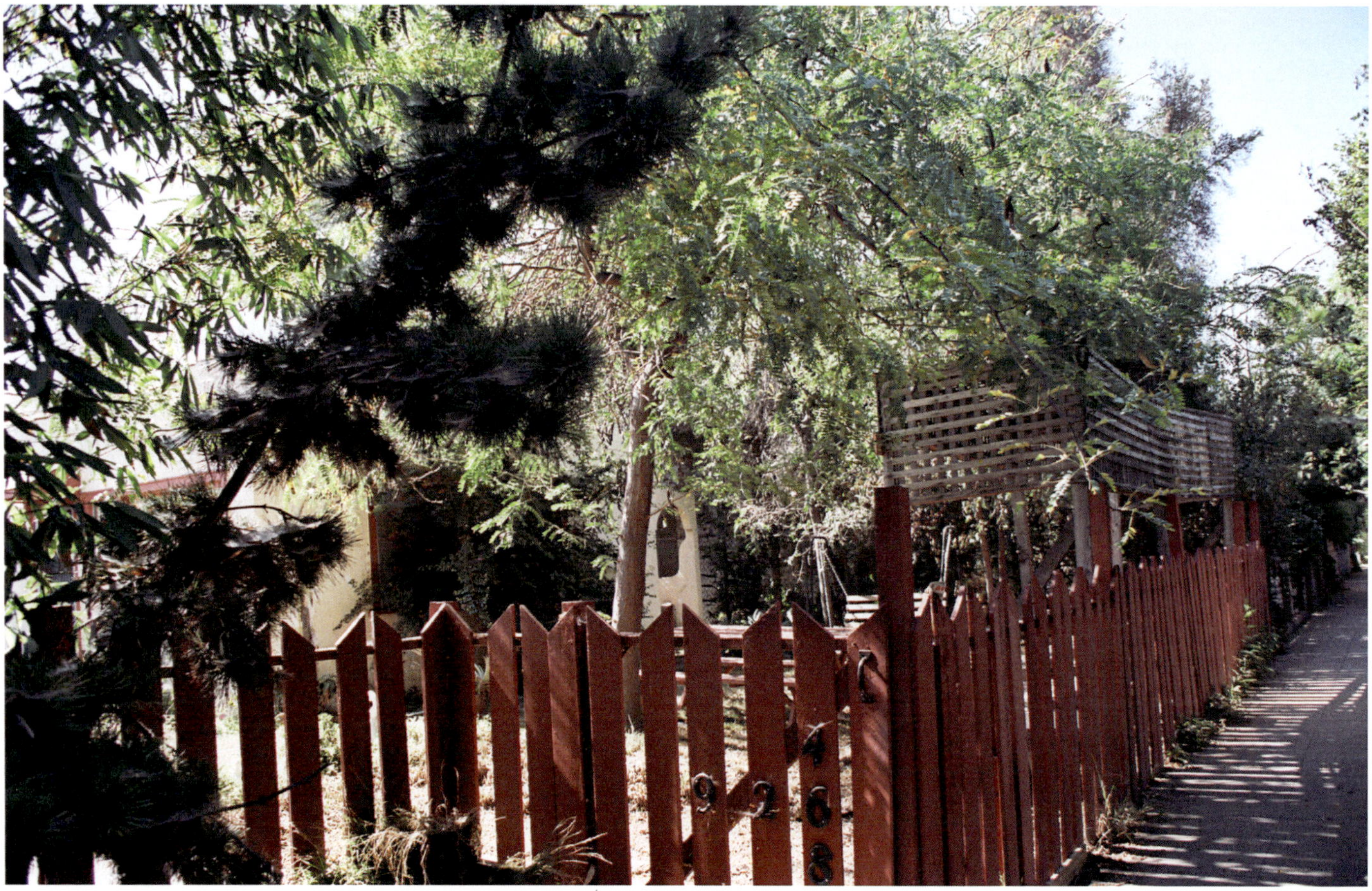

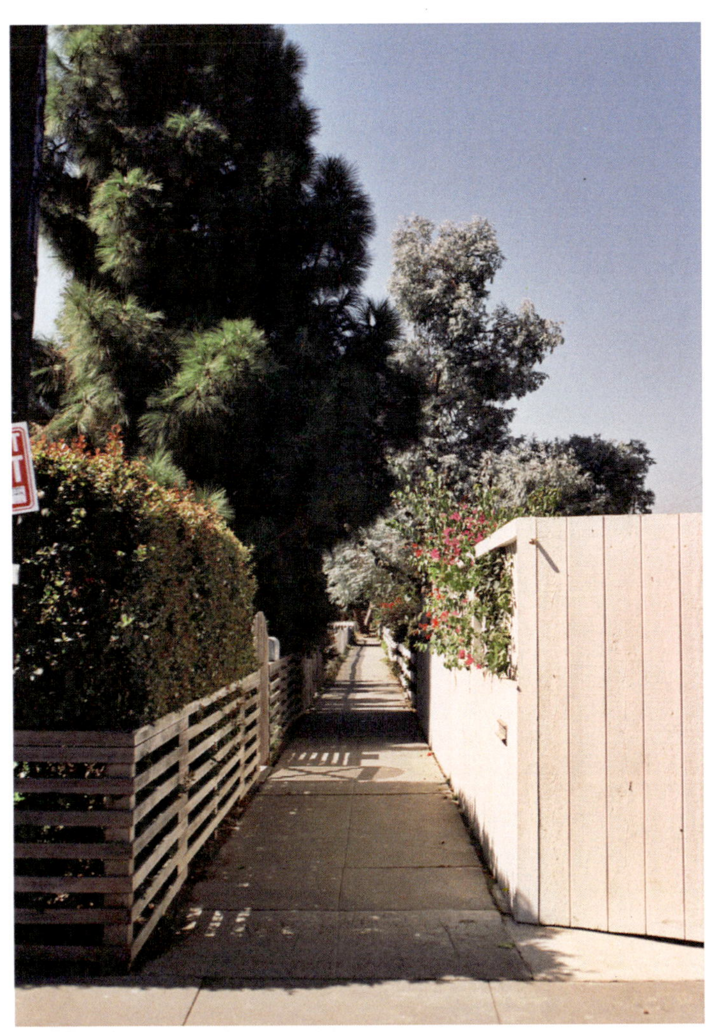
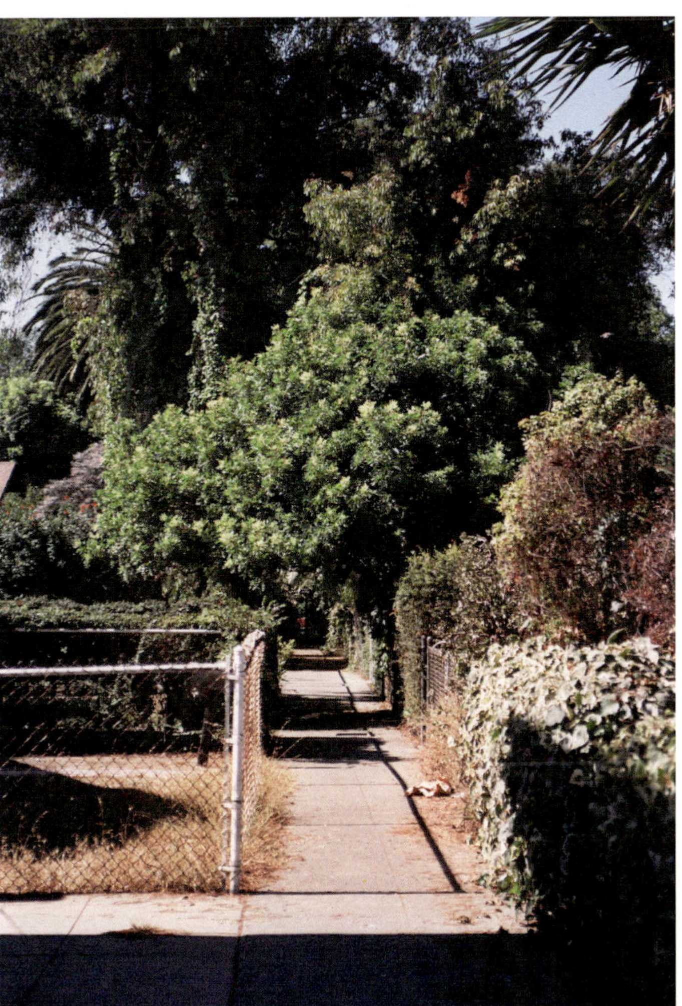

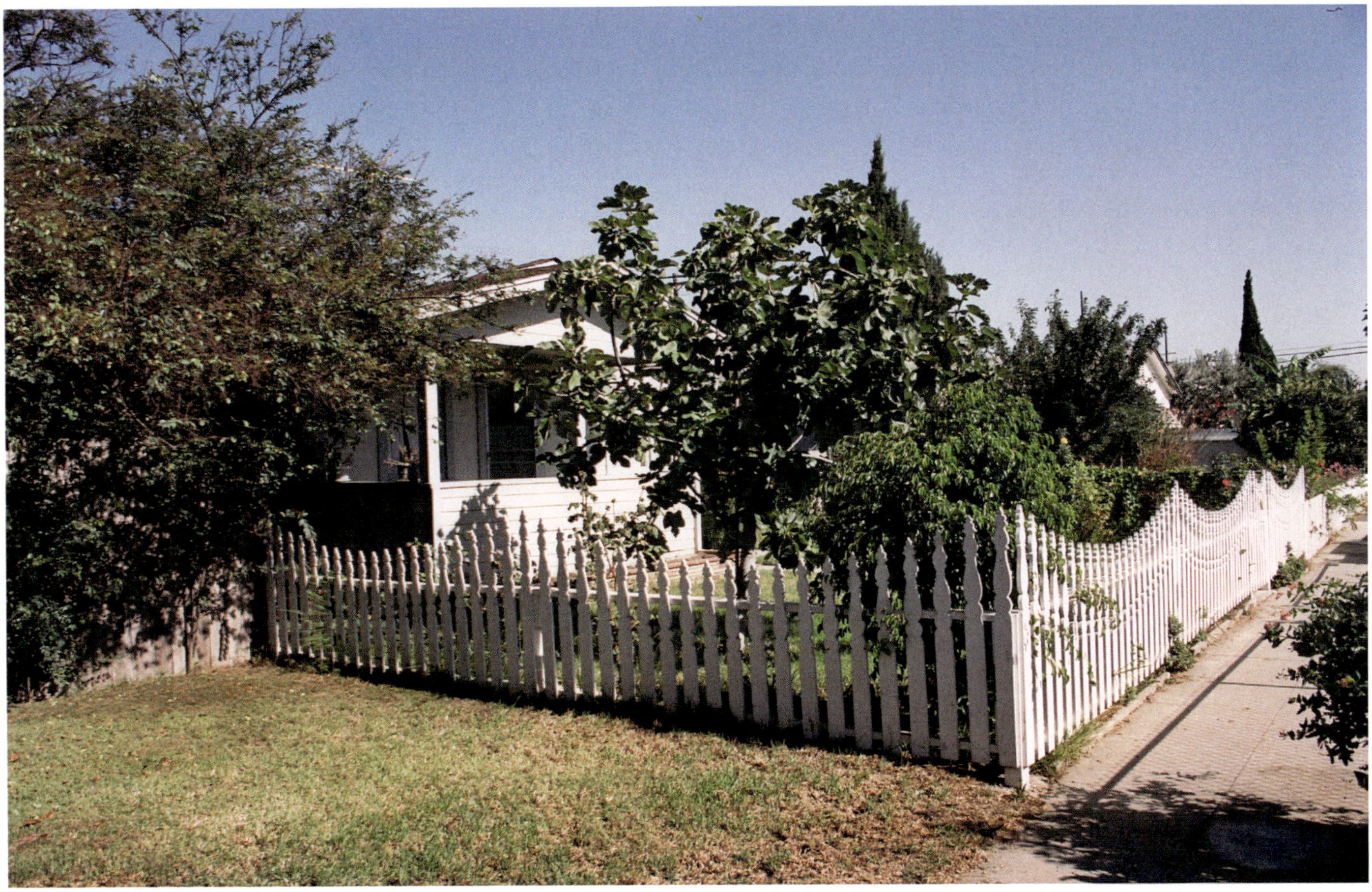

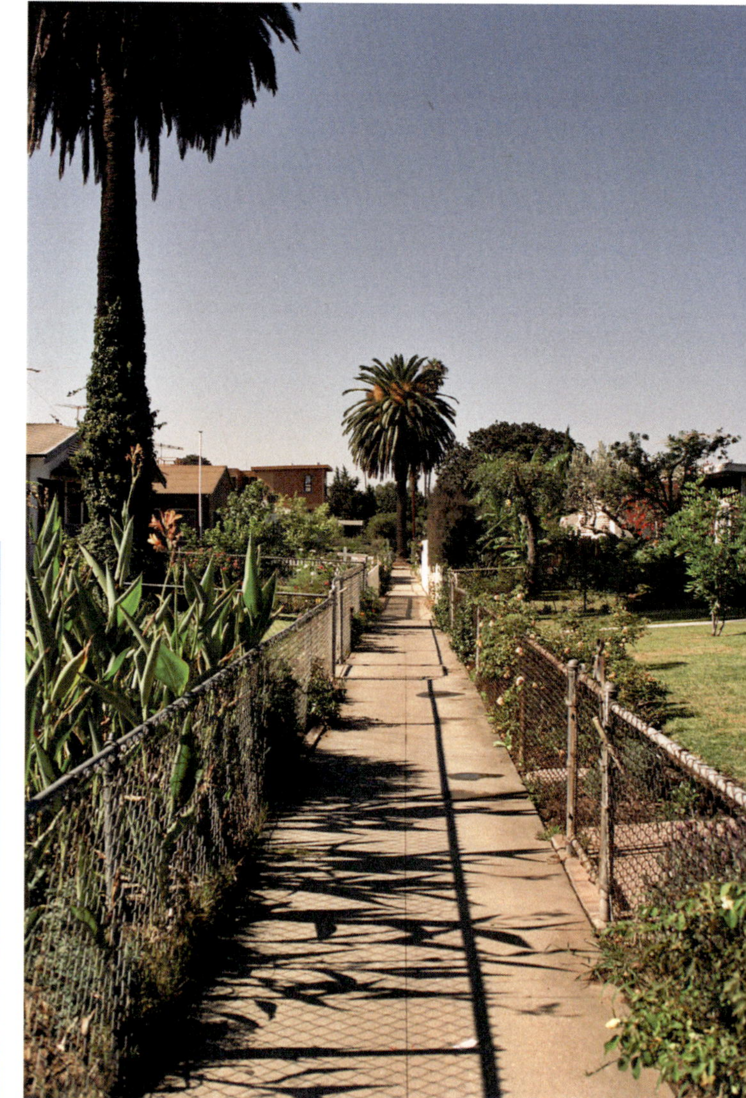

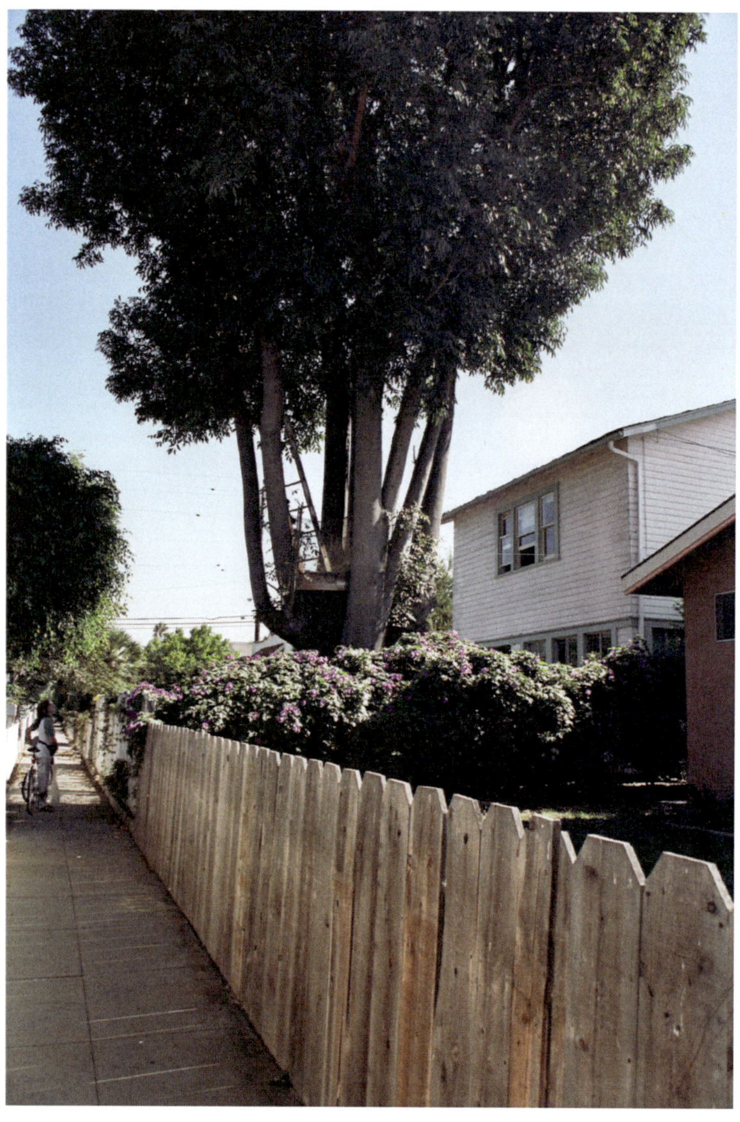

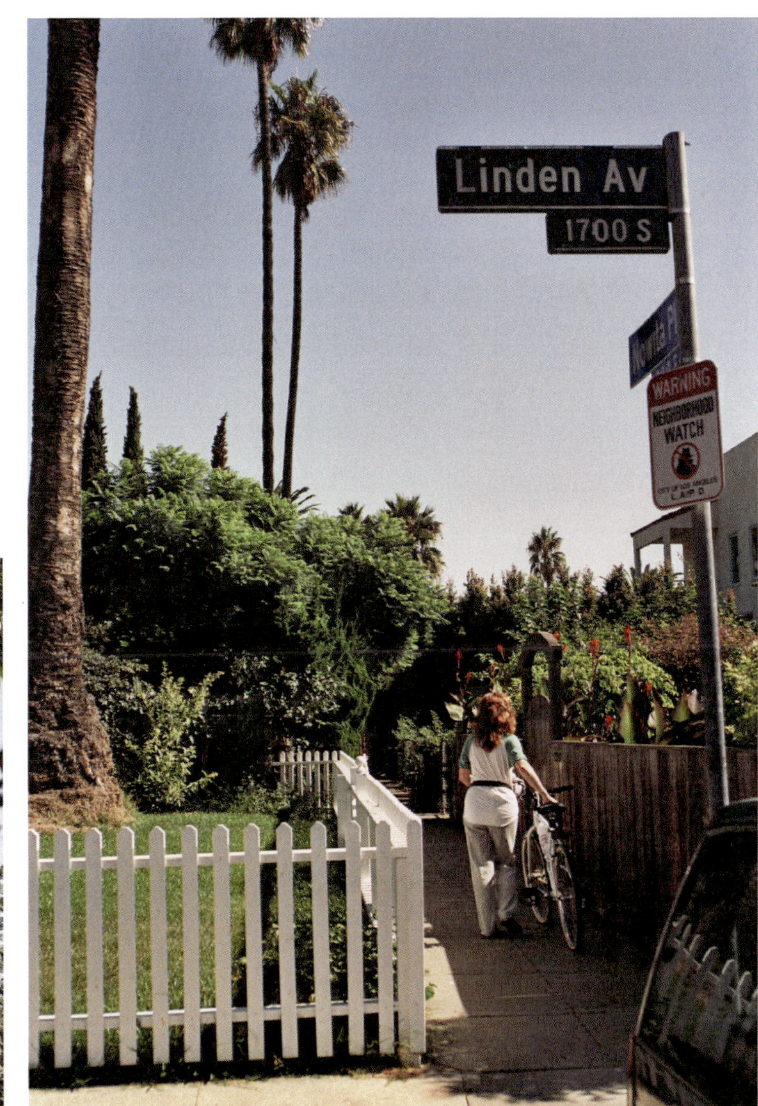

Linden Av
1700 S
WARNING
NEIGHBORHOOD
WATCH

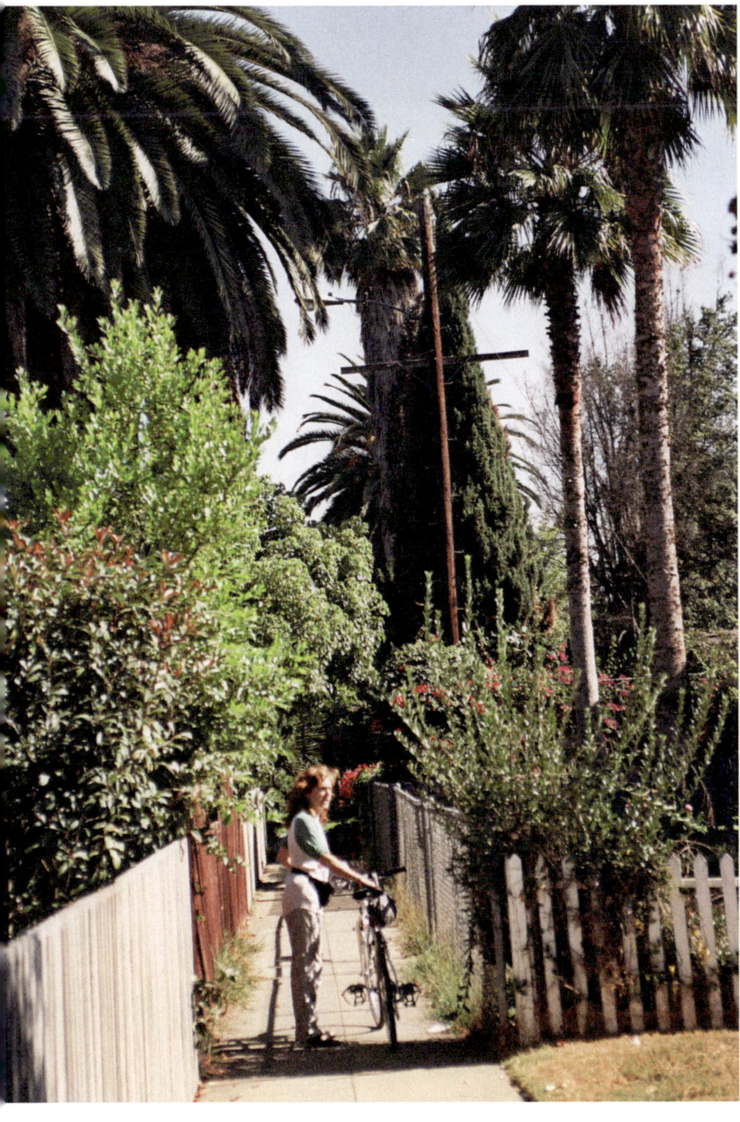